PLANT TREES CARRY SHEEP

A Woman's Spiritual Journey Among the Sufis of Scotland

A MEMOIR

S.A. SNYDER

The events written about in this memoir are as remembered by the author, who kept extensive diaries and detailed letters, which included some verbatim conversations. Most of the Scottish placenames and names of people have been changed to protect their privacy. Some characters are an amalgamation of multiple persons. The sequence of some events was altered for narrative continuity.

First Edition

Print ISBN: 978-1-7332925-1-1

Cover and book design by Melissa Williams Design
All Images by Adobe Stock 2019; house by drimafilm, roots by Alisa, mole by Tramper2, tree by Fotoschlick, Soay sheep by jamiehall, cross by dohee, English garden by forcdan, prayer beads by vasanty, turkey by veleknez, grass by kazy, Sufi spinning by uwimages, goose by cristianstorto, Star of David by Damian, mallard duck by taviphoto, Buddha by Francesc

Map by S.A. Snyder and Melissa Williams Design, based on an original drawing by John Boyd Brent (www.johnboydbrent.com)

Luna River
PUBLISHING, LLC

www.LunaRiverPublishing.com

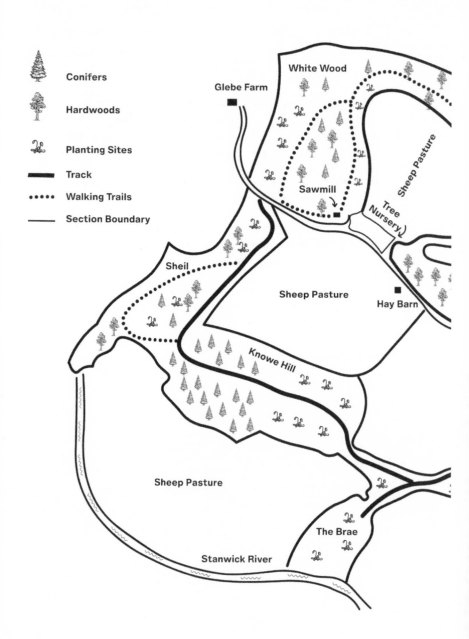

Conifers

Hardwoods

Planting Sites

Track

Walking Trails

Section Boundary

Glebe Farm

White Wood

Sawmill

Sheep Pasture

Tree Nursery

Sheil

Sheep Pasture

Hay Barn

Knowe Hill

Sheep Pasture

The Brae

Stanwick River

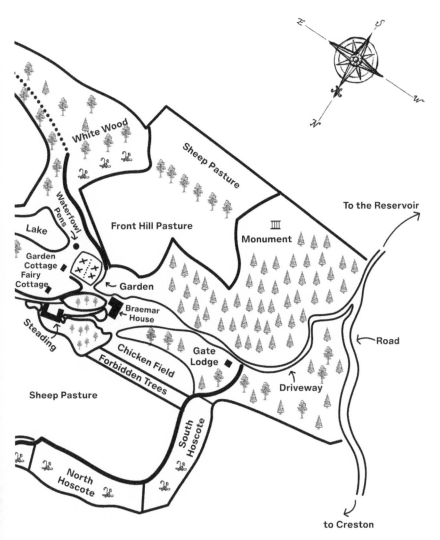

Your task is not to seek for love, but merely to seek and find all the barriers within yourself that you have built against it.

—Jelal ad-Din Rumi

PROLOGUE

O nly YOU would go to Scotland to plant trees and land yourself a nude modeling gig.

The thought occurred as I sat on a metal folding chair atop a paint-splattered table while five strangers interpreted my birthday suit in colored chalk on giant sheets of white paper. It was only the first of two times that I would remove my clothes for these artists. Even though my living expenses were nearly nil, having an extra twenty-five pounds sterling would be nice, although it wasn't a lot considering the effort to sit motionless for two frigid hours. How would I spend my cold-earned cash? A trip to the tropics would be nice! Thinking of warm climates didn't make me feel warmer. So instead, I began recalling what had brought me to these windy moors only a month earlier.

Ever since I was a young teenager I had been cultivating a deep love for Great Britain. Eleven years before my Scottish adventure, I had taken a break from college to live and work on a red deer park in England. My post-college dreams to tour the world and teach others about wildlife conservation led to Peace Corps service in Africa, which was cut short by civil conflict. I returned home to Montana to pursue environmental journalism instead. Freelance gigs barely paid the bills, never mind travel. Though blessed with mountains, sparkling rivers, and plenty of elbow-room, Big Sky Country began to feel isolating.

My midlife crisis began at thirty-four, an age at which most people were settling into careers and having families. I never wanted children, but I was lonely, and work was unfulfilling. Were there better opportunities elsewhere in romance and career? Montana's job scene was bleak; romantic prospects didn't exist; and thoughts of if-onlys and paths-not-trod invoked feelings of purposelessness and depression.

And then there was my spiritual crisis.

I was raised a Presbyterian, but in my early twenties I began yearning for more than the Church offered. Teachings of Buddhism, Taoism, and other Eastern mystical practices became more alluring, as did Christian mystics (Meister Eckhart, Thomas Merton, and Pierre Teilhard de Chardin) because of their transcendent views that bucked traditional religious dogma. Occasional retreats, workshops, and group meditations sparked something in my soul, yet mostly, life felt empty. I expected more divine guidance, signs to nudge me toward . . . something. Erratic prayers became missives demanding God improve my dead-end life. Unsure what I needed—or even wanted—I thought I might find it somewhere other than home.

In early 1998, I began searching the internet for conservation work in Great Britain in exchange for room and board. Volunteering was the only way, since I was an American and didn't qualify for paid work. By email I introduced myself to conservation-oriented organizations, listing my knowledge and talents: forestry, wildlife biology, all-around outdoor laborer. Of the half-dozen replies, one looked promising. A man named William at a place called Braemar House invited me to a two-hundred-acre private estate in Scotland. They needed help with a tree-planting project. I would have my own room, and all communal meals would be cooked for me. I excitedly read William's email numerous times. Pay dirt or just too good to be true? A follow-up phone chat with him persuaded me it was worth the risk.

Braemar billed itself as a "school of esoteric education" for adults, a spiritual retreat. Its website was filled with passages about the "Unity of Existence" and love and God. Here was a bonus: I could plant trees AND find my way through the spiritual forest at the same time! A few things on the website unnerved me though, mostly a lot of Arabic script and quotes from the Qur'an. Like most Americans, what little knowledge I had of Islam wasn't positive. On the other hand, the website also quoted the twelfth-century Sufi poet Rumi, whom I adored. His love poems to God had always stirred a longing in me for closeness with the Beloved. But who exactly were these Braemarites? What was their brand of esoterica? Personal reservations set aside, I accepted William's offer, secured the necessary visas, and began closing down my life in Montana. Five months later, I arrived in Great Britain.

The voice of one of the artists brought my mind back to the drafty studio.

"How are you getting on up there?"

"Fine," I half-lied.

"Well, I'm certainly impressed. Surely, you must be freezing."

Surely, she could tell.

"Can you manage for another hour, or do you need to give it a rest?"

"No problem," I said, immediately regretting it.

"It's a good job you are fit, my girl. I dare say you'll be doing plenty of hard work on the estate," Rafi said, scratching his chalk in large strokes across the paper on his easel.

Rafi, Braemar's maintenance man, had set up the modeling gig just a few weeks after I arrived to help me earn money, although he might have had other motives for wanting to see me *alfresco*. But never mind. Baring my body for the sake of art was nothing compared with baring my soul, I would come to find out. In Scotland, I would learn to love God, and Man—one in particular—though the path was nothing like I had imagined.

CHAPTER 1

First Impressions

A huge fan of British period films and American Public Television serials, I had always wanted to live in a British manor house on a massive country estate of bucolic pastures, ancient woodlands, and serene gardens. I imagined myself surrounded by antique furniture, dining in elegance on fine china laid out on crisp linen tablecloths. I would take daily restorative walks through field and forest, followed by afternoon tea. At Braemar, that fantasy became my reality, except the Jane Austen setting seemed populated with Star Trek characters. At least, that was my first impression.

My first visit to Braemar was a reconnaissance weekend in mid-September 1998. I had been staying with friends in Kent, England, and wanted to meet William, the man who had invited me to Braemar. He would be returning home to Australia before my planned move-in date, so I wanted to discuss the tree planting project before he left. I rented a car for the six-hour drive, bringing with me two steamer-trunk-sized bags stuffed with winter clothing. That way I wouldn't have to schlep them on the train the following week, when I was scheduled to arrive.

I parked behind Braemar's gray, pebble-dashed, Georgian-era manor house, which didn't seem as grand as those in BBC dramas. In Britain, they call these manor homes "the big house." Though smaller than those depicted on television—and a little shabbier—the big house was still impressive.

Not a soul was in sight. At the back of the house I stared at four doors, wondering which one to enter. I picked one, and inside was a red-painted concrete staircase with a dumbwaiter shaft next to it. The servants' entrance; how fitting for someone from plebian upbringing. I headed upstairs, calling out "Hello?" No one answered. On the next level I poked my head into a large kitchen. No one. The next two flights were carpeted in a threadbare maroon twill. At the top floor, I peeked into a couple of lived-in-looking sitting rooms before finding an office. Here, a petite, fiftyish woman sat at a desk. Her blond hair was cropped short, and her glasses rimmed her small facial features. I introduced myself. She stood and approached me.

"I'm Joanna," she said in a friendly English accent. "We've been expecting you."

"I'm relieved to hear that."

"Or Jelila."

I hesitated, confused. "Pardon?"

"Many of us go by two names. I'm also called Jelila. Would you like some refreshment? Tea is just being served."

She led me down the much grander front stairs to the dining room, a bright airy space with butter yellow walls and double-hung picture windows facing an enormous, croquet-perfect front lawn. A fireplace and mantle dominated one wall. An oval table filled most of the room; I counted twenty-two chairs. An assortment of seven men and women in a range of ages sat at the table silently sipping from delicate china teacups painted in tiny purple flowers. Little cakes and cookies were arranged on matching plates. A couple of people looked up as we entered;

others stared into space. Joanna-Jelila pulled out a chair for me, and another woman poured me a cup of tea. Joanna-Jelila quietly told me that I'd be staying on the top floor in the Victorian wing.

"When you arrive for good, Latif will assign you another room," she said.

Arrive for good had an eerie finality to it. Latif, I learned, was Braemar's head and currently out of town.

"You should visit the Monument before anything else," Joanna-Jelila continued. "Iskandar, our founder, is buried there. It's customary for new arrivals to pay their respects."

Up until that moment I had banished the notion that Braemar might be too out there for me. Some of my family had been mildly concerned. The word "cult" was never uttered, but it had been implied—and it rankled. Did my family think I was gullible? I didn't admit to having similar concerns and was confident I could resist attempts at potential brainwashing. Still, Joanna-Jelila's comment raised my neck hairs.

Out of politeness I agreed to pay homage at the grave of a man I didn't know, founder of an obscure religious group I knew nothing about. But whatever. I had come to plant trees, not drink the Kool-Aid. So after tea, I hiked up the hill that rose from the far end of the front lawn. A flock of fat sheep parted before me like synchronized swimmers. At the top of the hill, the circular Monument of poured concrete glowed white in the late afternoon sun. Three shallow steps wrapped around the base ring, with a grassy spot in the center. Four columns rose from its base to support another ring, about ten feet high and open to the sky. The Monument was about twenty feet in diameter, and the top step was engraved:

They are from Him and to Him they return.

I took off my baseball cap (I wasn't a complete heathen)

and stared at the words in agreement. So far so good. "Him" I took to mean "God." Feeling a presence behind me, I turned to see a woman standing several feet away and looking straight through me. She was dressed in colorful pantaloons and a white tunic. An elongated purple crystal hung from her neck. I introduced myself.

"I'm called Jelila," she responded, emotionless.

Another one? This Jelila reminded me of a Borg, the half-human, half-machine beings controlled from a central computer and bereft of individual thought. Great! My family was right! Soon I'd start calling myself Jelila after drinking drugged tea. Jelila #2 obviously hadn't climbed the hill to chat. She was still staring through me. Over her shoulder I spied a garden at the bottom of the hill not far from the big house. Departing with a smile and a nod, I hurried toward it.

The Victorian garden was huge and obviously had, at one time, been surrounded by a stone wall. Only one side of the wall was fully intact, about ten feet high, with a stone gazebo protruding from it. The other three sides had crumbled by varying degrees. One side was delineated by a fence, stone shed, and a long, stone lean-to. A small greenhouse occupied the opposite end of the garden. An enormous groomed beech hedge divided the garden into halves, with an archway in the middle for passage between the two garden sides.

There were eight square planting beds, each about fifty feet by thirty feet, which were overgrown in a tangle of orange and yellow nasturtiums and pastel cornflowers. Beyond the garden wall, ducks and geese paddled on the weed-choked surface of a large pond (which Braemarites called "the lake"). I passed through an iron gate and stood near the water's edge to watch the birds. Several minutes later, I was headed back toward the big house when a voice called out from behind me.

"You must be Sarah." A tall, somewhat well-fed man with short black hair and a boyish face approached. "Exploring the place, eh?"

It was William. We chatted briefly, and I was relieved that he seemed normal; that is, he didn't mention a Borg name. I was eager to talk about my Braemar role, but he wasn't.

"I won't be at supper tonight. Have loads to do before shipping out."

"Okay, but when can we talk about—"

"Gotta dash. I'll see you tomorrow."

He hurried off, his swinging arms carrying him swiftly away toward another grouping of buildings near the big house. I stood there with six hens, who clucked and scratched in the overgrown boxwood hedge nearby.

Supper that night was elegant, just as in my fantasy. Willow pattern dishes on white linen tablecloths softly glowed beneath silver branching candelabras. Vegetables with rice and noodles steamed in mounds on scalloped-edge china platters. Fresh salad greens complemented baskets of homemade bread, onto which we spread exquisite yellow curls of real butter. A bubbling, gooey chocolate pudding capped the meal. Tea and coffee followed. Even if they had plans to brainwash me, at least I wouldn't starve.

About a dozen people showed up for the feast, including a few new faces since teatime. I sat between Joanna-Jelila and her husband, Simon, whose Borg name was Rahman. He was Braemar's second-in-command, jovial and welcoming. A thick mustache danced on his lip when he talked.

"What does everyone do here?" I whispered, concerned about breaking the prevailing silence yet desperate to know more.

Rahman chuckled. "Whatever needs doing. Most of the people here now are just finishing a short course, which ends tomorrow morning. When you come back next week, you'll meet a whole new group."

"Meet" seemed a funny word, considering so far most people hadn't said a word to me, or anyone else.

After supper Rahman gave me a tour of the house. From the grand foyer we spiraled up the front staircase. I grasped the cherry wood handhold of the iron-spindled balustrade and imagined myself in a flowing gown, retiring to my suite after the gala ball. I promptly stumbled on the shallow steps, a reminder of my rather more humble place in society. Throughout the twenty-two-room house the floorboards beneath worn carpeting creaked and sagged noticeably with each step. Interestingly, on one wall in every room hung a framed Arabic calligraphy. The meditation room, on the ground floor, displayed the Qur'an in a framed picture, micro printed, so that the whole text could be read with a magnifying glass. Though beautifully accentuated with swirling lines and shapely flourishes, the Islamic accents seemed strangely out of place. I recalled the Qur'anic verses on the Braemar website. Were Braemarites Muslim converts? (So far, everyone I met looked like me: white, of Anglo-European ancestry.) I didn't ask Rahman, feeling that it might seem disrespectful. Also, I wasn't sure how I would feel about it if the answer was yes.

That evening I settled into my room. Three twin beds, each covered in matching pink quilts over down comforters, were carefully arranged to maximize space and privacy. On the nightstand my hosts had left a small plate with an apple and a pear, as well as a carafe of water and a little vase of cornflowers and fragrant sweet peas. Someone else was sharing the room, but I hadn't met her yet, and it was already after ten. I crawled into bed and began writing in my journal. Five minutes later, the bedroom door slowly opened and in stepped Jelila #2! Quietly, she prepared for bed.

"I'll try not to wake you in the morning," she said, gently pulling back her bed covers.

"Don't worry, I'm an early riser."

"Then you might like to know that group meditation is at seven. Full ablution."

An invitation or a command? Did full ablution mean everyone took showers together? I laid awake for a while even more concerned.

In my experience of spiritual retreats and solo hostel stays, I had never felt so out of place and alone as I did at Braemar that first day. How strictly religious were these people? Why did hardly anyone talk? Did they expect me to accept their beliefs—whatever they were? Would I have to change my name and worship the guy buried under the Monument?

In the morning, I joined a handful of people in the dining room for breakfast: a spread of cereal, fruit, porridge, yogurt, and toast. I sat next to William, hoping to glean as much as possible about the tree planting. Despite my having a forestry degree, I didn't feel confident taking over from him. My forestry knowledge was of the dry American West, not the damp European Atlantic.

"So what exactly will I be doing?"

"Baking bread, cleaning toilets, could you please pass me the toast?" William said.

Bread and toilets? Bait and switch? Was I about to be taken advantage of? I had agreed to plant trees, not be a scullery maid.

I handed him the bread basket and asked specifically about the trees.

"I want to learn as much as possible before you leave."

"No worries," William said.

"Actually, I have a lot of worries."

He stopped slathering marmalade on his toast. A glob of it plopped onto the tablecloth.

"Like what?"

"Like what exactly my role here is."

"The new estate manager can show you. You might meet him this afternoon."

"And he knows I'm here to plant trees?"

"Actually, there's not much tree biz at the mo. Plenty of other jobs, though."

He took a final bite of his toast, then rose from the table.

"Meet me at eleven behind the house. I'll show you around the estate," William said, and hurried out of the room.

I arrived early behind the house to find another man there sitting in a resin lawn chair, its front legs suspended precariously off the ground as he leaned against the house. He looked about my age and was dressed in grubby jeans and a T-shirt. A flour-dusted apron extended to his knees. He puffed on a hand-rolled cigarette, and when he saw me, a big smile split his face, revealing crooked yellow teeth.

"Oh, hiya! You must be the one from Montana," he said. He shifted forward, and the front chair legs hit the ground. He leaped up and thrust a hand toward me.

"I'm Shane!"

I shook his hand, appreciating his warm welcome.

"But you can call me Wakil."

"Okay." Another Borg name!

"Nah, go on, call me Shane."

"Shane is easier to remember," I said.

"Well, maybe you better call me Wakil 'cause that's what everyone else calls me. It might get confusin'."

"Wakil it is," I said, laughing.

"But I do like the way you say 'Shane.' Oh, never mind, call me what you like."

Then Shane-Wakil plunked a kiss on my cheek.

"Aw, you're sweet, I can tell. Glad you're here. Have to get back to me bread now."

He hurried into the house.

"I see you've met our resident hanger-on," William said, approaching. "Just tell him to bugger off if he gets bothersome."

Actually, I didn't mind Wakil's friendly welcome.

William and I walked up the long, gravel drive toward Braemar's entrance. Near a white stucco cottage, the Gate Lodge, we turned onto a single-lane dirt track and climbed a low rise. For an hour or so we trekked through muddy spruce plantations, crossed hillsides and pastures, and sank into the spongy forest floor. I became disoriented by the rolling landscape along the network of trails and vehicle tracks that circled the estate. My short legs tried to match William's pace while he offered a condensed explanation of the tree-planting project.

The Millennium Forest for Scotland project was a nationwide plan to revitalize the country's native woodlands. Centuries ago, Britons had hacked down their forests to build fortresses to protect themselves from neighboring brutes. These brutes also hacked down the forests to build forts to protect themselves from avenging brutes. Royalty and gentry needed wood for castle and manor home interiors and furniture. And everyone needed wood for heating and cooking. When Britain began building ships to conquer the world, the remaining forests hadn't stood a chance. During the twentieth century, the Forestry Commission planted vast tracts of Sitka spruce, a fast-growing North American species that provided lucrative earnings in pulp. Unfortunately, the non-native spruce sucked the life out of the soil and turned once bountiful wildlife habitat into virtual deserts. Conservationists began pushing the government to replant native trees, such as ash, oak, hazel, cherry, beech, and Scots pine.

Some parts of the Braemar estate had been logged in the 1980s, turning these areas into giant swathes of sucking mud and invading rushes. Other parts of the estate had been replanted a decade before my arrival. But without adequate protection for the new seedlings, the deer and rabbits had munched their way through any would-be forest. The newly minted Millennium Forest Trust had given Braemar a grant to replant certain tracts of land on the estate, and five months earlier, William had organized a hundred volunteers to plant eleven thousand native tree species on ten acres. They did it all in just two weeks.

"You should have seen the sleet on the first day of planting. Bloody buckets of it, but that didn't stop us." William said.

He pointed toward a hillside of new seedlings. The ground fell steeply away to the sinuous but narrow Stanwick River below. In front of us, the forest of green plastic tree tubes stood about two and a half feet high. Each tube protected a leafy seedling from hungry deer and rabbits.

"For the second phase of the project, you'll only have to plant six thousand trees," William said.

"What a relief," I said.

"Quite. It should be a piece of piss," he replied, ignoring my sarcasm.

Apparently, none of it would happen until the following spring. This explained his comment at breakfast about there not being much "tree biz at the mo"—in favor of baking bread and cleaning toilets!

We continued along the track, while William described the other projects they had completed. They had created a network of walking trails that circled the estate through the new plantings, dug drainage ditches in the boggy places, and built small bridges and boardwalks.

"Most of the work's been done, so you'll just be

bunging in a few more trees. Oh, plus weeding everything we've already planted."

By that he meant removing each tree tube, pulling out the grass, and putting the tubes back on. All eleven thousand. By hand!

"And the Millennium Forest Trust people want a written management plan as well, but I shouldn't worry about that," William continued.

Although he made it sound suspiciously simple—I knew it wouldn't be—learning more about the project eased my mind. There actually were trees to plant, even if it had to wait six months.

Also easing my somewhat dubious first impressions of Braemar was the departure of the somber group I had first encountered and the arrival of a dozen or so chatty new people who came for Sunday lunch. Some of this mix of British, Europeans, Americans, and Australians lived in the area. Some would assume Braemar staff positions, while others were former staff: cooks, housekeepers, office help, and estate workers.

"You'll all be living, eating, and working together," one man, Frank, told me. "We're one big family."

A Texan, Frank's face was creased with hard living. A hand-rolled cigarette teetered on his lower lip. He looked out of place in his cowboy boots and pearl-snap shirt, but to my Montana eyes, he was just normal. Frank lived in the village with his Braemar girlfriend and occasionally did odd jobs around the place. I told him I had come to plant trees. He suggested I take what was called the Six Month Course instead, which started October first every year. This course Frank talked about seemed to involve adopting a new name and, given what I had seen already, possibly converting to Islam. The way Frank promoted it as a "life-altering experience not to be missed" made me even more skeptical. I declined, saying I preferred to work instead.

"You'll want to take the Course eventually, though," he insisted.

His presumptuousness immediately turned me off.

Whether Braemar could offer me spiritual nourishment, it sure could deliver on the bodily kind. Sunday lunch was a gourmet spread of leg of lamb, roasted vegetables, broccoli-cheese casserole, Wakil's fresh bread, and salad. Wakil sat next to me and not too discreetly explained the relationship dynamics in the room.

"Our lamb's from the farm down the hill that belongs to that man. That's his girlfriend sitting next to him. Her mum manages Braemar's finances. The lady in purple was married to Latif, the principal, and those two teenagers are theirs. The one next to her was our cook before that bloke with the mustache took over. His sister was the girlfriend of that guy, but then she married Aziz instead. He lives in London, but you'll meet him eventually. That lady was married to the man sitting two down from her, but they broke up, and now he's with the lady on the left, but he's still like a father to her son, the one that's sitting at the end."

And around the table he went with the brain-boggling overview of the Braemar family tree. Afterward, I took advantage of the sunny afternoon to hike up the pasture in front of the house. Beyond Iskandar's Monument, the fern-flecked moors extended to the horizon. In the near distance rose a rounded high spot called Armstrong Hill, the highest point around at just over a thousand feet. From the top, I studied the 360-degree view of undulating landscape in more shades of green than imaginable, from the black green of the scattered spruce stands to the vibrant green pastures peppered with farmsteads and stout sheep.

The grassy hilltop was the perfect place for lying on one's back, staring at the sky, and pondering one's situation. For months I had been begging God for direction, throwing Scotland out there as a potential place to start. God had delivered the backdrop, but the Islamic theme . . .?

"Okay, now what do I do?" I said aloud to the sky.

Promptly, four blotchy gray cows ambled over and stared down at me. By all historical accounts, God used signs for doing business. Were the bovines harbingers of following the herd? Maybe Joanna-Jelila could help soothe my apprehension. I headed back down the hill to the big house, hoping to find her in the office. She wasn't there, but I did meet someone else.

"He's a genius with a chainsaw," William said, introducing me to his successor.

The new estate manager, Trevor, had been sitting with his stockinged feet propped on the desk, thumbing through the phone book. He stood slowly and approached me, his lanky, muscular frame towering above me at around six feet tall. His eyes quickly scanned me from foot to hat-messed hair. He was wearing a checked cotton shirt, and his beige jeans looked like they could have used a wash—as did his holey socks. He had brown-reddish hair that was beginning to bald on top, yet—I later learned—he was around my age. Not bad looking, either. He tipped his head, offered a faint smile, and shook my hand. It seemed like his loose grip was more a sign of disinterest than skepticism toward me.

"He'll be your boss," William said.

They both laughed.

"Oh, so we'll be working together?" I asked.

"You'll be the assistant estate manager," William answered.

This was news!

"What does that entail?" I asked.

Trevor mumbled something I didn't catch, and they both laughed again. I just pretended that I had heard his comment and smiled. Trevor sat back down at the desk.

"Do you know any good places to eat in Edinburgh?" he asked William in a soft English accent, effectively dismissing me.

The two of them hunkered over the Yellow Pages while I slipped out the door unnoticed.

That evening, about twenty staff and area Braemarites had a going-away party for William and his partner, Susan. We gathered in the Mead Hall, a handsome sitting room in the big house just off the grand foyer. I was not a big drinker, but what a relief it was to see alcohol! At least Braemar wasn't a dry cult. In fact, it was more like "ye olde pub" the way everyone was slamming them down. More than a dozen empty wine and whisky bottles littered the sideboard by evening's end.

William officially christened Trevor as the new estate manager and introduced me as his assistant. Neither Trevor nor I had prepared an acceptance speech, nor had Trevor many words of advice for me. I told him that, despite my size, I was a strong, hard worker.

He shrugged. "Do whatever you're able to. There's no sort of . . . pressure."

Part of me felt relieved that I wasn't expected to bust a gut. Another part of me worried that Trevor was less than thrilled about having me on board. Or maybe he truly didn't care either way.

That night I had the bedroom to myself; Jelila #2 had left. Before slipping under the covers, I stared at the bizarre Arabic script above my bed.

"I'm sorry, God. I don't know what it means, so don't blame me if you don't approve."

The next day, I set out early to return to Kent. I had one week to enjoy freedom with my friends, Ruth and John. I told them about my weekend, downplaying my anxiety in case they talked me out of going back. I half wanted them to. If the Braemarites did turn out to be a bunch of comet-chasing Kool-Aid drinkers, I would be on the first asteroid back to Montana, writing off the experience as another failed quest. Yet failure to commit to *anything* could doom me to an ever-shrinking field of opportunities.

I had to go back to Braemar.

CHAPTER 2

Arriving "For Good"

Many Braemar folk have an arrival story. You don't just show up, they say; you are brought there by God, Spirit, Divine Providence, whatever you choose to call it. You come for a reason, whether the catalyst is a crisis or a crossroads. God seemed to respond to my hesitancy by messing with my transportation connections.

My arrival story began on the Barnes Bridge train platform in London, near where I spent the night, on a Monday morning. Having already taken most of my luggage to Braemar the previous weekend, I had only a small backpack plus a large camera bag strapped around my waist. The plan was to take a train from Barnes Bridge to Euston Station, board another train to Carlisle, England, and catch a bus to Eltondean, Scotland, the town near Braemar.

The Barnes train never arrived, so I ran to catch a bus to the Underground station. The quickest route to Euston by subway included thirteen stops and a line change. The Carlisle train departed Euston in fifteen minutes. The odds of making it were not in my favor. Squeezing in with commuters on the Tube, I prayed for a delay of the Euston-to-Carlisle train. "Prayed" was a stretch; it was more like bargaining with God: *If you delay my train, I promise to be more faithful, maybe even listen to what cows have to say.* More faithful about what? I left it intentionally vague.

At Euston I pushed my way off the Tube and pounded up the three-story escalator, mumbling *please God!* all the way to the top. My pack pummeled my back; the camera bag, my front. Soaked with sweat, I reached the concourse four minutes after the train's scheduled departure time!

An unsympathetic woman at the ticket counter relieved me of thirty-five pounds for passage on a much later train. I meandered among the crowd in the cavernous waiting hall, wondering what to do for six hours. Then I heard a boarding call for my original train. It was late and hadn't left yet! So God had delayed it but failed to provide the ticket seller with the information—probably because of my hazy promise to be more faithful. Or maybe a test of my faith?

I plopped down in my seat for the five-hour trip, more than adequate time to worry whether going to Braemar was the right choice. In Carlisle, I asked an agent for directions to the bus depot, and walked to it a half-mile away. I asked a driver which bus was going to Eltondean.

"None of these, lass. That bus leaves from the train station." He looked at his watch. "In about ten minutes."

Groaning, I ran back to the train station, backpack and camera bag bashing the bruises they had created earlier. The Eltondean bus was just pulling away. I waved my arms at the driver, who stopped. I climbed aboard, breathless and sweat-drenched once again.

"Is this bus going to Eltondean?"

"Aye. I saw ye earlier and wondered if ye weren't coming back to me. I waited an extra couple of minutes just in case."

God sure did work in annoying ways.

The bus twisted along the A7 into Scotland, while the blue English sky turned a brooding Scottish gray. Towns thinned out, and civilization became scattered clusters of stucco cottages and lonely looking hillside farmsteads. In Eltondean I found a phone box and called Braemar for a lift to the house. Hamida, a woman I hadn't met before, fetched me and brought me back to my new home, eight miles from town.

Because I had driven myself to Braemar the previous weekend—and was preoccupied with keeping the car on the left side of the one-and-a-half-lane road—I hadn't noticed much about the narrow and tiny Creston valley, above which Braemar House perched. Now, as a passenger, I could take in the scenery of hillsides dotted with farmhouses and the occasional stately home. The pastures were stitched together with barbed-wire fences, reinforced by scraps of wood, corrugated steel sheeting, and bailing twine. Stone walls slithered up and down the rolling landscape through patches of woodland. Manure splattered the barnyards and, in places, the road; the musky odor of cows and sheep filled the air.

Hamida turned off the narrow road onto an even narrower lane, crossed a little bridge, and wound up the hill toward Braemar. We crawled down the long drive, past the Gate Lodge, and then past the big house to the Steading. The Steading was the original estate's stone barn, which had been converted into a dormitory. Guests, students, and some staff lived in the two-story building, which formed a C-shape of residences around a courtyard. Latif had assigned me to Room 10B on the northeast corner of the ground floor. A plate of fruit, a carafe of water, and a little vase of freshly cut flowers welcomed me in the Braemar tradition. I had arrived—for good.

After my near-missed connections, I was truly relieved to be there, despite the damp chill. I dropped my bags on the floor and headed straight for the radiator, cranking the dial into the red heat zone. Nothing happened.

I inventoried my new digs: dingy white walls scuffed by shifted furniture and marked by previous pictures; beige carpeting that had seen a lot of feet, and by the looks of it, a few spilled drinks; a small antique wardrobe, a double bed with oak head- and footboards, and a night stand; an Empire mahogany bureau with two top drawers nearly deep enough and wide enough for me to crawl into, plus an oval oak table with pedestal claw-foot legs and a single oak chair that had once been part of a dining set.

One large picture window offered views of the Creston valley, partially obscured by a young wood of ash trees and pine bordering the north side of the building. On the adjoining wall, a small door set in a little alcove was framed by two windows that looked out over an overgrown yard littered with toys and a simple, steel-frame jungle gym. During my previous visit, I hadn't seen any children, but someone mentioned that a few lived there.

Aside from the cold (the radiator had still not come on after twenty minutes), I would soon make my new room homey by taping up a few pictures of Montana. The framed Arabic calligraphy above the bed, however, would have to go.

In the dining room, just before supper, I finally met Latif. He was a handsome Englishman, fiftyish, with a slight build, dark wavy hair, and penetrating gray eyes. Whether it was his role as captain of this ship or his brevity with words, he made me nervous.

"How do you find your room?" he asked.

"Good, thank you. It's nice to be here."

"How was your journey?"

Sensing he wouldn't be interested in the animated version of events, I simply said that I had narrowly made all of my connections.

He nodded, then a great gong sounded from the foyer. At first, I thought this marked the end of my allotted time with him. But when Latif moved to stand behind a chair at the head of the table, I realized it was the dinner gong. After a brief prayer, spoken in what I guessed was Arabic, we sat. The table was as elegant as ever, chatter minimal and hushed. Only two of the twenty people present looked familiar. Trevor was absent, and for one panicked moment, I feared he may have quit, leaving me on my own.

That first night, I slept like the dead, waking absolutely famished the next morning. Uncertain whether I was supposed to report to work, I dressed in outdoor gear just in case and made my first of what would become countless short walks to the big house for breakfast. I was relieved to see Trevor sitting at the table that morning. He slurped his tea and stared across the room at nothing in particular. I greeted him and sat down. He managed a weak smile. He didn't seem any more pleased to see me than he had before.

"What's on for today, boss?" I said enthusiastically.

He took another slurp and set his cup down. Without looking at me, Trevor spoke.

"You may as well take it easy. It's best to arrive first, as they say here."

"Why relax indoors when I could be toiling in the cold drizzle?"

"There'll be plenty of days like this when you'll have to be outside. Today isn't one of them. Trust me, I've seen the hardest of men broken by the weather."

I tried to assure him that I was a weather-hardened Montanan. A little Scottish rain wasn't going to break me. He turned to look at me and raised his eyebrows. The corners of his mouth turned ever so slightly upward.

A half-hour later, we were slinging firewood into a large steel trailer attached to a farm tractor. We unloaded the wood behind the Steading, where it would be fed to the boiler. The boiler heated the Steading water supply, not only for showers but also for the radiators, which—allegedly—heated the rooms. Was this why Braemar was planting so many trees? For three hours, I shifted as much wood as I could, as fast as I could, to show Trevor how capable I was. After the second body-crippling trailer load, he handed me a set of keys.

"What are these for?"

"The tractor."

"What do you want me to do with them?"

"Drive it."

"I don't know how."

"What good is an estate manager's assistant if she doesn't know how to operate the machinery?"

So I climbed into the cab and sat behind the wheel, inching forward to the edge of the seat to reach the pedals. Trevor climbed up behind me, standing on the outside step. He leaned into the cab.

"Here's your clutch, here's your brakes, here's your gears. Keep this one in first and this one no higher than third. Here's your forklift controls. Don't forget to raise the forks before taking off and lower them when you park. Off you go."

He closed the cab door, and off we went, with Trevor standing on the step. It was easy once I got going, but ten yards into our journey he rapped on the cab window.

"Do you hear a scraping noise?" he asked through the glass.

I said no and drove on. He opened the door, reached across the steering wheel, and pulled down on a lever, raising the front forks. Oops.

We inched our way to the end of Braemar's long drive to arrive at neighboring Glebe Farm where we exchanged some firewood for a cold mound of old cow manure.

"How are you at growing vegetables?" Trevor asked me.

"I had a small garden at home."

"Brilliant. And reversing trailers?"

"Sorry?"

"Can you reverse the trailer through that gate, or shall I have a go?" he politely elaborated.

I gladly handed over the wheel.

"New assistant, then?" the farmer asked when I stepped down from the cab.

"Her first time at the controls," Trevor said.

"Oh, aye." The farmer chuckled. "She'll ken quickly, mind."

I hoped he was right that I'd catch on quickly. Trevor, of course, expertly backed up the trailer through the narrow gate with inches to spare on each side.

On the return trip, we stopped to explore Braemar's old sawmill, set back from the drive and about halfway between the big house and Glebe Farm. The small wooden building leaned precariously to one side, but that obviously didn't worry Trevor. He ducked under the beam of the main door. I followed, scanning for a potential exit just in case the thing started to collapse. Inside, a twelve-foot-high iron millwheel sat dormant. According to Trevor, for a century or so the millwheel had powered wood saws spun by water flowing from the tiny lake near the garden. The saws, long since gone, had sliced thousands of board feet of surrounding forest over the decades. The wheel was one of the few of its nineteenth-century kind still surviving in Britain.

Near the sawmill was a newly fenced enclosure, about the size of half a basketball court. This was the new tree nursery and would serve as a holding area for seedlings, Trevor explained. At the moment it was nothing more than a plot of weeds emerging from the scraped ground. A tall wire fence kept deer from leaping over the top, and chicken wire below kept rabbits from crawling under.

"We'll have to finish it this winter. Are you keen?" Trevor said.

Was I keen! Tending a tree nursery beat cutting firewood.

Trevor grunted. "Anything beats cutting firewood."

The next day, Trevor and I hung a wooden gate. When he spoke, his words were sparse, and I strained to hear his muted voice. Along with my determination to prove myself, I wanted to bring him out of what seemed like some sort of funk.

For the new gate, he loaded tools and a bucket of freshly mixed concrete into the massive steel trailer attached to the tractor.

"The keys are in it," he said, nodding at the tractor.

I took that to mean my driving skills needed more polishing. He said he would meet me down at The Brae. Noticing my blank stare, he gave me directions to a parcel of land on the estate known as The Brae (Scottish for "hillside"). The estate, I came to find out later, was divided into several named sections, each of which described that section in some way.

"Watch the downhill bit. It's a little steep," Trevor cautioned.

I climbed aboard and pulled the seat as far forward as possible, then sat on the edge of it to reach the pedals. Taking off at a crawl, I stopped to raise the forks after hearing the scraping noise. Learning already!

I soon discovered (and would continue to learn) that Trevor was a master of understatement. Phrases such as "the other day" could be any time from yesterday to six months ago; "a couple" could mean any number between one and infinity; and the hill's being "a little steep" meant your best option for survival was to get out and walk.

I skidded the tractor to a stop, perching on the hill's crest. From my vantage point high in the seat, I was tipped so far forward that the ground at the base of the front tires was nearly in view. I had visions of tumbling all the way down to the river a half-mile below. But showing a fortitude I didn't feel, I took a deep breath, shifted into granny gears, and talked my trembling foot off the brake pedal. Slowly, slowly, slowly, I eased the multi-ton vehicle down the fifty-yard drop, finally coming to rest at a level spot. I breathed deeply again to slow my pounding heart and wiped my sweaty palms on my knees before continuing along the track. Trevor came into view ahead, stubbing out a cigarette as I drew level with him.

He didn't ask how the harrowing drive had gone. Instead, silently, he gathered the tools from the trailer: a rock pick, level, and sledge hammer. He strode off to the gate, a dozen yards off the track. I lugged the bucket of concrete, following him to the long stone wall that snaked across the hillside. A narrow break in the wall allowed for passage between the neighbor's sheep pasture on one side and Braemar's land on the other. I steadied the wooden posts, and Trevor filled the holes with wet concrete. While we waited for the concrete to set, I admired the adjacent stone wall, a solid, two-foot thick, mortarless work of art. Mortarless walls (called "drystane dykes") run up and down the hillsides across Scotland's moors from coast to coast. Many have stood for centuries. Trevor casually mentioned he had spent the better part of that summer rebuilding large sections of it.

"Wow, you did all this? Impressive."

He smiled, more noticeably than I had seen previously, which gave me an opening to discuss what was really on my mind.

I asked him about Braemar's Six Month Course. After a long pause he spoke but was hardly enlightening.

"You'll soon find out. Starts in a few days."

"Have you taken it?"

"Only the nine-day version."

"What was it like?"

"A lot of navel gazing. Contemplate, read, discuss, repeat."

"What did you read?"

"All sorts."

He stood and walked over to the fence post, poking at the concrete to see whether it was set enough.

"They seem a little picky about stuff," I continued. "Yesterday, a lady told me there was a right way and a wrong way to stack the teacups."

"It's their way of doing things. The Braemar Order."

"I don't want to make mistakes or offend anyone."

"You will eventually. You'll be told if you do. As you've noticed."

After the concrete had hardened a little, we hung the gate. Trevor slopped some of the leftover concrete on the ground beneath it to form a stepping area. He squished a few fist-size stones into the gray mass with the toe of his Wellington boots.

"Should we carve our initials?" I said, kneeling down with a twig.

Trevor scribbled his initials a safe distance from mine. I etched the date.

"Forever in stone," he said.

I drove the tractor back up the hill, which was less scary than going down it but more difficult because I kept sliding back in the seat, my foot slipping off the pedals. I also couldn't see the road over the dashboard. The steel trailer clanked ominously behind. Trevor met me outside the back of the big house and suggested I take the rest of the day off. However, I was not ready to call it a day and was soon swept up by the housekeeper. Along with most of the other staff, I helped clean the big house and the Steading rooms to prepare for the students' arrival. It was a great way to see the other rooms without having to snoop.

While dusting the reading room in the big house, I had a closer look at the bookshelves. Copies of Meister Eckhart's observations shared space with the Chinese philosophy of the Tao Te Ching, Rumi's poetry, ruminations of early Sufi saints, and twentieth-century treatises on mindful living. I owned a few of the very same titles. Braemar was starting to feel less weird.

Later that afternoon, I was heading out the back door of the big house when I plowed into a man who was just coming in. I craned my neck to look up at his face. He reminded me of an extra-tall version of Omar Sharif, complete with a bushy mustache, though without the gap-tooth.

"Hello! Who do we have here, then?" he said.

I introduced myself to the grinning Englishman, who called himself Rafi, and said he was in charge of building maintenance. I told him about my recent deputization as assistant estate manager.

"I could use a hand with maintenance, if working outside isn't your thing," he offered.

I considered it for a second, wondering whether Trevor would prefer that.

"I'll stick with the estate for now."

"Suit yourself. At least join me in a glass of whisky at my caravan some evening," Rafi said.

Before I could reply, Dr. Zhivago was giving me directions to his mobile home, tucked in the trees near the garden.

"Why not," I said.

"Looking forward to it. By the way, have you ever modeled for an art class?"

CHAPTER 3

Fitting In

T he start of the Six Month Course on October 1 fell on a Thursday that year. Every Thursday was Ablution Day at Braemar, when we cleaned inside and out—in all literal and figurative senses—the big house, the Steading, the cottages, the grounds, and our thoughts and thoughtless habits. Never mind that we had just scrubbed every centimeter of the place the day before to prepare for the students' arrival. At the daily post-breakfast staff meeting, Latif reminded us about the staff's overarching role: to support the students, whom we hadn't yet met, since they were sequestered in their rooms, fasting until supper. I was glad I chose to come as a volunteer (enough of a commitment for me) and not as a student.

"Our hearts and minds must be focused on God in the act of service," Latif said.

Having volunteered for church and other charitable and nonprofit groups for much of my life, I was fully prepared to do what I could to support the students.

"We are required to be mindful of the Order," Latif continued.

Heads nodded, and everyone said they felt refreshed and joyful about a new course starting. Even though Trevor had mentioned the "Braemar Order," I still had no clue what it was—and felt uncomfortable asking—but I hoped to catch on. During lunch, clinking utensils outpaced the sparse and whispered conversation. Was somberness part of the Order? Would there be no more drinking parties?

On Ablution Day, I decided to help Rafi clean the barnyard of broken appliances, tools, furniture, and contraptions that were otherwise unidentifiable. We loaded the junk onto a flatbed trailer, towing it behind Braemar's communal Land Rover Defender for several trips to the local dump. Rafi's friendly conversation was a welcome break from Trevor's dispiritingly quiet demeanor.

"So what did Latif mean by the Order?" I asked Rafi.

"You'll understand when you take the Course," he said, heaving a roll of rusted barbed wire onto the flatbed.

I ignored his presumption. "Okay, prepare me for *when* I take the Course. What's this Braemar Order?"

He rested his elbow on an oak dresser battered beyond repair. "It's our way of doing things. For starters, the students will have a strict schedule of work, study, and meditation. No television, no newspapers, no radio, no drink, not even sex. They're not allowed into town unless they need to see the doctor."

"That sounds harsh."

"Not really. When you're on the Course, everything is so . . . delightful." He smiled broadly. "You find you don't want those things. They're just distractions from what's real."

"Television, radio, and sex aren't real?"

"I mean Real with a capital 'R.' The Reality of Realities. It's all about God."

"The Reality of Realities?"

"Take the Course, but in the meantime could you just give us a hand with this?"

We hefted the broken dresser onto the trailer.

"But there's a television in the staff lounge, and we had

a pretty boozy send-off for William and Susan last week."

"Yes, well that's different."

"So the staff don't abide by this Order, but the students do?"

"We do, but we can drink and have contact with the outside world."

"How are we supposed to support the students during their exile from modern life if there's a double standard?"

Rafi let out an exasperated sigh. "It's not exile. They need focus, free from worries of what's going on in the world. We mustn't talk about certain things in their presence, either. It distracts them."

"Like current events and pub crawling," I said.

"Exactly. There'll be some rough patches, but they'll muddle through."

He said the students studied nuggets of wisdom from many of the mainstream religions and schools of Eastern thought. That explained the varied books in the library. I asked whether they also studied the Qur'an, but Rafi said the Course's founder, Iskandar, felt it too complex and beyond the scope. They did, however, study much Islamic philosophy.

"So are you Muslims?" I asked.

"No, Braemar isn't about religion, per se. We're just . . . it's about knowing the deeper spiritual teachings of the prophets and messengers throughout the ages. It didn't end with Jesus. Muhammad was the last of God's prophets, you know."

I hadn't known, and his apparent annoyance with me triggered my defenses. Even though he hadn't expressly bashed Christianity, Rafi's comment played on my mind. I silently asked God to supply me with a useful response. Just then, several dozen sheep began gathering at our junk heap near the hay barn. Mud- and dung-caked wool hung in stringy lumps from their sides. They chewed their cud and stared inquisitively at us. The last time I had asked

God for an answer, cows appeared. A flammable shrub might have freaked me out, I suppose, yet so far the livestock hadn't been enlightening either.

"Look, why don't you just take the Course? It will all make more sense," Rafi said.

"I'll think about it," I lied.

"You won't regret it."

Later, I thought about what Rafi had told me. So Braemarites weren't Muslims. Or Borgs. Still, I wasn't entirely comfortable, but at least some of my initial fears had subsided.

Emerging from their fast, the six new students appeared at the table for supper that night. A few looked as apprehensive as I had felt during my first visit to Braemar. Getting-to-know-you conversations were subdued, although while hand-washing dishes after the meal, we got to know one another a little better.

Thirty-something Jerusha was an American living in Israel. She had brought her daughter, Nikki, a shy eight-year-old who didn't speak much English. A motorcycle accident fifty years earlier had left Diane, a seventy-year-old New Zealand Maori, with a stiff limp. Jill, an Englishwoman and former school head mistress and teacher, was in her late fifties and had recently moved to the Scottish Borders. Bridget, another twenty-something, had lived at Braemar as a teenager when her mother was on the staff. She worked in the film and theater industry. David, an Alaskan in his early twenties, had been excommunicated from the Mormon Church at age sixteen, but I never did find out why. He was a computer whiz kid and a national Yo-Yo champion. Mike, a twenty-something Australian, had a permanent smile on his face. He would dole out hugs to anyone who would let him (I always accepted). Mike and David could have passed for brothers; both had slight frames, dark hair, and small facial features. Eventually, we would affectionately refer to them as "the lads."

After the dishes were washed, I retired to the staff lounge to watch television. When the uninspiring program ended, I headed down the grand front staircase to the boot hall to get my coat and shoes and return to my Steading room. When I reached the foyer, however, I stopped. From behind the closed doors of the Mead Hall came chanting and foot stomping—rhythmic, pulsating, and purposeful. I listened to the strange, muffled phrases audible through the doors. Whatever they were saying, it wasn't in English: *whoom lala, whoom lala,* or something like that. It sounded primeval. My stomach leapt and my scalp prickled. It was obvious everyone but me was in the Mead Hall, chanting strange phrases and doing God-knows-what cultish things. Did they intentionally not invite me? I stumbled back to the Steading in the pitch dark. (Now I understood why there was a flashlight on my dresser.) Maybe Rafi was right. You had to take the Course to experience the full haggis. For now though, I took down the Arabic script from above my bed and tucked it in my dresser drawer. Until I could find out what it meant, I didn't want God to think I had crossed over to the Dark Side. So much for subsiding fears.

* * *

The students' fully scheduled days, filled with meditation, work, and study, had built-in continuity designed to support them while they experienced any type of emotional crisis. The schedule was part of the Order, and every single day for the students went like this:

—5:30 a.m.: Full body ablutions (wash every part of body, including hair)

—6:00 a.m.–7:00 a.m.: Group meditation

—**7:00 a.m.–9:00 a.m.:** Lay table for breakfast, prepare food, eat, wash dishes

—**9:00 a.m.:** Report to work or study (alternating every two days)

—**10:15 a.m.:** Lay table for morning coffee and prepare coffee

—**10:30 a.m.–11:00 a.m.:** Coffee break and clean up dishes

—**11:15 a.m.:** Report to work or study (alternating every two days)

—**11:45 a.m.:** Partial ablutions (hands, feet, and face)

—**Noon–12:45 p.m.:** Group meditation

—**12:45 p.m.:** Lay table for lunch

—**1:00 p.m.–2:15 p.m.:** Eat lunch and wash dishes

—**2:15 p.m.:** Report to work

—**3:45 p.m.:** Lay table for afternoon tea and prepare tea

—**4:00 p.m.–4:45 p.m.:** Tea break and wash dishes

—**4:45 p.m.:** Individual study

—**5:45 p.m.:** Partial ablutions

—**6:00 p.m.–7:00 p.m.:** Group meditation

—**7:00 p.m.:** Report to work

—**7:45 p.m.:** Lay table for supper

—**8:00 p.m.–8:45 p.m.:** Eat supper and wash dishes

—**8:45 p.m.:** Full ablutions

—**9:00 p.m.–10 p.m.:** Zikr (ritual moving meditation and chanting)

—**10:30 p.m.:** Bedtime

During study days, students read, reflected, and held discussions. During work days, they were assigned tasks according to the needs of the house or the estate, and according to their abilities and interests. The schedule seemed overly strict to me, yet my self-imposed schedule wasn't easy either. I worked from right after breakfast until well after supper just about every day, both outside on the estate and inside helping to wash up after every meal.

Staff had to attend a half-hour meeting every weekday in the Mead Hall after breakfast. The meetings were supposed to strengthen us to support the students, as well as flush out any of our own issues before they got out of hand. This confab revealed to me small pieces about the Course because the topics we discussed mirrored what the students were studying at any given time. The themes that ran through every study topic were a focus on service to God and that we are Love. The meetings could sometimes be excruciating, listening to others grappling with their own doubts, and sometimes getting angry, or not saying anything when you knew they were suffering or upset. As a distraction, I often focused on the front lawn and the hill pasture outside the picture window.

Gradually, I learned from conversations with students and staff that the Course was designed to deconstruct the old self by renewing the spirit. Braemar staff took care of the students' basic needs, while the students' inner worlds collapsed into black holes of despair before they were spit back out into the cosmic soup of humanity, ideally with a better understanding of their Divine selves.

In simple terms, the study focused on understanding what Braemarites called the Unity of Existence: the belief that God was everything and everyone. As Braemarites would explain, people erroneously believed themselves to be separate from God and one another only when they observed life through their minds and their senses alone. When we can transcend, through spiritual experiences, the chatter and nonsense of the mind, we can learn to know God as the sole essence of all things and beings with names and forms.

In moments of deeper self-reflection, I had been contemplating that concept for much of my adult life, though I could never put words to it. Upon arriving at Braemar, my own deconstruction had only just begun. Not that I had realized it yet.

CHAPTER 4

Finding Friendship

On the Sunday after the Course started, I was invited to go to Edinburgh Zoo with a handful of others to celebrate the fifth birthday of Colin, the son of one of the staff couples. Three other Braemar children, a teenage sister, and four adults crammed into the Land Rover on that rainy morning. Despite it being Sunday, I still felt compelled to ask Trevor for the day off. "Nay bother," he responded. He seemed relieved to be relieved of me.

When we returned later that afternoon, we drove past Trevor, who was slicing up firewood with a chainsaw in the cold drizzle along the main drive. His rubber rain jacket and pants glistened with water. The small bald spot on top of his head was a slick sheen. He glanced up as we drove past. I slunk down in my seat. Guilt drove me to put on my work clothes and head back outside. As I trudged up the drive, weighed down with my layered outdoor gear, Trevor was headed back toward me in the tractor. He stopped when I waved, and he motioned for me to climb into the trailer. The tractor started again with a jerk, landing me on my rump among the muddy wood pile.

We dumped the load behind the Steading. I stacked quartered pieces of soggy wood on the chopping block, while Trevor neatly spliced them into digestible bits for the wood stove that would heat the water in the giant boiler.

"Have you been at this all day?" I asked.

He split a length in two, holding his response for several seconds. "Pretty much." He leaned on the long-handled axe. "How was the zoo?"

"Great," I said, a little too enthusiastically. "I mean, it was okay. It rained most of the time."

He nodded and reached for another piece. The axe came down with a powerful thwack! The separated pieces sailed in opposite directions. I quickly set another one on the chopping block and backed away.

THWACK!

I recalled that William had told me Trevor's five-year-old daughter had been in the hospital in Edinburgh for several weeks. I wondered if worry about her was the reason for his melancholy.

"So how is your daughter?"

"She's back home now with her mum."

THWACK!

"Good to hear. What was wrong with her?"

THWACK!

"Some rare disease which made her intestines twist up. All her organs began shutting down. She was at death's door for weeks."

THWACK!

"Is she your only child?"

THWACK!

One of the pieces flew up from the chopping block and clipped me in the shin. Trevor said nothing. I put another piece on the block and waited for an answer.

"My boy is nearly three."

Between chops, I learned their names were Daisy and Brian and that they lived with their mother in a small village about an hour's drive away. Divorced, Trevor saw them every other weekend, though following Daisy's six-week stint in the hospital, he didn't know when they'd visit Braemar next.

"It must be fun for them to run around this place. Lots to explore."

"It's brilliant," Trevor said.

And that was all we exchanged for the next hour. It was going to be a long winter. I considered taking up Rafi's offer to work with him instead.

Fortunately, there were plenty of other people to make friends with. During that year, about thirty of us lived at Braemar, including children and teenagers. A handful of Braemarites lived in nearby cottages, or other Scottish Borders villages, and popped in regularly for a meal or to lend a hand. Other visitors arrived periodically; some were first-timers and others were Braemarites, mostly from the United Kingdom but also from other parts of the world.

Not only did Braemarites represent a cross-section of the international population, they covered all the personality bases, too. The pious and fastidious ones forever reminded others to keep their voices low, fold the bath towels properly, and lay the Willow pattern dinner plates on the table with the picture right-side up. The annoyed-by-the-pious-and-fastidious ones went out of their way to annoy the pious and fastidious by talking loudly, not showing up for meals, or bragging about drinking binges. Most of us fell somewhere in between. Differing social habits and customs, personal quirks and preferences, blended together like oil and water on moderate days, whisky and water on good days, and—though rare—gasoline and a lit match on bad days.

I connected deeply with a few staff, quickly forging close friendships. Wakil, the funny but friendly man whom I'd met during my reconnaissance weekend, was unkempt and sometimes crude. But his honest assessment of life was a refreshing counter pose to those who sometimes talked in spiritual jargon I didn't understand. He pretended not to "give a toss what that lot thought" of him; "that lot" being anyone who scolded him for making occasional negative comments or for not showing up to bake our daily bread or for generally failing the Braemar Order, all things he did with regularity. Yet, the slightest reprimand could send him to his bed sulking on a whisky bender for a day or two.

Our cook, Rashid, was a jolly Edinburgh chap, Santa and Jeeves combined. Behind a huge grin and sparkling eyes, he hid well his frustrations with communal life and the stresses of cooking two daily meals for a houseful of people. Another fast friend was Hadiyya, a tall, witty Manchester native, solid in body and spirit. Her hand in the office got business done. I spent the occasional evening in Rafi's caravan sipping whisky and enjoying philosophical discussions about what the students were studying and about life. Sometimes we bitched about the annoying behaviors of other staff.

The principal, Latif, remained an enigma to me. At meals, from across the table, he would sometimes focus on each of us, one at a time, monitoring our moods and seemingly amassing information with his eyes as they landed for a purposeful moment. When he and I met in passing, he rarely said hello, just smiled and nodded. His quietness intimidated me, and I avoided him whenever possible while at the same time looking for some sign that he didn't think me some heathen American. Eventually, I would discover another side to Latif. What at first seemed like cold indifference was really an ability to sense when his guidance was needed, or when he should let us sort out issues for ourselves. With a few simple words, or sometimes just an intense stare (and less often—but notable—a rebuke), he could steer us in the right direction without our even knowing we were being steered. Some treated him with sycophantic reverence, begging for guidance regularly. Some privately—and not so privately—begged for others to be guided. And still others (like Trevor and me) tried to keep off Latif's radar. It couldn't have been an easy job being the spiritual leader of such an eclectic group.

I quickly grew comfortable with the house routine, and, like the students, began to feel comforted by it. Laying the table for meals, washing dishes, abluting the house on Thursdays, and generally stepping up where and when needed all bestowed a sense of belonging. It soon became clear that the Braemar Order was, largely, this routine. I learned a lot from intimate conversations during dish washing. For one, the Borg names were actually referred to in Islam as the Beautiful Names. Each described a quality of the Divine. A name could signify a quality that someone either had or needed to work on. People could choose a name for themselves if they wanted one.

What I needed more than another name, however, was a defined direction in my role as assistant estate manager, especially since the promised tree planting was months away. Trevor's role partly involved caring for a coterie of forty chickens, twenty-five ducks, twelve geese, and seven turkeys. I was delighted when he passed that job on to me, a true lover of animals. My morning routine now included letting all the birds out of their pens and coops and feeding them. The evening routine included feeding them again and putting them back in their pens and coops to protect them from foxes. I was two days into the job when one of the turkey hens paraded six newly-hatched chicks through the garden, where she secretly had been sitting on a nest. The October nights were too cold for the chicks, so we marshalled mom and babies into the grain shed, a small cinderblock building behind the house where, appropriately, feed grain was stored. We rigged up a heat lamp in one of the empty grain bins and added straw for bedding.

The built-in bins were also built with cinder blocks and had sheets of plywood for lids. The bins were about ten feet long and four feet deep. A few days after we put the turkey chicks in the sheltered grain bin, Trevor brought me a tiny bundle wrapped in an old silk scarf.

"I thought you could keep it in your room for a while. It needs tender loving care."

"It" was a listless turkey chick, one of the four new babies. I named her Tana, for Montana, and put her in a shoebox kitted out with the silk scarf. I sprinkled in some grain and included a tiny water dish in case Tana woke from her near-death stupor with the munchies. Tana rallied for a little while but died the next morning. I felt awful despite Trevor saying it was no great loss. Chicks died all the time for various and unknown reasons, he said. We wrapped Tana in the silk scarf and buried her near the garden. I mumbled a little prayer and wiped my eyes, feeling the warmth of Trevor's hand on my shoulder. Unfortunately, she wouldn't be the last creature we would bury.

Trevor began sitting next to me at breakfast, sometimes describing his plans for that day's work, such as readying the greenhouse for starting seeds, clearing brush, or patching fences. And that was just for starters. He doled out work instructions like a health-conscious parent doles out sweets to his child: in small, controlled amounts, as if divulging too many details would somehow spoil things or scare me away.

Between his accent and soft voice, I often had to ask him to repeat himself and clarify the goal. Did he want me to dump the wheelbarrow of garden weeds on the pile of dead branches from the beech hedge we had trimmed, or did he want me to dump the weeds in the compost bins? Did he want me to hand him tools while he wrestled with stringing the fencing wire, or did he want me to start on my own section? To avoid seeming like an idiot, sometimes I just pretended to understand, then struggled to keep up, always fearing I would do something incorrectly. And sometimes I just did what I thought was best.

For two long weeks, I endured more of Trevor's non-demonstrative manner, torn between my love of the outdoor work and a strong need to enjoy the work company. Then one day, the ice cracked. We were fixing a fence near the front entrance, where the rotting wooden posts had only marginally been supporting strands of rusty wire. The neighbor's sheep had been getting through the sagging wires and helping themselves to a patch of succulent saplings on the Braemar estate. In true Scottish Borders fashion, we tried patching the mess with materials we had on hand. To shore up the posts, we gathered stones from an adjacent, and hopeless, drystane dyke and shoved them into the post holes to straighten the leaning posts. Trevor held taut a section of wire, while I pounded staples to hold it in place. I worked gingerly around the smooth wire, which was attached to the posts by telltale ceramic knobs: electrified.

"Don't worry, there's no power running through that," Trevor said.

"Are you sure?"

"Look at the state of it. It couldn't carry a current if it tried."

"Hmm," I commented, unconvinced.

I pounded in a few more staples. Trevor continued unrolling a short strand of new wire. Suddenly, he exclaimed a few choice words that would have sent any sheep within a mile bumbling for cover. He grimaced and shook his hand.

"Don't touch that wire," he said. "I'll just go have a word with the farmer."

The fence *was* electrified. I fell to my knees, laughing

to tears. "Thanks for the warning, boss!"

He picked up a clod of mud and playfully chucked it at me.

"Don't call me 'boss.' We're partners."

At last, acceptance! Partners, even!

The rest of that afternoon we jabbered nonstop. Trevor told me how he'd first discovered Braemar by bringing a group of conservation volunteers to install fencing and cut down dead trees. He was invited back to help with various forestry jobs, including planting trees that previous spring. Then Braemar offered him the estate manager position when William announced he would step down.

Before that, Trevor had supervised laborers in conservation-related work for the Scottish Wildlife Trust, such as fencing off sensitive wildlife habitat from livestock; building goose nesting platforms, bird blinds, and boardwalk trails; planting trees; and teaching chainsaw operation and safety. He wielded a chainsaw like a surgeon, and every tree dropped exactly where he said it would. A genius, just as William had said.

Trevor began to show another side to him, a wry sense of humor that you had to listen carefully for or miss ("I'd give my right arm to be ambidextrous," etc.). We finally bonded through our love of the outdoors, the birdsong that surrounded us daily, and the scent of the earth— to say nothing of the mud, wind, and rain. Maybe the autumn and coming winter would be tolerable after all.

Work was made more fun when we had the students to help. On their first full work day, I led them on a tour of the garden before tackling our first job, which was cleaning the garden shed. Far from the tidy picture-perfect grounds and gardens featured in travel magazines and coffee table books about Britain, some of Braemar's outdoor areas were littered with old machinery and tools, mountains of plastic greenhouse pots, and piles of old lumber.

And that was just the identifiable stuff. Overgrown hedges and gnarled weeds crept through the border gardens near the house grounds, while the walled garden plots were a frightening jungle of nasturtiums to rival Audrey II, the plant in "Little Shop of Horrors." Walled gardens were often called "kitchen gardens" in Britain because they grew produce to help feed the manor house. Braemar's kitchen garden hadn't fed so much as a waif in the past few years.

So while Trevor built his list of big-picture jobs, including reviving the kitchen garden to full food-providing splendor, my own list overflowed with tidying chores. After all, Braemarites claimed to celebrate beauty. At the very least, we could put things in designated storage areas. Frustrating were the hours we wasted tromping among two acres of grounds and outbuildings in search of a shovel or a pair of fencing pliers for what should have been a fifteen-minute job. The idea of an organized, clutter-free, smoothly running estate sustained me; the actual effort required to achieve it would, eventually, be my emotional undoing. Nevertheless, my self-appointed direction had started to take shape.

With the students, I surveyed the garden shed. Rotting wellies, gloves, and rainwear had been shoved under the work bench and stashed in other nooks and crannies. A rusted cabinet at one end had a collection of enough poisons to wipe out half of Britain's floral and faunal pests, as well as its precious wildlife. Tools were strewn everywhere despite the purpose-built hangers for them on the walls. Most were beyond identity, which made our scrubbing of the mystery implements something of a treasure hunt. Who knew what lurked under the caked mud and rust? Trevor warned us not to get too carried away with the cleaning in case some of the tools fell apart; rust being the only thing holding some of them together. I suggested we make a pile of things to throw away, while he suggested everything could be saved with a little oil, while I suggested there wasn't enough oil in the world to revive them from their cankerous affliction. He didn't even know what some of them were for. I held up a small fork-type thingy with three sharp prongs. One was bent like a beckoning finger and another was nearly rusted through.

"What about this?"

"Looks fine to me," Trevor said.

"What does it do?"

He stared at it, deep in thought.

"Tell me quick or I'm throwing it out," I said, dangling the Kung Fu-like weapon from my hand. Trevor snatched it and held it up for the students.

"The first person who can tell us what this is gets to leave early for morning coffee break."

Everyone stared in silence. (It wasn't such a deal either, seeing as how they left early anyway to help prepare for the break.)

"We give up," I said.

Trevor studied it briefly, biting his lower lip.

"You don't even know!" I accused.

"Of course I do. It's a . . . something which . . . uh, pokes holes in the earth so you can plant seeds." He turned to me and smiled. "See? Useful. We'll have plenty of seeds to plant in a few months' time."

"And if you accidentally poke yourself with it?"

"As long as you've had a tetanus jab, nay bother."

As we chopped wood or scrubbed garden tools or pulled weeds, the students and I discussed their course studies. (Latif often reminded us in morning meetings that we were all students, especially when the Course was in session.) Through our discussions, I grew more interested in this Sufi mysticism. I was on board with the Unity of Existence notion. But their jargon clouded other things, like the Reality of Realities Rafi had once mentioned. What did that mean? Depending on who would mention these concepts, I would either ask for an explanation or pretend I understood. The students would explain things to me without judgement; some of the staff would tell me to take the Course if I wanted to know more, or else they would answer using even more confusing jargon. Mostly, I just figured things would become clear to me over time. The good news was that with each passing day, Islam became less threatening to me. Over time I came to learn that Braemar wasn't about following one prophet or one savior, or even multiple gods, but about living life grounded in the universal truths of love, compassion, and forgiveness—the central tenets of all religions. Easy in theory; challenging in practice.

The students Mike and David, "the lads," were especially enjoyable. They always found a way to make arduous or boring work fun, such as re-enacting Monty Python sketches. Trevor pretended he wasn't amused and would try to refocus us on the garden. The Sisyphean task of rehabilitating it required wheel-barrowing load after load of weeds to a mountain of organic waste outside the garden wall, and wheel-barrowing load after load of compost into the garden to spread on the plots. Every bit of work clothing I owned acquired a cocoa-brown hue from the soil. My brand new bright yellow rain gear looked decades old within a month. My water-resistant watch developed moisture behind the face, and my pockets filled with fencing staples, nails, and baling twine.

Trevor was also engaged in hand-to-claw combat with moles that had taken up residence beneath the front lawn. For some reason, their presence caused him great personal offense, something to do with messing up his perfectly manicured lines of mowed grass. For a person who didn't care whether the garden tools lay on the shed floor in a hazardous heap of tetanus, he sure was picky about a few little mounds of dirt on the lawn. Our disagreement over poison-bombing moles versus tolerating God's creatures was just one of what would become many arguments about managing the estate. My fantasy of living in Britain was going to get worse before it got better.

CHAPTER 5

Seeking Warmth

Despite the chronic damp cold, the endless chores, and the cuts and bruises that never seemed to heal, I had grown accustomed to Braemar and couldn't imagine living anywhere else in the foreseeable future. For Scotland's cold and damp, I had come prepared with layering clothes. The estate team's turnout gear included at least two underlayers covered by waterproof over-trousers and a jacket, Wellington boots, and different types of hats and gloves, depending on the job. You needed gloves for warmth and protection, yet the type of gloves that protected your hands from hazards didn't keep them warm, and the type that kept them warm didn't protect them from the reality of farm life, such as barbed wire, splinters, and the occasional chicken beak. Headwear posed a similar problem. The type that protected your face from the wind and rain obscured your ability to see, while the type that allowed you to see failed miserably against the elements. It didn't help that physical labor raised your body temperature, but shedding clothes often chilled you when you stopped for the briefest moment. The constant layering and unlayering wore you out, never mind the labor.

Henry Ford supposedly said that chopping your own firewood warms you twice: once while cutting it and a second time while burning it. For me, only the first half of the aphorism proved true. My room never felt warm enough despite forever harvesting firewood for the Steading boiler to heat the water for the radiators and showers. When I complained about my cold room to Rafi, the maintenance man, he confessed that the radiators were on for only a few hours in the evening. Those hours happened to be when I was at the big house eating supper and washing dishes. And it didn't help that my room was at the end of the radiator line.

"When winter arrives, they'll be on all day," Rafi assured me.

I took "winter" to mean when the temperature fell from forty degrees to thirty-two degrees and asked for a portable space heater instead. Rafi scoffed and launched into a lecture about Braemar's electricity. We were off the grid, and power for the big house, the Steading complex, and the cottages was supplied by two propane-powered generators: the "big jenny" and the "little jenny." Part of Rafi's job was keeping them running, which sometimes required kick-starting. Literally. The lights often flickered under the work of our temperamental jennys, and sometimes the lights would blackout for several minutes. Rafi used mealtimes to remind us to turn off all unused lights and to forego hair dryers and electric kettles. After days of my begging for an alternative heat source, Rafi brought a propane-fueled space heater to my room. The thing looked frighteningly like something from a 1950s catalogue.

"What if the gas leaks during the night, and I wake up dead?" I asked.

"Don't be silly. It's perfectly safe." He lit the heater and cranked it to HIGH. "Why don't you come to my caravan for a glass of whisky while your room heats up?"

If nothing else, a good shot of whisky would warm the blood. So, I stumbled behind him in the dark on the muddy path through the trees to his caravan on a little hill above the lake. Once inside, I asked Rafi to tell me more about how a group of Britons had come to form this spiritual retreat at Braemar, and from where it got its Islamic essence.

He explained that in the 1960s, Iskandar (the Turkish founder buried under the Monument) had come to Britain to spread the inspired writings of a twelfth-century Muslim philosopher and Sufi saint called Ibn Arabi. Educated at Cornell and Yale, Iskandar helped fulfill the yearnings of people wanting more than what traditional Western religion was offering. He wanted to make the knowledge of great spiritual masters throughout the ages available to all, to help people shape their personal spiritual journeys.

He established a spiritual studies school at a much larger, and derelict, Downton Abbey-like estate in England, which the followers began to rehabilitate as part of their spiritual study. Later, some followers had discovered the similarly derelict Braemar House in Scotland and squatted it. Eventually, they bought Braemar—another relic for them to bring back from the dead. These early Braemarites set up a trust, to which people tithed, and began buying back parcels of the original estate, which had previously been sold to a timber company for logging.

Over the years, the devotees rebuilt the big house, transformed the old Steading barn into a dormitory, and built some cottages and outbuildings. The cozy Fairy Cottage was near the big house, where Joanna-Jelila and Rahman lived. Latif and his family shared Garden Cottage just outside the garden wall. Where cows and sheep had once sought shelter in the abandoned big house, residents now sipped tea at the elegantly laid table.

Courses were established, with Ibn Arabi's writings at their core. Latif, Rafi said, had been handpicked by Iskandar to take his place as Braemar's spiritual leader upon Iskandar's death.

"The Course teaches that we can all uncover who we are, who we truly are, for ourselves. We don't need preachers and rabbis and gurus or whatever," Rafi said.

Tiring of stories about Braemar, Rafi told me about the kit plane he had built and flown to Braemar that previous year. The wind had flipped the plane while it was tied down in a field, smashing it into several pieces. I pictured him in a leather flying cap and goggles winging over the Scottish Borders, making an emergency landing and ending up at this odd retreat on the moors, which he never got around to leaving. It wasn't quite how Rafi's arrival story went, but it was fun to imagine.

"When I put it back together, I'll take you flying," he promised.

Rafi was also a sculptor. One of his pieces was a cast of a nude woman, painted a gold color, which stood outside his caravan door. He was also taking a drawing class in town, and probably because of the whisky, I finally agreed to pose for the class.

After my visit with Rafi, I returned to my Steading room, which was as warm as a basket of toast but had a gassy smell. I turned the heater off and opened a window. As I took my pajamas out of the bureau drawer, I rediscovered the framed Arabic script tucked under my clothes. Wakil had told me it was a prayer of protection and should never be taken down. As a precaution against potentially deadly fumes, I hung it back up above my bed. The next morning I told Rafi to take the propane heater away. I would have to cope with the cold.

Firewood gathering began picking up steam—even if the task failed to ultimately produce steam in my room. Students Mike and David, and I, would shield our eyes from sawdust and wood chips while Trevor dug the chainsaw into a dead elm he had just felled. He could lop off the branches in no time before reducing the entire trunk into dozens of eighteen-inch lengths. When he let up on the saw, that was our cue to rush in, grab the pieces, and toss them in the tractor's trailer. The lads and I playfully jockeyed for the wood, like baby birds squabbling for scraps from our parent.

Next, we drove the load back to the Steading and dumped it behind the building, ready for splitting. All this work just to feed one ancient wood stove that heated the water in the boiler. We called the stove The Beast because of its voracious appetite. It needed stoking every few hours, day and night. If left too long, it would sputter and die, sometimes taking a while for the wood to get going and build heat again. The Beast had originally lived in the big house, and Rafi once boasted it had been in continual service for at least a hundred years. He was obviously under the illusion that it still worked.

Mike and David were in charge of keeping it fed around the clock. Their room was directly above mine, and I heard their alarm nightly at 3:00 a.m., followed by a pair of feet thonking out of bed, clomping down the stairs, and shuffling down the corridor to the other end of the building, banging through the three swinging fire doors along the way. Twenty minutes later, the sound effects would play in reverse: bang, shuffle, and clomp, ending with a flop back into bed. One afternoon they coaxed me into feeding the wood stove.

The lads led me into The Beast's lair, a tiny rock cave at the back of the Steading. It looked and smelled like a smokehouse. For some reason, Rafi had gone to the trouble of painting the walls white, which had quickly sooted up again. The Beast itself was a large, cylindrical iron blob with nicely wrought legs and a door that had to be propped up when opened to keep it from falling off its one remaining hinge.

Despite having grown up camping and living in a wood-heated house for two years, I had never gained a knack for starting fires.

"Careful with the door," Mike said.

Just as I touched it, the door crashed to the stone floor.

"Leave it. Just get the wood in first," David said.

As soon as I threw an armful of split logs on, the fire died.

"No worries. Kindling," Mike said to David.

"Kindling," David repeated. He grabbed a bundle of sticks and handed it to me.

"Matches," Mike said.

"Matches," David repeated, handing me the box.

Half a box of matches later, a flame finally took to the kindling. When the lads gave me the go-ahead, I put a few more logs on the fire. Soon after, the three of us tumbled out of the little room, coughing and wheezing. I had doused the flames again with too much wood, causing the room to fill with smoke. The shower water for personal pre-meditation ablutions that day was only just tepid. From then on, I was forbidden to even *look* at The Beast.

One potential solution to my lack of heating issue was a hot bath. With the lads at the helm of fire duty, the Steading water was usually hot. But the Steading had no bathtub, and the showers were more misty than showery. Worse, adjusting the shower knob just right required a neurosurgeon's precision to find that perfect temperature somewhere between frostbite and steel-forging. One day, Wakil offered his bathtub in the Steading Bothy, a tiny cottage at one end of the Steading. So I put together a little bag of special scented bubbles, a loofah, and a few votive candles I had found in a Steading cupboard. Off I headed for warm, watery bliss. Alas, only lukewarm water trickled from the hot tap. I returned to my room, a sodden, sorry soul, and basked under the glow of my hair dryer—generators be damned.

Feeling bad about my bath experience, Wakil suggested that he, Trevor, and I go to a pub in Eltondean, where Wakil could buy me a drink instead. The only ones in the pub, we sung to eighties hits blaring from the juke box. It was fun to see Trevor loosening up more. (I didn't have him down for knowing the lyrics to Madonna's "Like a Virgin.") Lately, while working on the estate, he would occasionally gently touch my shoulder or give me a side hug to thank me for a job well done. It didn't seem forward, given that friendships forged quickly and deeply at Braemar. Besides, I didn't mind the touch. And once, he brought me a small bouquet of the last of the garden nasturtiums. I wasn't sure what to make of his sudden affections, but I welcomed them, and was open to seeing where they led.

Oddly though, at our pub outing Trevor began encouraging Wakil to brush up on his pickup lines, using me as a guinea pig. Wakil had never had a girlfriend—at least not for a very long time—despite that he was nearly forty years old. Gently pulling back the collar of my shirt, Wakil pretended to read the tag.

"So it is true. You were made in Heaven."

His lame line made me laugh and Trevor slap his own forehead.

When he was in his early twenties, Wakil had succumbed to meningitis, which, in his Yorkshire words, "made me brain all funny." It's possible that he contracted the disease after jumping into the water one night at the docks in his home of Hull, England, to save someone who was drowning. For his bravery he received a police medal and a lifetime illness. He could behave like a child one minute and a remarkably insightful man the next.

After the pub we took a scenic drive up the hill behind Braemar and wandered into a sheep pasture near a small lake to gaze at the stars. The lake was the same one I had looked down on from the top of Armstrong Hill during my first visit to Braemar; the same scenery I took in while sitting among cows and asking God what was expected of me now that I had arrived.

"I remember that caravan," Wakil said, pointing to a small trailer parked by the lake.

Its aluminum sides glistened under the quarter moon. It belonged to a local farmer who rented it to holiday campers in summer.

"I did a runner during my first Course and slept under that caravan one night," he said.

"You never," Trevor said.

"It's true. I got really cheesed off with the Course and chucked it in."

"You could've frozen to death," Trevor said.

"Nearly did. That's why I came back to the Steading in the middle of the night."

"Plonker," Trevor said, playfully tackling Wakil.

They tussled for a minute, then we all lay down on our backs to look at the Big Dipper, barely discernible among the sea of stars.

"What did you think of the Course?" I asked Wakil.

"It's brilliant! Are you gonna take it?"

"No, it's too restrictive. I want to get out and explore while I'm here."

"You'd do really well!"

Trevor laughed. "It's not school, Wakil. You don't get marks for it."

"No, I mean she'd like it. She knows God and all. Don't you?"

"I'm trying," I said.

"It's not for everyone," Trevor said.

"You didn't even take the Course," Wakil shot back.

"I took the Nine Day Course."

"Just because you didn't like it, doesn't mean she wouldn't."

"It's not that I didn't like it. It's just . . . I like being outside, not sitting in a stuffy room and talking," Trevor said.

"Plonker," Wakil said.

"You're a plonker," Trevor retorted.

They tussled again, and I moved out of their way, suddenly noticing I had lost one of my earrings. It was my favorite pair, a silver bison with a silver feather dangling from its belly, which I had bought from a Blackfeet Indian at a Montana powwow. We crawled on the ground looking for it among the sheep droppings.

"It's too dark, love. We'll never find it," Trevor said.

Even though the British commonly called perfect strangers "love," hearing Trevor say it seemed to up the stakes of his affections, stirring something in me. But I was so upset about my earring that I started to cry.

"We have to find it!"

"It's just an earring, you big crybaby," Wakil said.

"Wakil, she means it! Don't be such a bastard," Trevor said.

He put his arm around me, promising to come back the next day to look in the daylight. I moved closer into his arm around my waist. He wiped the tears from my cheek, further heightening was turning out to be an interesting evening.

We drove back to Braemar, and the guys escorted me to my room. I asked them to stay awhile, but the only comfortable place for the three of us to relax was on my bed. So we all crawled under the covers—fully clothed, me in the middle—and chatted about nothing in particular.

"Sorry I called you a crybaby. It's the alcohol. Does funny things to me 'ead."

Wakil's Yorkshire accent made me laugh.

"Forgiven," I said.

"Come on, Wakil, let her get some sleep," Trevor said, getting up to leave.

"I'm not bothered," Wakil said, snuggling up to me.

Trevor grabbed his arm and yanked. "Oy, she doesn't want you in her bed."

As they headed out the door, Trevor glanced back at me and coyly smiled. What did that look mean? More than two years had passed since my last serious relationship. I was both excited about and wary of starting down that path of romance. If that's what was happening.

After breakfast the next morning, the three of us trudged back to the pasture to look for my earring in the pouring rain. I called off the search after twenty minutes, touched by their effort. I had lost an earring but gained two devoted pals.

As the only two staff that hadn't taken the Six Month Course, Trevor and I could talk to each other without the spiritual scrutiny and analysis of a situation that other Braemarites often engaged in. If, for example, your day included breaking a teacup while washing dishes, cutting a finger while chopping onions, and tripping on the stairs, a Braemarite might say it was the "nafs drawing your focus away from the Real." (Translation: the ego distracting you from contemplating God and being mindful.) Trevor and I would just call it having a crappy day. Nevertheless, the Course, and its intense examination of the nature of God, intrigued me, even if the language Braemarites used to describe the human–spiritual experience was sometimes annoying and pretentious sounding. I began asking more questions about it, but the answers weren't always forthcoming.

"Are you going to zikr tonight?" Trevor asked me. We had volunteered to clean the Steading bathrooms during Thursday ablution.

I stared at him blankly.

"It's in the Mead Hall at ten o'clock every Thursday night. The students do it every night, but Thursday is when the staff join in. Some of the other lot that live round here also come."

Something suddenly made sense.

"Would zikr happen to involve a lot of stomping and chanting?" I asked.

"So you do know."

"What's it about?"

"Go find out for yourself."

"Why can't you just tell me?" I asked.

"It's best if you just find out for yourself."

So in succession, I asked Wakil, Rafi, and the lads, Mike and David. They all told me to find out for myself. It felt like they were trying to trick me into going. I refused out of stubbornness.

In this place, where the focus was supposed to always be on God, I had quickly forgotten about my promise to be more faithful. Every once in a while, though, I had the niggling suspicion that I was supposed to be paying more attention. I hadn't yet caught on that something like zikr might help.

CHAPTER 6

The Birds

One of my main, and favorite, tasks as assistant estate manager was looking after the poultry. Braemar's chickens were a unique breed developed by Iskandar, Braemar's founder. The hens and cockerels were black with flecks of light gray, and the cockerels had white and sheeny green tail plumes that cascaded over their rear ends in a feathery waterfall. The chickens freely strutted and scratched for grubs around the house grounds, in the border gardens, and among the leaf litter beneath the ash, beech, and conifers near the big house. Sometimes they gathered behind the house, hanging out with the resident smokers and looking bemused at the comings and goings of the humans. At night the chickens divided themselves among three coops located in what we called "the chicken field." Every couple of months we repositioned the coops to prevent rats and stoats from nesting beneath them.

In the mornings, I let the chickens out of the coops and filled four long wooden troughs with kitchen leftovers and plate scraps, which I lugged to the field in a large bucket. It wasn't long before I started developing chicken-bucket elbow. As soon as the coop doors were opened, my little friends would rush out, swarming my legs and scrambling underfoot, as I dumped the scraps in the troughs.

At night the turkeys roosted on the coop roofs and always won the race to the troughs in the morning. It was no contest when a turkey wanted a soggy dinner roll; a chicken didn't stand a chance. The more greedy birds stood in the troughs, shoving others out of the way for dibs at a chunk of day-old anchovy pizza. The free-for-all left many birds with food-splattered feathers. Mashed potatoes were particularly sticky, and for a few hours after breakfast, they enjoyed one another as walking smorgasbords.

While they ate, I collected their eggs, brown-shelled gems with rich yellow yolks. By mid-morning the hunger games were over, and the birds peacefully moved on to scratching among the shrubs. The jackdaws would then swoop in for the remains. Whenever I was in the chicken field or near the big house, the bolder hens would strut over to greet me (though their "friendliness" was probably more a Pavlovian food response).

In late afternoon, the chickens would loiter at the grain shed waiting for their second feeding of supplemental barley. Here they would swarm around my legs, squawking excitedly. When I opened the grain shed door, they bumbled over one other to get in. Some would hop onto the bin ledge to watch as I scooped the grain into a bucket. I tried to spread the barley evenly in the troughs, and often accidentally stepped on little toes in the frenzy. By dusk, the chickens returned to their coops. After dark, I shut the hatch doors.

The male turkeys frequently tried to court me, gobbling and strutting in circles around me with puffed chests. The blobby things on top of their heads dangled in a shock of bright red.

The geese and ducks lived by our little lake outside the garden wall. The ducks were mixed breeds, mostly part domestic and part mallard, compliments of the wild mallard drakes that frequently dropped in. The geese hissed at anyone who ventured too close to their gaggle.

When I first arrived, the waterfowl had been used to staying out all night after their caretaker had left Braemar. No one else had bothered to call them into their pens for the night. They had to get used to the pen routine again to protect them from foxes, so I had to call, "C'mon, ducks, c'mon!" while shaking a bucket of grain. They quickly associated my voice with food, and the lake would become a choppy sea of flapping wings and paddling feet, as the flotilla surged out of the water onto the muddy bank.

The ducks got used to me, and occasionally I would pick one up and hold it. Gaining their trust instilled calmness among the flock and made capturing them easier if they ever needed medical care, or when it came time to kill them for eating, a job I never got used to.

Cleaning the birds' sleeping quarters had its challenges too. Every week the students and I pitched mucky straw out of the duck pens and chicken coops to spread fresh bedding. We also had to scrub the chicken coops, a labor-intensive responsibility. We shifted tons of sodden straw in wheelbarrows to the garden compost and scrubbed slime from the ducks' water basins. During winter, when the garden spigots froze, I stomped through the ice on the edge of the lake to fill their water basins and to clear a path so they could access the ice-free zone in the middle of the lake.

Cleaning the coops took most of the day. If the weather was dry, we could drive the tractor with the trailer into the chicken field and transport the straw that way. But usually the field was too wet for the tractor, which meant transport by wheelbarrow, load after load.

For obvious reasons, straw was a hot commodity. Ours came from neighboring farmer Angus who agreed to keep us supplied in exchange for some piece of unusable farm machinery that Braemar had given him the previous summer. Judging by the historical collection of dead apparatus in his front yard, Angus had a passion for useless equipment. Our problem, however, was fetching the straw from his barn. Initially, Trevor thought it best for us to fetch it ourselves using a flatbed trailer towed by the Braemar Land Rover.

Angus's straw was bundled into huge rolls and stacked five high in his barn, a tall building of sheet-metal and wood that didn't look at all sturdy. To retrieve a bale, Trevor and I had to push one down from the top of a stack, sometimes from fifteen feet high. This required clambering up the bales and nudging the one we wanted, inch by inch, toward the edge of the stack, where it would teeter precariously before crashing down.

Getting the rolled bale up on the trailer was the next step and really required a ramp, which we didn't have. Instead we scavenged a rotting unused wooden gate we had found in the barn. Then we heaved, pushed, and cussed the round bale up the gate-ramp and onto the trailer (requiring several attempts). We broke the gate on our second trip to get straw, so we jerry-rigged a beam and fulcrum to heft the load. The trailer could hold only two bales, and sometimes we used as many as four bales a month, requiring multiple trips.

Trevor was determined to teach me how to properly back up the Land Rover with the trailer attached. I could only just see over the Land Rover's steering wheel and was a little nervous my first time behind it on one of our straw outings.

"Reverse it into the barn," he instructed.

What Trevor had meant, of course, was reverse so that the trailer went inside the barn and not so that it bashed *against* the barn. We both concluded later that (a) Angus would never notice the huge dent on the side of his barn and (b) it was a good thing I hit it in a reinforced section, otherwise the whole building might have collapsed.

There were easier—and safer—ways to get the straw, though playing in the barn took us away from the sometimes-over-serious atmosphere at Braemar. But, after a half-dozen trips, we decided it was more efficient to leave our trailer with Angus so that he could load it with bales at his leisure using machinery appropriate for the job. We would then go back later to collect it.

We also needed feed grain. Always looking to save Braemar some money, Trevor didn't want to pay the twenty-pound delivery fee. So on our first—and only—trip to collect it ourselves, which was a thirty-minute drive, we waited an hour for the merchant to fill a gigantic nylon bag with barley. They loaded the bulging bag onto the Land Rover trailer and weighed it. We paid our money and drove off. As we headed down the narrow country lanes back to Braemar, I glanced out the back window and noticed the bag was sagging to one side.

"We should stop and adjust it before it spills."

"It weighs half a ton. It's not going anywhere," Trevor said.

We continued along the winding road up and out of the river bottom, twisting our way to the top of the hill. I cringed at every turn. The bag sagged more.

"It's going to fall," I said.

"Stop worrying," Trevor said.

We turned onto a busier A road. I looked back at the grain bag and covered my eyes.

"It's fine," Trevor said.

He glanced into the rearview mirror, swore, and hit the brakes.

We scooped up what we could of the barley and brushed about another twenty-five kilos onto the road verge. From then on, Trevor paid to have the grain delivered. But we still had to transfer it from the giant nylon bag to the grain shed bins. Bucket by bucket, we would wheeze and choke from the grain dust. Fortunately, it was a quarterly, not a monthly, procedure.

For the pleasure the birds gave, the trouble of their care was worth it: watching the ducks and geese paddle through a morning mist creeping across the lake's surface or listening to the soft clucks and coos of the chickens scratching in the brush. At times, it was unclear who relied on whom for their well-being.

CHAPTER 7

Joining the Flock

Braemar celebrated food, using nothing but the best ingredients. No substitutes or fakes, no fat-free or skimmed, no boxed sawdust. The cook personally selected fruits and vegetables during weekly trips to an open-air produce market in Newcastle, England, just south of the border. Potatoes, cabbages, celeriac, lettuce, tomatoes, parsnips, carrots, apples, pears, bananas, oranges, broccoli, cauliflower, onions, aubergines (eggplant), peppers, and mushrooms formed the basis of our diet. Organic as much as possible. We made our own yogurt with full-fat milk, delivered twice weekly in pint bottles from a local dairy. Wakil baked our daily bread using flour, salt, yeast, and water. Some of our eggs came from our own chickens, ducks, turkeys, and geese; one goose egg could make an omelet for three. We ate locally raised lamb in various forms, and morning coffee and afternoon tea breaks featured homemade cakes and cookies.

Certain foods were forbidden, not even allowed in the house: pork, shellfish, and garlic, primarily. The first two were banned on Islamic and Jewish traditional grounds, the latter because, as Jelila had told me, "the odor frightens the angels away." I found the explanation interesting, considering some Braemarites consumed tobacco and alcohol as if they were major food groups. When I asked Jelila about those unpleasant odors, it gave her honest pause for reflection but no response. I adored garlic (maybe that partially explained my spiritual crisis!). Perhaps at garlic-free Braemar my angels would come around again?

Getting enough to eat wasn't a problem; getting too much was. I had been primarily a vegetarian before setting out for Scotland, but had I not indulged in meat there, the climate and my physical laboring in it, would have left me starved and weak. At least that's what I told myself every time I reached for an extra helping of lamb shank stew or enjoyed just one more, no three more, chocolate biscuits before heading out to split wood in the rain. It wasn't long before my jeans grew tighter and my sweet tooth gnawed to shreds what little willpower I had left.

Braemar also beatified food. Reverence and presentation were paramount. Anyone helping in the kitchen was required to read a short treatise on how to prepare one's mind before cooking (an ablution of the mind) so that the food was treated with love, care, and respect. This was especially the case for all animals that gave their lives. Braemar founder Iskandar, a gastronomique himself, had believed that cooks who brought emotional strife to the kitchen transferred that energy to the food, affecting those who ate it. In short, mealtimes were a treat, a wholly intentional gathering to rejoice in God's bounty and gratitude for nourishment.

Despite the food fortification, I came down with a virus a few weeks after my arrival. Because there was so much to do, I felt guilty for taking time off to be ill. But fortunately, it happened while I was house- and cat-sitting in the charming Fairy Cottage for Jelila and Rahman while they were away on business in England. And although it had central heating, because that was powered by the temperamental Braemar generators, the cottage was only marginally warmer than my Steading room. A wood stove provided supplementary heat, but the catch was it required someone with fire-starting skills.

During the ten days of my illness, three main caretakers dropped by in shifts, each with unique talents to cheer and entertain me. Braemar maintenance man Rafi's talent was fire-starting and conversation, which he liked to enhance with a dram of Famous Grouse whisky. Having heard about my misadventures with the students Mike and David in trying to get a fire going in the Steading Beast, Rafi introduced me to firelighters, a novel invention that any ten-year-old could use to start a fire but that thirty-four-year-old Americans who are crap at fire building should avoid. Basically, they were lighter fluid in solid form, about the size of a butter stick. After a dozen butter sticks, I had managed to create a roaring blaze for just long enough to singe my hair and fleece pullover, before the flames sizzled and died. Thankfully, Rafi took charge of fire-making, stopping by periodically to stoke the wood stove.

Wakil, our bread baker and kitchen prep cook, was another regular visitor. His talent was making me laugh. He brought me a hand-painted get-well card, which the children had signed, and another of his paintings. Slightly larger than a postcard, the scene depicted a sunrise over mountains with a lake and boat in the foreground. Wakil framed his watercolor and hung it in my Steading room. He also read me some of his poems, most of which celebrated the spiritual side of food. In one, he compared getting to know God to peeling onions. It wasn't clear whether he meant that God was a many-layered concept, or that the more you got to know God, the more God made you cry. Probably both.

Throughout our conversations, I learned that Wakil had come to Braemar fifteen years earlier with a couple from Yorkshire. He had been homeless on the streets of Hull, England, and the couple took him under their care. In Hull he worked various jobs, including at a fish factory and bartending in a pub near the docks. That work was before contracting meningitis in his twenties. Braemar was his lifeline.

"I can't have a proper job on account of it," he said.

His chosen name, Wakil, meant guardian, or one who looks after someone's affairs.

"So I'm gonna look after you," he asserted.

His sincerity was touching, and I often asked him to explain more to me about the Course and Islam.

"Iskandar believed that union with God was the sole purpose of our existence. Iskandar was brilliant!"

"So how do Braemarites feel about Jesus?" I asked Wakil, thinking why not just throw it out there.

"Jesus is brilliant!"

Wakil thought a lot of things were "brilliant."

He reminded me that many of the Sufi poet Rumi's writings ecstatically praised Jesus. He also said that, supposedly, when Rumi died more Christians than Muslims came to his funeral. Students of the Braemar Course studied Jesus, and even Ibn Arabi wrote extensively about him as God's most exalted prophet. The discussion satisfied me, and I slowly began to understand that my initial fear of Islam was really prejudice borne of ignorance.

My third visitor to Fairy Cottage was Trevor, whose gift was care. He made me a large pot of vegetable stew because I wasn't well enough to go to meals in the big house. He never talked much nor stayed long. He often just sat next to me wherever I was lying down, on the bed or the couch. He would put his hand on my forehead to check my temperature and gaze at me with doleful eyes. He brought gardening magazines for me to read. It felt suspiciously like a hint, seeing as how I had told him planting trees appealed more than weeding vegetables. His quiet, gentle manner was a nice tonic to Rafi's and Wakil's more lively company.

After ten long days, my virus was a memory, just in time to move back into my Steading room when Rahman and Jelila returned. How comforting to once again be part of the group, eating meals in the big house and reconnecting with people. Oddly, in my absence, I had become more prized in the hearts of the children. Thus began an obsession with sitting next to me at weekend lunch times, the only meals the children were allowed at in the big house. I also met Trevor's children, whose visits started again after five-year-old Daisy recovered from her frightening illness.

"I was in hospital and nearly died," she said, when her dad introduced us.

She happily tore around Braemar with the other children, while Brian, nearly three years old, didn't want to be away from his mother and spent much of his first return visit crying for her.

Mostly I was grateful to be back outside working again, even on days of relentless rain and gloom. I soon got back into the routine, forgetting about being wet and cold or achy and tired ... until I came back inside and was reminded how wet and cold and achy and tired I really was. The weather was less challenging, however, than letting go of work expectations. Trevor and I had no formal plan for the estate, no set to-do list. Each morning, he made decisions about work based on the weather, available help, and his mood. He easily flowed with whatever haphazard thing took his fancy at any given moment. I, on the other hand, craved a plan for tackling jobs in an organized way. I craved what seemed rare in these parts: a sense of completion.

For example, if we were patching a fence within sight of mole mounds, Trevor was reminded that he needed to shovel up the mole dirt and wheelbarrow it to the garden. On his way to the garden, he would be reminded that we needed to spread compost on the garden plots. While getting compost, he was reminded that we needed to fix several broken boards on the compost bins. In turn, this reminded him that we needed to split more wood for the boiler, which reminded him that we needed to cut down the dead tree by the lake and haul away the wood. In doing so, the tractor would get stuck in the soft ground by the lake, which led to spending the rest of the day trying to get the tractor unstuck. In the meantime, the fencing we had initially set out to do a week earlier would be abandoned for a series of other, never completed, tasks.

The size of the place, alone—nearly 200 acres—could be an issue. Sometimes, we'd be in the middle of a job at the far end of the estate and realize we needed more tools or supplies. I would drive the tractor back to the garden shed to fetch the items, only to have to walk three-quarters of a mile back to the job site to tell Trevor that the tractor had gotten stuck in the mud-sucking hole outside the garden shed. (Fixing the drainage problem that caused the mud-sucking hole was at the top of our priority list for three months.) Oftentimes, just when we were getting into the rhythm of the work, we would break for tea or lunch. All of this added up to what would be, in theory, simple jobs lingering for months, if completed at all.

Most of the time Trevor and I worked together, but sometimes I peeled off on my own to accomplish a task I could no longer stand to leave undone. Usually these were jobs that would prevent future headaches. For example, putting the sloughing heap of plant pots, which had been carelessly dumped outside the greenhouse, into organized stacks not only tidied things but prevented the pots from being blown all over the place by the wind—which we'd have to collect again—and prevented the pots from getting stuck in our wheelbarrow tires every time we pushed a wheelbarrow past them.

Every time I cleared up junk in the hay barn, or in the garden lean-to, someone would dump more junk there: piles of used carpeting and industrial shelving units salvaged from an office somewhere; milled boards for woodworking projects no one would ever get around to; or broken furniture and equipment no one would ever repair. (Rafi and I had only made a dent the one day we abluted the barn.) If only Braemarites cared as much about the estate as they did about their perfectly laid table. It was enough to make a clutter-phobic neat-freak like me go bonkers.

When the tasks piled up even too much for Trevor to bear, we drew up a plan for the estate. Clean up the rusty equipment outside the garden shed. Weed the garden and spread compost. Prune the old apple orchard, fix fences, and repair stone walls. Fill the driveway potholes and fix the drainage problem on the perpetually flooded track by the garden shed. Bring the old mill wheel at the sawmill back to life to generate electricity so we wouldn't have to rely on the generators anymore. Create a mole-free lawn, etcetera, etcetera. All we had to do was find time between the weekly cleaning of the chicken coops and duck pens, firewood harvesting, spot-patching fences to keep the neighbors' sheep out, etcetera, etcetera.

Laying out a plan for the estate didn't seem like such a good idea after all. It only showed us how much there was to do. I began looking forward to Ablution Day every Thursday. At least with cleaning, there was a sense of accomplishment. Latif, the Braemar principal, often reminded us staff at the morning meetings that completing a task wasn't the point. I wasn't convinced. I also wasn't aware of it yet, but the constant to-dos were part of God's plan for me.

* * *

At the end of October Braemar's board of directors and trustees arrived from all over Britain for their quarterly weekend meeting. It was easy to picture them as the 1960s hippies Iskandar had first inspired and organized into a spiritual community. Only in place of long hair and love beads, they now sported comb-overs and bifocals on strings. The added guests vexed the sputtering generators, a problem that grew worse each passing week. Flickering lights were Rafi's cue to lecture us about electrical vigilance. He was rabid about no electric kettles, hair dryers, or space heaters. If he caught anyone using forbidden appliances, they would be publicly flogged with an extension cord. Though I wasn't using my hair dryer much now (having grown more used to the cold), nevertheless, I stuffed it at the bottom of my wardrobe just in case Rafi decided to launch a search-and-destroy mission.

Trevor and I met with Sam Banks, the board director in charge of estate affairs. With a walrus mustache fringing a bright smile, and brown shaggy hair creeping toward his eyes, Sam looked like he had just walked off the cover of a 1970s issue of Mother Jones magazine. As the three of us strolled through the garden, we told Sam about our dream to turn the Braemar estate into the miracle we had outlined on paper. Sam thought it a "lovely plan," without overtly commenting on its near impossibility, given our lack of financial and personnel resources. We also reviewed the tree-planting project, and I learned a few things William had failed to mention. For one, we had to file monthly expenditure reports in order to get the next forestry grant installment, which had already been promised to us but which we'd have to prove we were using. Put another way, we had to spend money we didn't have in order to get reimbursed with money we were promised.

We thumbed through ten binders of estate information,

which William had meticulously catalogued, three binders alone for the tree project. He had saved every scrap of paper he ever jotted notes on. Every transaction, decision, job performed, money granted and spent, random thoughts about life, were stuffed into the binders. He even saved six versions of a "final" monthly expense report for September, none of them with specific dates. Serious office time would be required to unravel many of these mysteries. So when my thirty-fifth birthday arrived at the end of October, I was reluctant to take the day off; however, Trevor offered his car for the day and suggested I go have fun with Wakil.

"He'd be over the moon if you asked him," Trevor said.

I was a little disappointed that Trevor didn't want to go. But nevertheless, Wakil and I headed down the Creston valley road to Eltondean. Still not used to driving on the left-hand side, I swerved to miss a logging truck, which forced us toward the embankment.

"Try to keep the car on the tarmac," Wakil advised, though he'd never driven a day in his life.

"We'd be pancakes now if I had," I said.

He imitated my accent: "We'd be paan-cakes. Oh my gawd."

I thumped his leg with my fist. "Plonker."

"You're starting to sound like one of us now," Wakil said.

In Eltondean, we laughed and skipped arm in arm up the High Street in the drizzle. We ate lunch at a café that was a throwback to the 1940s and full of elderly ladies smoking their lungs gray. In this woe-begotten town a third of adults were out of work. In the 1950s, Eltondean had claimed its title as cashmere capital of the world. It once buzzed with woolen mills that churned out knitwear for the frozen masses. Now, most of the mills sat empty, while pubs churned out pints of beer for the unemployed masses.

Wakil and I called in at all eight thrift stores on the High Street to poke through the goods. I found a new pair of black stockings, and Wakil begged me to let him buy them.

"I've never bought anything naughty for a lady before."

I handed him the package.

"I don't want to touch them. I just want to buy them for you," he said, recoiling.

The cashier stifled a chuckle. Like many of the older women in town, she was dressed in a conservative dark-colored skirt and buttoned-up white blouse. Bifocals hung from a silver chain around her neck. She put them on to read the price tag, then cooed in her Scottish Borders accent.

"Find everything all right, then?"

"We did," I said.

"That's grand," she said, a common local reply. "That'll be one pound fifty."

"I'll just have these shoes as well," Wakil said.

"Right. Another three pound, for four and fifty," the lady said in her sing-song accent.

Wakil dug into his shabby pants pocket for the cash and handed her a fistful of coins.

"That's grand, thanks," the lady said, her "thanks" sounding more like "thonks."

Wakil held up his old smelly loafers. "I'll just leave these here, only I don't need them now I got smart new ones."

Judging by the way the lady grimaced, this wasn't so grand. Nevertheless, her voice ushered us out of the store with a friendly, "Cherioooo."

It was not unusual for Wakil to leave his shoes behind.

He had few possessions, and where clothes were concerned, he owned only a few different outfits at any one time. He would wear them for several weeks before rummaging through the Steading jumble for something else to wear, though he assured me he did wash his clothes. Sometimes. The jumble was a large wooden chest where guests and residents left their unwanted clothing for others to use. It was always a treasure hunt.

Whenever someone gave Wakil a gift, he'd keep it for a week or so—a month if he really liked it—then give it away. Every year for Wakil's birthday, Rahman and Jelila bought him the same style watch. One year, he had kept the gift for as long as six weeks before giving it to someone else. When I mentioned wanting to buy a boombox so I could listen to the radio in my room, Wakil gave me his.

"Everything I own fits in one bag. You know, in case I need to bugger off some day," he once told me.

Following our sweep through the thrift stores, we stopped at a pub. After Wakil's fourth pint of Guinness, he made a confession.

"I'm not supposed to drink on account of me medication."

"Oh? Maybe you should stop drinking until you're done taking it."

"I'll be taking it for the rest of me life. It's the meningitis," he said, tapping his temple.

"What happens if you drink?"

"I could peg out."

"Meaning you could die?"

"Yeah. I'll just have one more."

He stood to go to the bar. I grabbed his arm and whisked him out the door. If he had pegged out then, it certainly would have gone down as a memorable birthday.

Back at Braemar, a birthday tea party awaited me, complete with the special china reserved for such occasions.

Two teenage girls—one Latif's daughter, the other belonging to Sam Banks—had baked a "fallen angel" food cake. (How had they known it was so fitting for me?) Some people gave me gifts, which was totally unexpected, making it all the more touching. My haul included a woolen scarf, a book about Ibn Arabi, a pair of earrings, and two little pink soaps in the shape of ballerina shoes, which eight-year-old Esmé had picked out herself. Trevor gave me a collection of various scented bath bubbles, which raised a few eyebrows, including my own.

Feeling less of an outsider and more part of the flock, I was growing quite fond of my Braemar family. And especially of Trevor.

CHAPTER 8

Discovering Love

Just six weeks at Braemar felt more like six months, my days were so full. I now had a strong sense of purpose. Animals needed caring for, firewood needed splitting, the garden needed clearing, and trees needed planting. Overall, the estate needed loving, and the students needed unconditional support in their quest for an understanding of the Unity of Existence. Despite all my questions, and my attempts to grasp more of the Course specifics, one thing was clear: I belonged here.

Trevor insisted I drive the tractor at every opportunity to improve my skills at lifting, bucketing, loading, and unloading. I had managed to scrape up several yards of the gravel driveway (would I ever remember to raise the fork lift before driving off?), knock down three fence posts, and destroy an aluminum saw table that someone had left in an inconvenient place. I got plenty of practice reversing the tractor with the trailer attached by moving six trailer loads of scrap wood from the sawmill to the barnyard, where Rafi wanted to burn the scraps in a giant bonfire. I had even more practice when Trevor made me haul it all back to the sawmill, where he wanted to burn it instead. Just when I had had enough tractor practice, Trevor decided to donate the wood for the local celebration of Bonfire

Night, which required hauling it into Creston village.

On November 5, the entire Creston valley—about two hundred people—gathered to celebrate Bonfire Night (a.k.a. Guy Fawkes Day), which is a bit like American Independence Day, but only so far as fireworks and outdoor partying are concerned. In 1605, the Catholic rebel Guy Fawkes set out to assassinate the Protestant King James I by attempting to blow up the English Houses of Parliament. To this day, the British burn Fawkes' effigy to celebrate his failure. Braemar's contributions of scrap wood transformed the local bonfire into a ten-foot-high, teepee-shaped firestorm.

Most Braemarites attended the celebration; however, the students were forbidden to because of their exile from such things. Valley residents, many of them farmers or forestry workers, appeared to be a fecund group, evidenced by the dozens upon dozens of children running among the crowd in the soggy pasture. Trevor's children had also come for the weekend. Everyone oohed and ahhed at the fireworks, while Gustav Holst's "The Planets" blasted from speakers lodged in a second-story window of the hosts' farmhouse. Mulled wine contributed to a lot of tripping over the carved pumpkins and was likely also a contributing factor in the singeing of jackets from the numerous tiki candles. Whisky flowed like, well, like whisky at a Scottish country village affair. Children flitted among the crowd with fistfuls of sparklers, and teenagers tried to conceal flasks of booze in their jackets. To keep warm, everyone—many dressed in flammable synthetic fibers—crowded near the towering inferno, which was helped along with generous splashings of gasoline. (PLEASE, don't try this at home!)

Later, we gathered in the village hall for food and more fun. For the first hour or so, the children glissaded across the polished wooden floor, while the adults sat on the sidelines drinking, smoking, and visiting with neighbors. A massive game of Musical Chairs left some of the younger partyers in tears. Eventually, the sporadic crying was drowned out by music and Scottish country dancing, accompanied by a three-piece band of local farmers.

Trevor wanted to get his children to bed, so he didn't stay for the dance. Daisy and Brian were disappointed because they wanted to stay up late and party. I was disappointed because I wanted to swing and twirl and dosie-do with their father. Yes, somewhere between pounding fencing staples and slinging chicken poo, I was growing quite fond of Trevor. As far as I could tell, the attraction was mutual. He sometimes brought me a small bouquet of flowers scavenged from what remained in the garden from summer. From time to time, he'd leave a box of chocolates or gummy candies outside my door. (I didn't have the heart to tell him I couldn't stand gummy candies.) Sometimes he would look at me and smile just a little longer than acceptably normal after relaying instructions about how to properly spread compost.

For the time being, however, any openly expressed affection on my part was directed at my feathered charges. The only problem with loving the winged creatures at utilitarian Braemar was that they were eventually destined for the table. When the time came to dispatch the chosen ones, my role was to capture them. As execution day drew near, I tried bargaining with Trevor for the lives of certain chickens and ducks. In particular, I wanted to spare "Skippy," a young cockerel with deformed feet. (Advice to would-be keepers who raise animals for food: Don't name them!) The other chickens picked on Skippy, and Trevor wanted to get rid of him so he wouldn't pass on his "imperfect genes" and "pollute" the flock.

In an effort to poke holes in his reasoning, at lunch the day before the slaughter, I said to Trevor: "I'm nearsighted and therefore imperfect. Why don't you just chop my head off?"

"I'll consider it," he said.

A better argument was needed: "He can't compete with the big cockerels, so he'll never get a chance to fertilize eggs anyway."

"He could sneak in and get a leg over while the other cockerels were preoccupied," Trevor said.

"The hens won't let Skippy near them!"

"Ah, but you don't know the male chicken psyche." Trevor tapped his temple with his index finger. "Where there are hormones, there's a way."

"You're not killing him," I said.

Soon, several of us at the communal table were pleading for the lives of other favorites; the vegetarians for all the birds. Outnumbered, Trevor grew exasperated.

"Okay, but just Skippy! Tomorrow, I don't want you saying, 'Oh, please, spare this one, and this one, and this one.' Is that clear?"

I promised, and by teatime that afternoon, I had persuaded him to add a dozen more birds to the "spared" list.

On the morning of my first bird cull at Braemar, I entered each chicken coop to capture, one by one, the hens and cockerels that Trevor had selected for the larder. They were calm in my arms, until I handed them over to the axman, at which point they seemed to sense their fate and began squawking frantically. Those students who could stomach it plucked the birds behind the garden shed, which looked like a pillow-making factory by morning's end. Silent contemplation replaced the usual friendly banter during the chore. In all, we sacrificed ten chickens, four geese, and six turkeys for that year's cull. Most of the ducks were too small and not worth the effort, a fact I pointed out to Trevor in the ducks' defense. I accepted my Judas role as part of an omnivorous existence and farm living.

As our attraction for each other grew, so did Trevor's and my desire to get away from Braemar now and again. Sometimes a getaway was simply picking up supplies in town, then stopping to search for treasures in the ubiquitous thrift shops. Other times, getaways were more adventurous: a long drive through the country and a stop at a tiny chapel on the moors, or the odd village museum, or a modest castle ruin. Even an outing to the local supermarket cafeteria for tea and scones was a treat sometimes. Occasionally, we would attend a lecture by the local chapter of the Geographical Society.

Trevor started calling me "love" more often and doling out frequent hugs. He had a sincere desire to see to my outdoor comforts too. He bought me new boots, specialized for chainsawing in wet climates. The bright orange steel-toed Wellington-type clodhoppers matched the bright orange fleece jacket and bright orange waterproof chainsawing gloves he also bought for me. Nothing says *love* like chainsaw gear.

One unusually sunny morning, we drove an hour to the North Sea, passing through the Borders' market towns and across undulating pastures sliced by rippling streams. On the way, we stopped at a tiny Norman church, a lone sentinel to Britain's ancient Christian roots, holding its own in a bleak vale below the road. We ambled through the eroding cemetery among long-forgotten folk; names once carved sharply in granite now dull and lichen-covered.

At the coastal town of Seahouses, England, we enjoyed lobster bisque and fish and chips at a posh pub overlooking the water.

"Thanks for suggesting this," I said.

"Thank you for appreciating it. I enjoy seeing you so pleased and shall make it my goal to see that you're happy."

Wow, what a romantic! I stared at this new person

in front of me, dressed in jeans and a plaid wool shirt, instead of his usual sage-colored cable-knit sweater, combat fatigue trousers, and waterproofs. He sure did clean up nicely.

After lunch, we strolled along a coastal path to a fortress ruin, bracing ourselves against the brisk wind. Trevor subtly reached for my hand as we walked, surprising and delighting me. Later, we drove to Lindisfarne Isle across the sand- and seaweed-covered causeway to the abbey ruins. Here, I learned about St. Cuthbert, a seventh-century monk who at one time had been the Bishop of Lindisfarne. I would learn more about him in months to come.

Crossing back to the mainland before the tide rose, we headed back to Braemar as the sun was setting. Trevor dropped me off at the big house in time for supper. He never ate supper at the big house, preferring to retire to the seclusion of his cottage in the evenings.

"I had a really lovely time. Thanks for sharing it with me," he said.

I lingered for a few seconds in case he leaned in for a kiss. When none came, I got out of his Peugeot sedan and watched him drive back toward the Gate Lodge. Maybe someday I would be going back there with him, I thought.

With each passing day, Trevor gradually grew more affectionate, and I let him set the pace. He seemed to want to move slowly, which was fine with me. My approach to relationships had always been cautious, preferring to make sure the other party was keen also, in order to avoid embarrassing myself over misinterpreted cues. Besides, I was more concerned with how a budding romance between us would be viewed by the Braemar community, although I later learned it wasn't a big deal. It happened a lot.

Work ground on, and we turned our attention toward longer-term projects, like developing the tree nursery to prepare for the spring tree planting, which was still five months away. We also tried making things more fun. As we unrolled four giant straw bales across the nursery's bare ground to smother the weeds, we buried each other in the straw. And now that I was an expert at reversing the tractor and trailer, Trevor taught me how to scoop and dump with the tractor bucket. We hauled tractor-trailer-loads of topsoil from the barn to the tree nursery. Eventually, the soil would be shaped into giant blocks to temporarily hold tree seedlings. He also taught me how to round up our neighbor's sheep when I forgot to close the gate after scooping and dumping dirt.

The neighbors' sheep were a constant bother. Nine rams were forever finding weak spots in Braemar's fence and munching tree seedlings that had been planted that previous spring. As soon as we'd patch one weak spot, the sheep found another one. Another group of lambs regularly slipped through the fence wires and made for the garden. After rounding up the truants a half-dozen times, I developed a great respect for sheep dogs, to say nothing of an appreciation for good fencing. The spectacle of trying to herd three lambs, which would scatter just before we succeeded at getting them back into their pasture, must have been comical to witness. It usually took three or four attempts. The fencing was Braemar's, so it was our responsibility to keep the sheep out rather than the farmers' to keep them in (the law of the land in Scotland).

Chasing animals always called for a hot bath. Actually, working on the estate in general always called for a hot bath. In my never-ending quest for the perfect one, I gave Wakil's bath in the Steading Bothy another try. Wakil shared the separated Steading rooms with one of the students, Jerusha and daughter, Nikki. My previous bath attempt was a bust because of cold water (which had led to our pub experience followed by the romp on the moors at night with Trevor, when I lost one of my favorite earrings). This time Wakil promised that the water was hot because neither he nor his Bothy mates had used any hot water since that morning. When all I could milk from the taps was barely lukewarm water, I returned to the main Steading and endured the scalding mist of the shower room, then shivered under my bed covers until supper.

After complaining to Trevor about my cold bath experiences, he offered his in the Gate Lodge. The bath bubbles he gave me for my birthday would finally come in handy. It was also my first good look at Trevor's home, a cute, yet worn, place with a large sitting room and closet-size kitchen on the ground floor, and a bathroom and two tiny bedrooms on the second floor. I wondered whether his ploy was to see whether I'd emerge naked from his bathtub. Maybe he was waiting for some signal from me? But I didn't have the nerve, and he remained a perfect gentleman, staying downstairs while I bathed.

The only problem with the divinely hot Gate Lodge bath was having to return to my cold room afterward, which is why I shrieked with joy when Rafi told me the Steading was going to have a brand new oil-burning boiler in December. No more harvesting firewood! No more suffering the one-hundred-year-old wood stove Beast! Even better, Trevor had talked to Principal Latif about my warmth issues, and Latif agreed to let me move into another room in the Steading. Room 5 was being renovated, and new insulation had already been installed. All it needed was paint, carpet, and lighting. The deal was I had to help finish the job.

On the Steading's upper floor, Room 5 had a steeply peaked ceiling and walls only four feet high. Rough-hewn wooden beams pocked with bug holes stretched across the ceiling and down the walls. One small window at floor level in the corner overlooked the Steading yard. A skylight provided additional light. Trevor and I took advantage of a rainy afternoon to paint my new digs. We drove into town to buy white paint. Just as I finished applying the first coat, Rafi came by to see how we were doing. Not well, apparently. He scolded me for getting the wrong brand of paint. Trevor had gone to get another brush, so I was left holding the forbidden can.

"We thought you'd be pleased because it was on sale, twenty quid cheaper," I said.

"You're not saving anything if the paint is crap. You must go back into town and buy Dulux brand, eggshell white."

He was touchy because the big jenny had crashed four times that week. And it had just crashed at lunchtime that day.

Oddly, the jennys often crashed during lunch. The dining room lights would go out and suddenly everyone would be dead quiet, making more pronounced the sound of Rafi's fork and knife clanking on his plate and the shoving of his chair away from the table to get up and take care of it. Minutes later, the lights would flicker on, and Rafi would return, lobster-faced and pleading:

"Please, I must beg you. Stop using electric heaters. If you have one in your room, you mustn't use it. These take a tremendous toll on the generators."

Electric heaters? I thought no such thing existed at Braemar. So after he had mentioned it, I sidled up to him while he washed the lunch dishes.

"Can you grant me an exception to the electric heater rule?"

He stopped scrubbing a plate to glower at me, which I interpreted to mean no.

"I'd prefer electric to that deadly gas thingy you brought me a few weeks ago."

I knew I was pushing his buttons, but I hoped he might

bend. He plunged a stack of plates into the sink, sending soap bubbles aloft.

"If I catch anyone with an electric heater, they'll be hooked up to a treadmill and forced to supply the electricity themselves," Rafi snapped.

"At least I'd be warm."

I finished painting my new room (with the sanctioned paint) alone because Rafi needed Trevor's help with some heavy-duty job (probably dumping the generators over the hill into the river). The next day, Trevor and I installed the floor underlayment and the carpet. The carpet had been salvaged from some office building somewhere, and a Braemarite had stored it in the hay barn for future use. Because the neighbor's sheep also had access to the barn, we had to carefully pick through the poo-covered scraps in search of the cleanest ones. None was big enough to cover the entire room, so we pieced them together. Growing up in a cash-strapped frugal family had prepared me well— along with my dumpster-diving college days—for Braemar life.

After three hours of fitting, cutting, tacking, and gluing carpet, Trevor and I grew dizzy and lightheaded. He half-leaned, half-sat on a table in the room. I turned to face him. We looked at each other; I took a step closer. He reached out, took my hands in his, and gently pulled me toward him for a kiss. There amid the toxic fumes and darkening late afternoon sky, we kissed again and again. It was divine! Would this budding relationship fulfill one of my reasons for leaving Montana? Time would tell. For now, it felt right. Later, we agreed to keep up a charade in front of others of being only work companions just to keep it simple.

The next day I drove Trevor's car to Eltondean to shop for luxury essentials to transform my new room into a homey retreat. Most needs were met in a deceptively sprawling department store tucked away off the High Street near the bus stop. The store, another throwback to 1950s Britain, was more like a museum than a shop. On the dusty shelves, mousetraps mingled with hair curlers, Wellington boots, and wind-up egg timers. I bought candle sticks, a cotton print cloth to cover the overstuffed chair, and a faux antique Asian-style vase with an arrangement of dried flowers. I also bought an electric kettle in blatant defiance of the Geneva Convention on Electrical Items Prohibited at Braemar. When I returned with the contraband, Rafi was in my room doing some last-minute adjustments to the radiator and hooking up the overhead light. So I had to wait until after dark to smuggle the kettle in. Rafi tested the light, which worked, and then he climbed up the ladder to hang the Japanese lantern shade over the bare bulb.

"There you go. Quite lovely. You should be happy now."

He climbed down the ladder, and I switched the light back on. At that very same moment, in the big house, one of the students had just switched on the old-fashioned hot press to iron the linen table cloths. It wasn't yet 4:30 p.m., the time when Rafi switched power from the little jenny to the big jenny to carry the heavy load of evening lights and other energy-sucking appliances—like old-fashioned hot presses. The little jenny did its usual tailspin thing, the light in my room went out, and Rafi stomped off to the generator shed, leaving me in the dark.

Eventually, this room would be perfect. And now I had someone whom I hoped to share an occasional overnight with.

Chapter 9

Grumbling

The trouble with volunteering at a place where something always needs doing, and you are in charge of setting your own work hours, is that it clouds your judgment. Whether you have something to prove, are motivated by a martyr-like sense of duty, or are just plain stubborn, you never stop doing things, ignoring all the warning signs that you are overwhelmed. Some Braemarites seemed to know their limits and abided by them, guilt-free. Others (ahem) had to learn.

Each day for me usually began with helping lay the table for breakfast, then continued with physical labor outdoors, ending around 9:30 p.m., when I helped clean up after supper. Then I would go to bed exhausted, and typically slept well. But I was always tired.

"You had better start pacing yourself," the office manager, Hadiyya, warned one day.

I had been complaining to her about my growing resentment directed at a few of the staff who rarely raised a hand to wash so much as a tea cup. I wasn't the only member of staff who had begun griping. Everyone had something to say about somebody else's annoying behavior or habits. We each sought allies to bitch to about others' shortcomings: control freak personalities, forthrightness, pious scolding,

physical ailments, too much drinking, not enough partic-
ipating. Some were even annoyed by Rahman's perpetual
cheeriness. From talk around the chicken shed, the usually
merry students were also beginning to show signs of wear.
Such was communal living.

Trevor, too, warned against my being one of the last
ones standing night after night.

"But the work will never get done if we don't all pitch
in," I said.

"It'll never get done, full stop," he emphasized.

Being well attuned to prevailing moods, Principal
Latif chose the subject for each morning staff meeting
based on the issues he was observing. Overwhelm came
up frequently.

"What is service?" he asked us one morning.

Dead silence.

"Any ideas?" Latif said.

We stared at our feet. He paused several long minutes
before speaking again.

"Does no one have anything to say?"

Finally, one of the staff found the courage to answer.

"Serving others is serving God."

Latif elaborated: "Our focus should be on service to
God. And we do that by serving others."

Exactly. Which is one reason I couldn't stop myself
from working so hard. At the time, I had taken Latif's
message to mean that we all had to pitch in. Although that
might have been part of it, in retrospect, I think he had
meant that grumbling wasn't going to solve our issues.
Grumbling would infect the students, too, if we weren't
careful. And, it was clear, our mission was to serve them
while they contemplated the nature of their spirits. That's
not to say that the students were the only ones learning.
As Latif frequently reminded us, we were all students, all
learning, as long as we walked the Earth.

Where the estate was concerned, it seemed, the harder Trevor and I worked, the more there was to do. In my mind, it was down to inefficiency. Part of the problem was financial. For example, Braemar couldn't afford to buy a leaf-sucking contraption for the riding lawn mower, so we had to pick up leaves the old-fashioned way. There was a certain charm in hand-raking two acres of leaves under the mature canopy of beech and oak trees on the grounds of a Georgian manor house. The charm quickly waned, though, when a relentless wind from the moors scattered dozens of carefully raked piles before we could pick them up. Poof! A week's worth of back-breaking work undone overnight.

At times I believed that inefficiency was supposed to be teaching me a lesson. After dragging sodden bags of kitchen waste from the house to the compost bins outside the garden, a one-hundred-yard trip, Trevor appeared and asked why I hadn't loaded the bags into the tractor trailer and driven them to the compost bins instead. This from the man who insisted on hefting million-ton bales of straw before thinking to ask the farmer to help with his machinery. And so the Braemar Order, I learned, also involved learning to pay attention to things like this.

Trevor's inefficiency-buster was to strategically place tools all over the estate. When we needed a shovel by the chicken field, for example, it was handy to get it from the nearby grain shed instead of walking a quarter mile to the garden shed. But it had its downside too. More than once, I had opened the grain shed door to fetch feed for the chickens and had to jump out of the way before a cascade of shovel, pickaxe, sledge hammer, and iron bar crashed down on my feet. And his tool-placement strategy didn't always work. Inevitably, when we needed the fencing pliers for a job near the garden, one of us had to walk a half-mile round trip to the sawmill to retrieve the pliers, which we had left there the previous day because we thought we'd be returning the next day to that particular job. Alas, we were usually consumed with a completely different task in a completely different part of the estate, which defeated the purpose of leaving tools lying around everywhere. Not to mention, we could never remember which jobs we had been working on the day before. Was the pickaxe at the sawmill or in the grain shed? Answer: It was always in the place you looked last. By the time you found your tool, it was time to break for lunch.

Another more personal challenge was spending all day, every day, working with the person you had just started a relationship with. When it came to priorities and methods, Trevor and I were, as the Brits would say, chalk and cheese (in Americanese: oil and water). Sometimes we separately attended to whatever we each thought more important. For me that might mean fixing a broken chicken coop door. For Trevor it usually meant prepping the garden in autumn so we could begin planting crops in February. Yes, *February.* I didn't believe it either until I later witnessed its value. (In Montana you can't plant many vegetables until late June, after the last frost.) His other priority remained waging war on moles. What began as a few homesteaders on the front lawn had reached mole metropolis proportions by mid-November. Despite all his efforts to stop them, he had managed to catch just one in a trap.

The drainage problem by the garden shed was the object of our first blowup. The mud wallow was forever devouring wheelbarrows, the tractor wheels, and occasionally boots if you stepped in the wrong place. Fixing it would mean no more wasted time digging out whatever had gotten stuck. The plan was to drain the swampy area, which was fed by rainwater pouring from the hill above the garden. We dug a French drain by hand but had to contract someone else with the necessary large machinery to help build up the gravel track as a water barrier.

We waited two weeks until Contractor Guy could come. When the day arrived, I never thought I could get so excited by large machinery. Finally, our drainage problem would be solved! However, his backhoe was the size of something you'd use to dig holes for a backyard jungle gym. It would take him potentially forever to do our big job. To make things worse, Trevor decided to loan Contractor Guy to Rafi's cause: digging a large hole behind the Steading to house the fuel tank that would replace The Beast. Contractor Guy would be occupied digging the fuel tank hole for the rest of the day. He'd have to come back another time to work on the garden swamp. Later, I cornered Trevor in the garden shed about this change of plans.

"I've been waiting weeks for this guy, and you loan him to Rafi without even asking me!"

His eyes darted from side to side, as if determining which exit door was closest. I decided to throw in additional complaints about the inefficient way we worked.

"I thought you'd be happy. We're digging the hole for the new fuel tank. You'll be warmer in your room," Trevor said.

He was right, but it didn't make me feel better. I wanted to drain the swamp.

A good walk usually calmed my soul, and Braemar's network of tracks and paths circling the estate was the perfect balm. The main track coursed through woodlands, pastures, clearcuts, and emerging thickets of aspen and willow. Several side paths presented peaceful diversions. During my first explorations with William back in September I had felt so lost. Now, I knew intimately each section of the estate. About halfway around the main track, in the Knowe Hill clearcut, was a tree stump, the perfect spot to sit and admire the view across the narrow valley. Latif's message about service came to mind. Yes, fixing the garden swamp would largely benefit two people, while a new Steading heat supply would serve more people. Maybe coming to Braemar wasn't about me. Maybe I was here to serve a larger purpose? Not that a new fuel tank was part of some cosmic order, but a small-scale representation of what it meant to think beyond one's own needs.

It was nearly teatime, so I walked back up the hill toward the big house. Latif was coming toward me down the hill with his arthritic yellow Labrador. He stopped, his gray eyes seeming to penetrate my soul. I said hello.

"How are you getting along?" he asked.

"Good. I enjoy being here," I said, mustering as much sincerity as I could.

He said nothing, a remarkably good tactic for drawing feelings out of a person.

"I work a little too hard sometimes," I confessed.

"Mm. Well, we're certainly pleased you came."

He smiled, nodded, and walked on, leaving me to wonder what he knew about my present emotional state and general level of frustration. And about mine and Trevor's relationship.

The next morning, Trevor approached me gingerly in the garden shed, extending his arm and gently touching my shoulder. We hugged, and I buried my face in his cable-knit sweater, flecked in sawdust and smelling faintly of two-stroke oil. We apologized to each other for the previous day's flap over Contractor Guy.

He invited me to the Gate Lodge after supper. I slipped out during the washing up, hoping no one would notice. I had forgotten my flashlight, so I literally had to feel my way up the driveway by tapping a foot in front of me before taking each step. Thinking I knew where the driveway curved, I stumbled in the shallow ditch on the verge and fell into a mossy tree stump. I picked myself up and carried on, only to twist my ankle in a pothole farther along. In daylight, the walk to the Gate Lodge took about three minutes. In the pitch dark, it seemed an eternity. Finally, the glow of light from behind the little cottage's windows came into view.

Trevor and I cuddled in front of the wood stove in the sitting room.

"Do you ever get lonely here?" I asked.

"I have a ghost to keep me company."

"Oh? How do you know it's a ghost?"

"Just a feeling I get. Maybe somebody who used to live here once."

On cue, the windows rattled.

"Sometimes it just feels like a dark cloud looming over my bed."

If he was trying to persuade me to stay, he wasn't doing a very good job. Later, flashlight in hand, he walked me back to the Steading. The clouds had parted, and we stopped at the chicken field to gaze at the star-pocked sky.

"For both your sakes, I hope your ghost gets out to enjoy the view," I said.

As we passed by the generator shed, we heard the big jenny sputter and die. Lights in the big house and Steading went dark. Rafi would be emerging soon from his caravan to work his magic on the blasted thing. God only knew what that entailed, but he (Rafi, not God—or maybe both) always got the jennys working again. A lesser man than Rafi would have given up and left months ago.

I was no longer using my hair dryer as an alternative heat source and had only used my new electric kettle twice (neither crashed the jenny). Nevertheless, Rafi was convinced an electricity-sucking appliance lurked under every bed, and that at any given time somebody, somewhere, was using one. Yet, the jennys crashed mostly during mealtimes when we were all gathered in the dining room behaving ourselves.

It was easy to recognize when he'd spent long hours in the generator shed praying to the churlish gods of voltage. He gave himself away by the homicidal look on his face and the way he snapped, "Are the lights turned out in your room?" when you asked him to pass the salad at dinner. Attempting levity, I once replied, "Well, the generator isn't working right now, so I imagine my lights are out." He hadn't found it funny.

Knowing people were still using electric heaters, Rafi went hunting for them, rounding up the illicit items and sequestering them in an undisclosed location in the Steading. While looking for a new lamp for my room one day, I stumbled across the coveted creatures held hostage behind an obscure door outside of Room 2. The captives' coiled veins were cold with dormant electrons; their cords wound around them like rope to prevent their escape. For a moment, I was tempted to nab one, but resisted.

A few nights after my discovery, I tried to persuade Rafi to willingly relinquish just one to me, as a special case. No way, he said, but he admitted that the radiator in my room was too small. He said he would install a second one. I asked if in the meantime he could bring me back the old gas heater for another try.

"I suppose the Steading is drafty enough that gas wouldn't have a chance to build up and kill me," I said.

"Don't be silly. I keep telling you it's propane."

That meant nothing to me.

"Well at least if I die, I'll know whom to blame."

"You can't have it anyway because I gave it to someone else. Besides, if you can sit still in a drafty studio naked for two hours, I daresay you can put on a few more layers to stay warm in your room," he jibed.

"What's this?" Bridget, one of the students, asked. We

had been washing the supper dishes.

"Naked?" students Mike and Jerusha said in unison.

"For the sake of art. And a little bit of money," I said.

"Hmm, interesting," Bridget said.

"What is?" David asked, coming into the servery with a tray of dirty water glasses.

"Sarah's taking her clothes off for money," Mike said.

"You sure do have all the fun," David said.

Sure I did.

CHAPTER 10

Little Lambs

To be a child at Braemar would certainly have been worth giving up my entire GI Joe and Hot Wheels collections for. Acre after acre of woodland and pasture, creeks and ponds, gardens and grounds all ripe for exploring, collecting frog spawn, finding treasures, and burying dead birds and other poor creatures stumbled upon. Though full of adventure, my childhood had been suburban. Mom never knew my whereabouts; the only requirement was to show up for supper on time. If Braemar had been my kingdom, Mom wouldn't have seen me for days, possibly weeks. I could have foraged for my own food.

While I was there, five resident children lived at Braemar. Principal Latif's oldest daughter was fifteen and lived with her mother during the week in the valley but lived at Braemar on weekends. Matea was her five-year-old half-sister and Latif's youngest child. The other children included siblings Esmé, aged nine, Colin, aged five, and Libby, aged eighteen months. They were children of two people on staff. Nine-year-old Nikki was the daughter of student Jerusha.

Evidence of the children lay scattered around the grounds: trikes and wagons, balls and Hula Hoops, and toy trucks and baby doll prams littered the Steading courtyard. Mini wellies in bright colors and tiny coats were often carelessly tossed on the floor of the boot hall in the big house on weekends, the only days the children were allowed inside the big house. Forts of varying sizes and configurations made of scrap wood or downed tree branches were found farther afield in trees and below trees. A non-permanent fort periodically appeared near the big house and was made of old bed sheets draped over the unusual drooping limbs of a giant horse chestnut tree. The kids called it the spider tree because of the way its lower limbs spread from its base like spider's legs. The kids sometimes invited me inside their "castle" for "tea." I was the only adult allowed inside, or so they said. One particular time, I accepted their invitation (anything was better than weeding the surrounding border gardens). Crawling inside for some make-believe refreshment, I was surprised, and delighted, to discover that the little scoundrels had nicked some chocolate cookies from the big house. Together we scarfed down their dirty little secret.

For someone who never wanted kids of her own, I never understood why they found me so irresistible. It appeared I had set an early precedent with Nikki. Despite having an American mother, Nikki spoke almost no English when she first arrived from Israel. She struggled to learn English while attending the local village school, where the farm children's thick Scottish Borders accents challenged even native English speakers. One day, Nikki shyly approached me in the garden, pointing at the last of our Little Shop of Horrors nasturtiums that I'd been ripping from the ground. She indicated that she wanted to help. We loaded the weeds in the wheelbarrow and took them to the burn pile outside the garden wall. On each return trip, I pushed her in the empty wheelbarrow up and down the mucky garden path (making them even muckier and later getting a stern rebuke from Trevor). Her giggles turned into full belly laughs, as she clung tightly to the rocking wheelbarrow's sides.

When dusk fell, it was time to bribe the geese and ducks into their pens with a bucket of grain. This was shortly after my arrival at Braemar, and the birds were only just getting used to me and used to being put away at night after their lax summer schedule. I showed Nikki how to hide behind the garden wall because the birds were especially wary of children. Just as the waterfowl waddled in from the lake, Esmé, Colin, and Matea arrived, looking for Nikki. Esmé was pushing Libby in a large pram across the muddy lawn.

"Can we help?" she shouted.

The birds did an about-face, fleeing back to the lake in a chorus of quacks, honks, and flapping wings. Before I could scold all creatures feathered and non-feathered, Matea's mother called from the adjacent garden cottage, and the children retreated to their respective homes. I tried coaxing the birds back, but they weren't taking any chances.

At supper that evening I sat next to Jerusha.

"Nikki couldn't stop talking about the fun she had with you today."

"Pulling weeds?"

"Whatever you did, she's really come out of her shell. Coming to Scotland has been a difficult transition for her. Tonight she was a different person. Thank you."

From that point on, I was the prize quarry at Saturday and Sunday lunch, the only regular meals the children ate in the big house. As soon as I entered the dining room, Matea, Esmé, and Nikki would rush to grab my hands, or cling tightly to my arms and insist I sit next to one of them. Their devotion was endearing, and they were all too cute for their own good, but I didn't always have the mental stamina to indulge their constant questions and chatter.

Matea and Esmé would begin fighting over me. When Trevor's children, Brian and Daisy, visited every other weekend, they took precedence. After all, I was their dad's girlfriend now. Occasionally one wailing soul—one who didn't get the coveted seat—would have to be removed from the dining room. Sometimes I deliberately arrived late for meals to avoid the trouble.

My company was also in hot demand outdoors on weekend afternoons and during school holidays. So they wouldn't disrupt the students and peace of the indoors, the children weren't allowed in the big house without an adult, and not in the Steading at all except in the nursery room. They often waited outside one of the Steading doors, pouncing on me as I emerged and insisting on "helping" with any work I was doing. They seemed to have special sensors that could detect me from anywhere. As soon as I would step outside the Steading or the big house, their war cry would echo throughout the grounds:

"Saaaaarrrrraaaahhhhh, wait for uuuusssss!"

It wasn't enough to just say hello.

"We want you to spend the whole rest of the entire day with us," Matea once made clear.

Occasionally, I would indulge them by examining whatever treasures they had uncovered, including dead birds and other deceased creatures. ("You just have to see it. It's got bugs and everything!") Once they saw a "scary animal" in the woods and insisted I investigate. The three girls clung to my jacket as I dragged them along in search of the beast of the moors.

"I'm not afraid," Colin said, casually bringing up the rear.

The "scary animal" turned out to be a stray calico that had been fighting Ruby, one of our resident cats, and stealing her food. The children wanted to put out a bowl of milk for the stray, tame her, and teach her to be nice to

Ruby. Before I could object, they ran off to get some milk.

They loved to tag along when I fed the chickens their afternoon grain. That is, until one of the cockerels began attacking them whenever they entered the chicken field. The cockerel's sudden aggressive behavior was a mystery, but it came in handy whenever I wanted to ditch the kids. All I had to do was excuse myself to the chicken field on pretend business.

The ruse was short-lived. After the offending cockerel also attacked me one day, Trevor dispatched it and took it to the kitchen for that night's soup. In another Orwellian moment, later that same afternoon, a second cockerel attacked me. Had we killed the wrong one? The second cockerel also ended up in the soup pot, leaving us with a sole surviving male, whom we named Rambo.

If the chickens weren't friendly to the kids, at least their grain bin provided some fun. It was just big enough to hold a half-ton of barley and four children. I caught them playing in it one afternoon, taking turns burying one another up to the neck, pretending to be trapped in desert sands. They coughed and laughed in the rising dust. I humored them for a few minutes then told them to get out before they all got lung cancer.

For all the times I had ditched the children, the karma was repaid one evening at an art show at the studio where I had modeled nude. Just about every one of the Braemar staff attended, as well as many area Braemarites and the whole of the Borders arterati—about a hundred people in all. Imagine my surprise when I saw a colored chalk drawing of my unclad self, framed and hanging on the wall. The asking price was four-hundred-fifty pounds. All I got was twenty-five pounds to freeze my keister off. It had occurred to me while sitting for that portrait that the public might see an artist's version of me one day. But at the time, I didn't actually know anybody in the area. Now my list of friends and acquaintances had swelled by the dozens.

The not-so-modest drawing had been hung on the top floor at the back of the studio. Surely most people wouldn't see it. If they did see it, surely they wouldn't notice the simple title (my name), or they might think the naked woman just *looked* like me. I hoped that if they did know it was me, by the time they reached that point in the gallery, the wine would have gone to their heads, and they would have forgotten all about it by the next morning. All scenarios became irrelevant when Esmé and Matea breezed down the open staircase, which overlooked a large room, and announced their discovery to the entire gallery.

"Sarah, we saw your naked drawing, and it looks just like you!"

Several people turned to look at me, asked where they might find the likeness, and under the careful guidance of two little pipsqueaks, were led directly to it. Not exactly how I had imagined my fifteen minutes of fame, but I guess it did say something for the artist's skills. Trevor was impressed but short on cash, otherwise, he said, he would have bought it. (If it ever did sell, and the buyer is reading this, I hope you got your money's worth.)

My interactions with children didn't end at Braemar's borders. One day I visited the Creston Village School to talk to the class of fourteen about trees. The idea was to prepare them for a little project planting seedlings along Braemar's main drive in honor of National Tree Week. Trevor suggested I take the lead since I was "so good with children."

The school had only one classroom for ages five through eight. I brought a tree tube and a seedling for show-and-tell. The children were duly unimpressed. Unbeknownst to me, every single one of them knew all about having to plant tree seedlings in the protective plastic sleeves to prevent deer and rabbits from eating them. Many had planted trees on their own farms or had dads that worked for the Forestry Commission in Glenmeade Forest at the end of the valley road. Duh.

Surely I could dazzle them with my knowledge of photosynthesis instead. When I asked who could tell me what that big word meant, ten hands shot into the air. I picked the youngest looking one, hoping to trip him up. The little smarty pants began reciting the whole process, even throwing in some minute details I had long since forgotten, like how the process creates energy by splitting hydrogen and oxygen atoms. I couldn't shut him up. I flopped my hands in my lap with exaggerated annoyance (although I truly was annoyed that he seemed to know more than me, who has a forestry degree!).

"I don't know why I bothered to come today. You already know everything."

They laughed. Then, in true grade-school form, they began raising their hands to tell me more. Only this time we veered away from trees into off-topic anecdotes about their babysitters, siblings, dad's bunions, and how one of them had seen a badger.

Because my visit was at the end of the day, I had driven the Land Rover to the school in order to bring the Braemar kids back with me, saving a parent the trip. Esmé, always the boss, sat in the front seat and begged to help drive. A week earlier I had let her sit on my lap in the tractor and steer us down the drive and back. Six times.

"Please? My dad lets me drive sometimes," she said on our way back from the school.

"Yeah, right," I said.

"He lets me steer."

Normally I wouldn't allow a nine-year-old to operate a half-ton, ten-passenger motor vehicle on hilly, winding roads. But since this was the middle of the country, what harm could it do? At first, I let her steer, but after thirty yards of veering too close to the verge of the narrow road, which dropped off steeply to the creek below, I let her shift gears instead. She was quite proud to shift from second to first when we slowed down to take the turn into Braemar.

When we drove slowly up to the big house, Principal Latif was standing by the back door, waiting to use the Land Rover. I smiled and waved. He returned with a half-wave of his own and a puzzled expression. That's when I glanced in the rearview mirror and saw Colin swinging like a commando between the side windows from a piece of nylon webbing that he had hooked over a bar across the back door. I parked, and the kids hopped out.

"Colin, it's best to stay belted in your seat when we're driving," I said.

He looked at me like I'd just spoken Egyptian and ran off. In the meantime, Esmé was talking excitedly to Latif. "First I steered, then she let me shift gears."

"Hmm, wow," Latif said. He turned to me and smiled. "May I have the keys, please?"

I was never asked to pick up the kids from school again, but I did get kudos for organizing the valley school children to plant trees. The next morning they arrived in a little bus, and our own adult students each chaperoned two kids in the task. They were so eager, they planted fifty saplings in two hours, plus tubed and staked them. Which is more than I could say for Trevor, who suddenly realized he had to fix a fence on the far side of the estate that morning. He reappeared only after all the children had gone home.

Two photographers from local newspapers also came to record the event. When it was over, we scraped two inches of mud off little wellies and packed our underage workers off to the Steading nursery for cocoa and biscuits. While they tucked into their goodies, many talked about how they had named their planted trees (three of them after me).

I was exhausted, and it was only just lunchtime. But not just any lunch. American Thanksgiving, which, thankfully, had crossed the pond to Braemar. All the trimmings were present, except the cooks had underestimated the popularity of stuffing. I had made four pumpkin pies the day before from scratch. Unlike the other school children, the Braemar kids didn't have to return to the classroom that day. Both Matea and Esmé got to sit next to me at the Thanksgiving meal, one on each side, for which they were truly grateful. Me, I was just thankful to be so loved.

CHAPTER 11

Shepherding

As our relationship progressed, Trevor and I took a day off a week to explore the countryside, the Borders towns, and abbey ruins. During occasional trips to Edinburgh, we poked around shops, cafés, bookstores, museums, and galleries. Off campus, we held hands and stole occasional public smooches. At Braemar, we pretended our relationship was purely professional, though most everyone knew otherwise. A few nights a week, I would slip out after supper and stumble my way to the Gate Lodge in the dark (always forgetting that dang flashlight). Not only did I have to sneak out after supper, I would also have to sneak back to the big house for breakfast in the morning. We always tried to walk into the dining room separately just to keep up the charade.

Trevor would have the wood stove well stoked whenever I arrived, and we'd snuggle on the couch to watch TV or a video rented from town. Inevitably, the Gate Lodge generator would crash at the most exciting part of the film, and Trevor would have to trudge up the short hillock out back, following the oft-trod muddy path, to get it going again. He would return smelling of diesel and muttering obscenities under his breath.

Though we enjoyed ourselves during our down time,

working together didn't get any easier. Our differing priorities and approaches rarely meshed. Our eventual downfall began in the cheese and meat aisle at the Safeway grocery store in Eltondean one Saturday morning. Amid the cheddar and minced lamb, we ran into an old acquaintance of Trevor's. Cecily and her husband, Tom, lived on a big farm about thirty miles away. Cecily told us that they had started a new venture raising rare livestock breeds for the organic food market. They had White Park cattle, Dutch Bantam chickens, and Soay sheep. I was familiar with Soays because there had been a small band of them on the red deer park where I worked in England eleven years earlier for six months (a break from college). I mentioned this to both Cecily and Trevor.

"Aren't they lovely things? Would you like to have ours?" she said.

"You don't want them?" Trevor asked.

"It's just that we . . . well, we need to get rid of them for now."

I told her we didn't have anywhere to keep them. What I really wanted to say was that not only would Hell have to host the Winter Olympics before I ever adopted Soay sheep again, but pigs would have to grow wings, mules would have to talk, and all of this would have to take place over my rotting carcass.

Soays are native to a Hebridean Island of the same name off the northwest coast of Scotland. Supposedly, they are the species from which all domestic sheep are descended. Only thigh-high when fully grown, and with little horns, they look more like goats than sheep. They are also so crafty that not even blue-ribbon sheep dogs can herd them, making them extremely difficult to manage. And they're smart. Sometimes animals with brains are a bad thing.

Cecily said she'd sell all seven ewes to us for only

twenty-five pounds. Trevor said he'd have to clear it with Principal Latif first. I repeated that we didn't have anywhere to keep them. Trevor ignored me.

"I'm certain it won't be a problem," he said to Cecily, then turned to me. "My assistant, here, would be pleased to look after them."

"We don't have anywhere to keep them," I said a third time.

"We can put them in the chicken field."

"What little fencing the chicken field does have is a poor excuse for an enclosure," I said.

I began to explain that the Soays we had had in England were in a pasture with a six-foot-high electrified fence. Trevor interrupted me.

"Twenty-five quid for the whole lot?" he confirmed with Cecily.

"Yes, that's what we paid for them at auction."

"Sounds reasonable," Trevor said.

"Why are you getting rid of them?" I asked.

"Could you collect them at Loch Farm as soon as possible?" Cecily asked Trevor, ignoring my question.

"I don't think Latif is going to go for this," I said.

"I'll talk to the Braemar Principal and give you a ring," Trevor said to Cecily.

Her face lit up. "Wonderful! I know they'll be going to a good home!"

"We can't take care of them," I said.

"Sarah loves animals," Trevor said, smiling at me.

"Oh, and these sheep are so lovely," Cecily cooed. "I do hate to see them go."

"So why *are* you getting rid of them?" I asked again.

"We just need to sort out a little fencing problem." She looked at her watch. "Must dash. I'm so pleased! I'll wait to hear from you."

And with that, she fled.

"Raising sheep will be a fun little project for you," Trevor said.

Because, of course, we didn't have enough fun little projects.

"What will we do with them?" I asked.

"We could eventually use them for meat, once we have a little flock going."

"I'd rather have moles," I said.

Trevor scowled. "You'll love them."

"We're not getting Soays."

"Let's just see what Latif says."

Confident Latif would say no, I left it at that.

Latif said yes, agreeing with Trevor that twenty-five pounds was a steal.

The following Saturday Trevor, his children, and I drove in the Land Rover to Loch Farm, near the Cheviot Hills, hauling a borrowed horse trailer. Cecily and I waited outside with Brian and Daisy, while Tom and Trevor wrestled the ewes in the steel-sheet barn. Much banging and muffled swearing came from inside before each of the men emerged carrying a wriggling wooly package. The routine was repeated until all seven had been nabbed and shoved into the horse trailer. Cecily was tearful as the last of her little babies was captured.

"I do hate to see them go, but I know my darlings are in good hands," she sniffled.

Looking a bit bashed around, all Tom had to say was, "Good luck."

On the drive home, Brian and Daisy were delighted with Daddy's new flock.

"Can we name them?" Daisy asked.

"Course you can, darling. You can name them whatever you like."

"Me too?" Brian asked.

"Course you can, my son."

"I'm calling the one that's a bit whitish Snowy," Daisy said.

"Aw, don't you think that's a lovely name, Sarah?" Trevor said.

"Lovely. Are you going to take care of them, too, Daisy?"

"Yeah!"

"Me too!" Brian added.

Sure they would.

Back at Braemar we had to temporarily hold the Soays in one of the duck pens until we could upgrade the chicken field fence. We could drive the horse trailer only within fifty yards of the duck pen, which meant having to carry the beasties the rest of the way. But first they had to be captured. Again.

The horse trailer was partitioned into two levels. The sheep were on the lower level, which was only about four feet high. Trevor wasn't small enough to crawl under it, so I was elected. The "adorable" fleecy monsters ran from one end of the trailer to the other, while I lunged at them, on my knees, in six inches of straw, soaked with sheep poo. I nearly lost an eyeball from their sweet little horns, cursing a certain estate manager to the fiery depths of Hell, along with seven of the Devil's hoofed agents. One by one, I caught each ewe and wrestled her to the trailer door, where Trevor grabbed them and carried them to the duck pen.

"That's Snowy! You caught Snowy!" Daisy squealed. "And that one I'm calling Ginger because it's gingery," she said of the next.

It wasn't long before the rest of the wee rascals picked up the activity on their radars and joined us. Brian, Daisy, Matea, Colin, Nikki, and Esmé all watched as our terrified new arrivals bounded around the small enclosure looking for an escape route.

"Let's call that one Biscuit," Esmé said.

"No, she's called Shadow," Daisy said.

"I think we should call it Roundy because she has a round tummy," Matea said.

"Roundy?" Daisy and Esmé said in unison.

Soon, a few of the staff wandered down to the pens to check out the fuss. One suggested naming them after Scottish isles, while another suggested wildflowers.

"I'm going to call them a mistake," I said, thoroughly annoyed, knowing this was the extent of anyone's input, and I alone would be looking after them.

Once inside the pen, the Soays formed a tight group and darted around the perimeter. I liked the suggestion of Scottish Isles and decided on Iona, Islay, Isabelle, Flora, Kilda, Skye, and Morag (Mo for short). The latter wasn't an isle, but Morag seemed to fit. She was the most wary and the obvious ringleader. When she bolted, the others followed close at her kicking heels. She was larger and leaner than the others, with notable chutzpah. If they were to be tamed, it was clear I would have to win Mo's trust first. I didn't know how to do that, since I didn't exactly have the patience of Jane Goodall nor endless hours to sit with them, hoping they'd get used to me.

That first week, I spent snippets of time every day in the pen with the sheep, speaking quietly to them and strolling around the perimeter. Because they were nervous, I pretended to ignore them, fiddling with the feed bin or the water pan or the fencing. Inquisitive creatures, they followed me at a safe distance, sniffing where I had just bent down to pull on the fence wire or shift the feed bin. After a few days, Isabel and Iona came close enough to sniff the alfalfa pellets in my hand. By day five, all of the ewes, except Mo, were cautiously eating out of my hand. Isabel even let me scratch her ears from arm's length. Whenever Mo got edgy, she leapt into the air, and the others scurried away.

We had to worm them, which meant I had to catch them. Again. Even though they were eating from my hand, they wouldn't let me handle them. So, in three inches of mucky straw, I lunged at them while they ran circles around me. All the trust I had engendered in the fleecy beasts that week went down the drain. They would not soon forget me as the lady who tackles them. Trevor enjoyed watching, especially when I missed one and splatted on my belly.

"You'd make a better rugby player than some of the lads on the England team."

I took that as a compliment, wishing I had a pro athlete's salary to go along with this job.

Eventually, I managed to catch them one at a time. Trevor restrained them, while students Mike and David, and staff member Derrick, force-fed the ewes their worming pills. Their eyes glistened with fright as they gagged on the tablets. But they got them down and were soon prancing about again.

When not playing the sheep whisperer, I spent hours in the chicken field assessing and repairing the fence in preparation for moving the Soays there. With the help of the students, we patched holes, shored up sagging wires and leaning posts, and erected a new partition fence across the middle, giving the Soays a half-acre plot to share with the poultry. After a week, Trevor declared the fence good to go and suggested we move the sheep as soon as possible. But I wasn't convinced. The chicken field fence still had small holes, which the sheep could make larger by poking at them. The fence also wasn't high enough.

"How much longer is this fencing project of yours going to take?" Trevor asked.

I knelt in the mushy grass and twisted the ends of a wire mesh bandage around the smooth host wire. One end punctured my fingertip, adding another wound to my scabbed hands.

"Until we patch the last hole. And it wouldn't hurt to add more barbed wire at the top," I suggested.

"They're sheep, not kangaroos," Trevor said.

"If I'm going to look after them, I want this fence Soay-proof."

"But I need you and the students for other things. You can't spend the whole time on fencing."

"Then I'll finish it on my own tomorrow."

Just then a fence staple popped off, and a section of barbed wire sprang from the rotting post, bouncing to a sag. "Or the day after that," I amended.

So I worked alone for another day in the gusty winds and occasional horizontal sleet. My arms ached from pounding fencing staples; my hands were swollen from accidentally pounding a finger here and there while pounding staples. I hadn't wanted these blasted sheep, and there were plenty of other things to tend to. Still, I convinced myself, I was working outside in Scotland, not sitting behind a desk in Montana. The weather and the work enlivened me even if both were challenging. And now that we had the sheep, I was determined to see they got due care.

After ten days of my working on the fence, Trevor insisted it was good enough. I was certain it was still too low in places.

"I know sheep. I've worked with sheep for years, and there is no way they can get over this fence," Trevor declared.

For a few minutes we argued about the acrobatic abilities of Soays. He didn't think they would feel the need to jump the fence as long as there was enough grass to eat on their side. He had a point, and I reluctantly agreed to move the sheep the next morning. But my resentment over buying them in the first place was growing.

The next day we had to catch the Soays to move them. Again. With Mike and David's help, we rounded them up and bunged them into the back of an old work jeep. Inside, the ewes clamored at the windows in search of an escape as we drove them into the chicken field. The second we opened the back door, Mo leapt out like a ballet dancer flying through the air. The others followed, and soon they were all scampering around their new digs. Within a few minutes they settled down to eat grass, contented. The chickens and turkeys regarded their new field mates with skepticism.

Several days later, new holes began appearing in the fence. One day, while pouring a bucket of barley into the feed troughs for the chickens' afternoon snack, I saw Mo pawing at the fence. The other Soays came running toward me, scattering the chickens out of the way to scarf the grain. I set the bucket down and inspected Mo's obsession. It appeared the Soays had been plotting their escape for some time. I found a dozen more small holes that hadn't been there days earlier; not big enough for a Soay to escape yet, but they would be soon enough.

Trevor thought I was being ridiculous. We argued about whether patching the weaker spots and the new holes was worth the effort. When it became clear neither of us was going to persuade the other toward our respective viewpoint, we avoided each other for two days.

We weren't alone with troubles. By the end of November, the students had hit what Hadiyya, the office manager, called the "pre-midcourse blues." It occurred when certain aspects of the Course dredged up fears and heated debates about the nature of God. Tensions among the staff were also getting worse. There was little chatter during meals, and the silence at morning coffee and afternoon tea was deafening. Squabbles erupted over inconsequential things, like someone putting out the wrong towels for a guest, and others hogging the laundry room washers. Rafi was still routinely snapping at everyone for abusing the electricity rules, and the housekeeper complained about the quality of the bread, which sent Wakil, the bread baker and kitchen helper, to his room for two days on a whisky bender. The cook was then shorthanded in the kitchen, which meant another staff member—despite her bad back—had to help cook until Wakil was ordered back to work. Others had borrowed tools from the workshop, forgetting to return them, which not only angered Rafi, but also Adam—one of the Course teachers—who had decided to try his hand at carpentry. The daily staff meetings grew more excruciating too.

"Silence again?" Principal Latif commented one morning.

He studied each face, going around the circle of chairs and trying to capture a pair of eyes, all of which were fixed somewhere other than on Latif. When the meeting was over, most people couldn't leave fast enough. I sat in my chair another minute, hoping Trevor would approach me to talk, but he was the first one out the door. I followed Wakil to the kitchen. Usually he could cheer me up.

"What's for lunch today, Wakky?"

"Whatever I bloody well put on the table," he snapped.

He grabbed a fifteen-gallon stainless steel pot and slammed it on the stovetop. I turned and hurried downstairs to the boot hall. I put on all my outdoor gear, grabbed a pair of soggy work gloves from the radiator where they were supposed to be drying, and ran outside to find Trevor. We needed to call a truce.

He emerged from the grain shed, shovel in hand, ignoring me as I approached.

"Can we talk?" I said.

He paused. "Let's go to the garden shed."

We walked in silence to the garden, and in the dank

and private confines of the little building we hugged each other tightly, agreeing that our communication skills, and the sheep fence, needed more work. There would be much patching up to do—on both counts.

The next day, we woke to a valley suffocated in fog so thick that visibility was only about ten feet. Our world had suddenly gone eerily quiet, except for the crunch of gravel underfoot as people walked to and from the Steading and the big house. You could hear the footsteps several seconds before seeing the person who was making them. Latif decided to implement a silent day, which was ironic because nobody was speaking to anybody anyway. Making it official, however, had an amazingly transformative effect. Our swaddling in a cloud of stillness and silence kept us focused on what was only directly in front of us, literally and figuratively. In front of me was the chance to remember why I had come here. It wasn't to get caught up in complaint and anger because people, and animals, weren't behaving the way I wanted them to. I had left home to pursue something different. Braemar did me one better by offering the opportunity to know, and practice being, my better self. I definitely got the different. But I was slow to catch on to the rest. The act of doing was so ingrained in me, and I was clueless about the art of being. I liked the work at Braemar only because it felt satisfying to put in a good day's labor toward a common purpose—that being of service to my new-found community of friends. Also, just living a different life in Scotland was still more desirable than what I had had before. But unseen forces continued to seep into my soul.

* * *

Part of the Six Month Course included a two-week pilgrimage to Turkey timed to coincide with the anniversary of the poet Rumi's death in mid-December around the year 1273. I was invited to join the students on the trip, along with some of the staff and other global Braemarites. During morning meetings leading up to the journey, Latif talked exclusively about preparing ourselves for the journey to saints' tombs and other sites of spiritual significance, both Muslim and Christian. Conversation both in and outside the meetings picked up. Everywhere there was chatter about it, and the staff reminisced about their past trips. Wakil, Rafi, and Hadiyya were excited for me, claiming the adventure would not only solidify the Course's study topics for the students, but also help me better understand some of the Course concepts and the Muslim saints whose works were read at Braemar.

To help "prepare our hearts for the trip," as Latif put it, one evening everyone gathered in the Mead Hall to watch a 1973 video called "Turning." Filmed mostly in Turkey, the story traced the evolution of spirituality up through Rumi's day, culminating with Sufi mysticism. After the film was over, the students appeared moved by it. I didn't know what to think, or feel. The message was too esoteric for me to pull together, and it made me realize that the students and I no longer shared the same unknow-ingness that we had when the Course first started. I was beginning to feel isolated. The students were moving on without me.

I began to wonder whether I should even go to Turkey. What could I possibly learn by visiting the tombs of Muslim saints? Initial doubts and fears about the "Islam thing" began to resurface. I took my concerns to Hadiyya. She told me not worry.

"Remember that great Sufis, like Rumi, lived in the realm of the heart. They transcended religious boundaries by keeping their faces turned toward God. That's what the video is about."

I would try to heed her words.

CHAPTER 12

Abandoning "Mr." God

We landed in Turkey in the evening during a cold rain. The crush of civilization ushered us from a retreat of relative calm to a loud metropolis of honking, impatient drivers and zipping throngs of people crowding the streets. The students hadn't left the confines of Braemar for ten weeks. But if our arrival unnerved them, they didn't show it. It did unnerve me, and I realized how much I had grown used to the quiet sanctity of Braemar.

The next morning we ferried across the Golden Horn to visit the tomb of Hudai Aziz Mahmut Effendi, a sixteenth-century saint and follower of Ibn Arabi. Hudai was also one of Turkey's most celebrated Sufis.

We removed our shoes outside the plain cinderblock building—we women covered our heads with scarves—then joined dozens of other people in the packed space inside. About the size of a tennis court, the tomb was divided into two separate rooms. At the head of the main room, Hudai's sarcophagus was behind a wrought-iron fence. Eight other sarcophagi formed a row in front of Hudai, each painted in bright colors. Some sported fiberglass turbans, comically large, like something you would see at a carnival. One woman not from our group ran from one sarcophagus to the next, throwing herself at each one and grasping the turbans while she wailed, shrieked, and swooned. I wondered about her suffering and hoped God would relieve it. With less flourish, the Braemar students approached Hudai's sarcophagus. Principal Latif invited me to come forward to pay respects, but I declined, already feeling out of place.

From the tomb we headed to the 1,400-year-old Hagia Sophia, built to honor the goddess of wisdom. This nod to the feminine had been absent from my own religious upbringing, not to mention my 1970s upbringing in general. My memories of Sunday school stories about women in the Bible were either as handmaids or whores, with few exceptions. God had been co-opted by a masculine-centric world.

We spent the rest of the day visiting a museum and two mosques, where the absence of icons, altars, organ pipes, pews, and pulpits made the space—and me—feel empty. I longed to feel some connection to God, to feel something warming and comforting inside. But I couldn't.

On our second day we visited another Sufi tomb before touching on more familiar ground: a Greek Orthodox church dedicated to the Virgin Mary. Inside, a natural spring channeled water through faucets into basins, from which the nuns invited us to sip. I lit a candle for my foremothers, taking comfort in the familiar icons. In my consideration for the feminine face of God, Mary had suddenly begun to occupy my mind. How little I had known about her, and how sad that, given her role, in the Protestant Church she was more like an addendum, brought out at Christmas then put away with the other ornaments until the following year.

At Chora, a church-turned-mosque-turned-museum, dazzling 1,500-year-old frescoes and mosaics told stories from the Bible. One series featured Mary's life, but our guide didn't know the stories, so he brushed past them in favor of others. Mary, the unsung codicil. The guide really seemed to get into Adam and Eve, though. Eve, the betrayer. Latif gathered our group to talk about the significance of Chora and its religious art. I tried to find a place in the circle so I could hear him, but our group closed in around Latif. When I tried to politely squeeze in, not a soul gave me leave. Though I'm sure the group hadn't intentionally pushed me out, I grew annoyed, feeling excluded by those I had thought were my people.

Our next stop was the cavernous underground Basilica Cistern, which once provided water for much of Istanbul. A sopping, dismal snow had begun to fall, the cold creeping into our bones as we waited for tour tickets. Two girls, about eight years old, caught sight of us foreigners and began hustling their trinkets. The sleet improved their ability to win hearts, and I walked off with pockets jammed full of tissue packets, paying five times the asking price at street stalls.

We were eating lunch at the sprawling Topkapi Palace, once home of great sultans, when the sun finally shone through the parting clouds of sleet. The light lifted my spirits, and I anticipated visiting more mosques, hoping to find something that would move me more deeply. Unfortunately, as I stood in the dead center of these pewless worship houses, my stocking-clad toes digging into the plush Asian carpets, I could not feel God's presence. Instead, the vast austerity made me feel vulnerable, empty. Was it something missing in myself? Visitors silently prayed on their knees, while Braemarites gazed about in awe and wonder. I wanted to feel what they felt. I wanted to experience God everywhere, not just in a church. I approached student David, a recovering Mormon. What did the mosques do for him? He smiled blissfully.

"I love these places."

I confessed my own feelings of emptiness, my inability

to feel God's presence.

"When the student is ready, the teacher will appear," he said.

"No, you don't get it. I feel God's presence in other places, just not in these mosques."

He shrugged. "If you were on the Course, it would make more sense. You won't feel God until you're on the path."

I wanted to slap him. How dare he presume I wasn't on a spiritual path just because it didn't look like his. For someone whom Braemarites had been praising for having grasped the complex esoterica of the Course with unprecedented understanding, he sure offered me no wisdom. But despite my irritation, I had a niggling feeling that maybe he was right.

I asked Jerusha, our Jewish student, how she felt about visiting mosques.

"Like I'm home again. The Christian churches feel uncomfortable to me."

When I asked her why, she simply stated that they were unfamiliar. Maybe that was my problem too.

"What does Latif mean when he talks about the Reality of Realities?" I asked one veteran Braemarite who had joined the trip from his home in England.

"Ahh," he intoned, smiling sublimely and looking heavenward. "The first step in which the absolute is removed from its absoluteness in the process of our knowing."

I stared at him blankly, waiting for further explanation. When none came, I nodded in feigned understanding and walked away. I began asking a few other Christian-raised Braemarites about their experiences in mosques; everyone said that mosques brought them peace, that God's presence was strong, and that I would understand if I took the Course. Something told me Latif would have had more to offer my dilemma, but I lacked the confidence to ask him. He felt unapproachable to me.

After the third mosque, I was ready to return to the hotel. I had developed a crippling migraine, but we made yet a fourth mosque stop. While everyone else went inside, I curled up on the seat of the bus and tried, fruitlessly, to will my headache away. I longed for a good cry in Trevor's arms. Instead, ridiculous thoughts tortured me: God didn't like women. There was no such thing as God-loving bliss. If God is everywhere, in everything, why couldn't I feel it? Something was wrong with me. I'm obviously not on a spiritual path. I wanted to go home, not to Scotland, but to Montana.

When the group finally returned to the bus, everyone was flush with excitement. The imam, they all said, had been a treasure, pleased pink to welcome the group. But a local worshipper had called our group "infidels" because they weren't practicing Muslims. Christians were bad enough, but some in this group were Jews! The imam had defended the Braemarites, exclaiming, *They are lovers of God!* Maybe I would feel God's presence everywhere when I became God's lover. What did that mean, exactly? Did I not love God enough? I didn't even know how.

The next day we ferried across the Marmara Sea to the Asian side of Turkey. The snowcapped mountains in the distance reminded me of Montana. For two days, our stay in Bursa was shrouded in fog, mirroring my spiritual fog. Our tour guide hustled us through Bursa's maze-like marketplace, while I tried to keep up. Suddenly, the entire group disappeared, melting into the ocean of humanity in front of me among the dozens of marketplace alleyways. Which alleyway had they taken? I didn't know where we were going, so I couldn't ask for directions. I didn't even know the name of our hotel! (The first rule of foreign travel: Carry a matchbook or card with the hotel's name on it.) I was lost, not only figuratively but now quite literally.

Panicked, I scurried down each arm of the labyrinthine market looking for the group. Ten minutes later, I spied a familiar purple jacket slipping around a corner and ran to catch up. What would have happened if I hadn't found them? Would anyone have even noticed I was missing? Maybe this was God's way of reminding me to not only pay attention, but that even when we feel lost, we will be given a sign to find our way back.

During some free time later that afternoon, I joined the two older Braemar students, Jill and Diane, to explore the marketplace. As we strolled, Diane admitted she hadn't felt overcome by any of the holy sites. A New Zealand Maori, she was an animist, with no particular affection for, nor negative feelings about, Islam. She just wanted to enjoy Turkey and wasn't concerned with the spiritual purpose of the pilgrimage. She had joined the Course because she wanted to explore other spiritual concepts. Jill, a Quaker, had one foot in each caravan. She welcomed being steeped in Islamic tradition yet was reluctant to pay homage at the saints' tombs, uncertain about some of their teachings. I hadn't been alone after all.

From Bursa, we headed south to the captivating ruins of Pergamum, near the Aegean Sea. As long as we stayed away from the religious places, I found I could enjoy visits to historical sites. Yet, the Virgin Mary still occupied my mind. Soon came time for a pilgrimage to the place believed to be where St. John had brought Mary after the death of Jesus.

Situated on a hillside across the valley from the ancient city of Ephesus, Mary's House stood discreetly among a grove of trees. We packed ourselves into the austere one-room cottage, where candles flickered around the room's perimeter. Some people sat on low wooden benches that faced an altar, while most stood shoulder to shoulder in the cramped space with other groups who had come to visit this early morning. The altar was a simple table adorned only with a statuette of Mary surrounded by flowers. The carved stone statuette, graying with age, stood about two and a half feet tall. Her hands were missing, broken off at the wrists. Mary gazed toward the onlookers, her arms open at her sides, ready to receive. I returned Mary's gaze, wanting to silently pour my heart out to her but at a loss for words. As I stood staring at the statuette, the thought occurred to me that Mary's love was so boundless it couldn't be contained in two small hands. She didn't need them.

Overcome, I began to shake. My body burned from head to toe. Sweat trickled down my sides. I put my hands over my face and sobbed until dizzy. Someone—I never looked up to see who—put an arm around my shoulder and held me. In a moment that transcended time, my understanding of absoluteness, that elusive Reality of Realities, became clear: The enormity and simplicity of God's love is all there is. It isn't packaged in Christianity or Islam or Judaism, nor in a church nor a mosque nor a temple. Being a lover of God is a club to which all are welcome. And God loves us whether we return the affection. Loving God is about loving others. I had a long way to go on the latter.

I stepped outside. The sun glinted through the pines; birds chirruped and twittered. Several white cats hung around Mary's house, scrawny, battle-scarred, and flea-bitten. Yet oddly, none of them begged for food like the feral cats at other tourist sites did. I washed my face in a spring from the mountain, which was piped to a row of marble basins below the house. Jill approached me.

"You're a beautiful person, Sarah."

Her words took me by surprise. I started to cry again, and we embraced. We both agreed that we needed Mary in our lives. A short time later, Latif gathered the group around, and again I was on the outside of the circle. But this time it didn't matter. His soft voice was carried to my ears.

"Mary is a vessel, the ultimate symbol of complete receptivity of God and from whom pours forth perfect and unconditional love," he said.

I understood completely. While the masculine may bring order and discipline, Mary opens her arms and says, "Come." She asks nothing and gives everything. God's chosen vessel accepted me with nothing but welcoming love. It was time to abandon the masculine idea of a punitive, judgmental God and focus on the She of welcoming, unconditional love.

That evening, I sat with David (the one who implied I wasn't a ready student) in the hotel lobby and told him about my experience at Mary's House. Latif joined us halfway through the conversation.

"Was Mary's House moving for you in a good way?" Latif asked.

"Astounding. I feel much lighter," I said.

"I'm pleased to hear it."

"The teacher has arrived," David said.

Praise God the teacher had been a woman: Beloved Mary.

CHAPTER 13

Re-Baptizing

The Sufi poet Jelal ad-Din Rumi referred to the day that he would eventually die as his "marriage with God." That day finally came around what is believed to be December 17, 1273. He was about sixty-six years of age. Rumi lies entombed in a grand mosque in Konya where we were now headed. The exact spot is marked by a conical dome on the mosque, aqua-colored, with blue Iznik tiles surrounding its base.

My epiphany at Mary's House confirmed that my spirit needed wooing back to God more completely, but in my own way, in my own time. I began to crave the sacred feminine, the experience of unconditional acceptance, whoever you are, whatever your path. Rumi understood this, and that is why I loved his poetry.

I had hoped for a quiet moment with Rumi at his tomb, but the Konya mosque heaved with his admirers, including many dignitaries. Every year, television cameras recorded the weeklong celebration of his death, and if ever a tomb could be a happy place, this one certainly buzzed with joy.

Jostled by the throngs, I stood for a few moments in front of the master's sarcophagus. Arabic script in carnival colors whipped up the walls from floor to ceiling, like Jacob's Ladder carrying souls to Heaven on words of praise. The stylized writing seemed to frolic in an electrifying dance of the spirit. The pulsating crowd, euphoric and yearning, gathered in a mix of brown, black, and white skin; long robes and covered heads; short skirts and high heels; designer gowns and diamonds; jeans and tattered kaftans. All gathered to heed Rumi's call:

> *Whoever you may be, come.*
> *Even though you may be*
> *An infidel, pagan, or fire-worshiper, come.*
> *Our brotherhood is not one of despair.*
> *Even though you have broken*
> *Your vows of repentance a hundred times,*
> *come.*

After just a few moments in front of his tomb, I was swept away in the crowd, like a jellyfish on the outgoing tide. Soon, we filed into an indoor sports arena, with hundreds of others, and watched as Rumi's order of whirling dervishes, the Mevlevi, practiced their meditation, called a sema, a symbolic journey of the spirit from Earth back home to God. The dervishes pivoted clockwise on their right feet, heads tilted to the right and arms opened up to each side. Their right hands turned upward to receive blessings from God; their left hands turned downward to bestow blessings on Earth. Black sashes accentuated their long white robes, which ballooned and floated as they spun. Their heads were covered in tall, brown beehive-shaped hats with flat tops. The camelhair hats represented tombstones for the ego, while the white robes were ego's cloak. Each part of the seven-part dance represented the spiritual journey from the ego to union with God. By revolving in the cyclical nature of life, the dervishes not only turned like all things in the universe, they were shaped—molded as on a potter's wheel—spiritually sculpted until their hearts turned toward God.

I recognized some of the metaphors from the video, "Turning," that we had watched at Braemar before the trip. Also, student Jill pointed out that the video featured noted feminine characters: Cybele (Anatolian mother goddess), Puduhepa (Queen of the Hittites), the goddess Diana, and Mary. More about Braemar's raison d'etre had begun to make sense. The roots of its own zikr were embedded in this ancient Sufi form of moving meditation. Zikr, Jill told me later, was the act of remembering God. It was the first clarity I had been given on the matter since I started asking around shortly after arriving at Braemar.

Our two-week pilgrimage was nearly over. I missed Braemar, Trevor, my birds, and even the Soays. We had one final free day in Istanbul, where the weather had warmed and brightened considerably compared with the first week. It seemed like a lifetime ago that we had been there, when I had first felt isolated from the Braemar inner circle. Now more at ease, I accompanied Latif and four others on a shopping expedition to the Grand Bazaar to buy specific items for Braemar: Turkish delight (a jelly candy that I seemed to be the only who despised), special salt, cinnamon sticks and other spices, olives, dried fruits and nuts, Turkish cologne (which Braemarites liked to use before and after zikr), rose water, pocket calendars that included Islamic holy days, framed Arabic calligraphies, and kitchenware.

Like a pro, Latif navigated the market stalls. Sellers hawked everything imaginable, from jewelry, rugs, scarves, shoes, clothing, and pots and pans to bushels of nuts and fruits, ancient books with yellowed pages, knives, chess sets, poultry—living and dead—animal entrails, and textiles. From the rows of unidentifiable spices and medicinal herbs wafted sharp, signature aromas that filled our nostrils and made us sneeze. Everywhere browsers and buyers haggled, chatted, argued, laughed, and hustled. It was a dizzying expo for the senses and thrilling to witness. Latif seemed more relaxed than his usual self. He even joked with us, a side of him I hadn't seen at Braemar.

As the sun set, some of us joined Latif on a ferry across the Golden Horn to stand at the tomb of Hudai, the saint we had visited when we first arrived. The tomb was closed, but we hovered outside the gates and silently contemplated our trip. Breaking our calm reflection, the sound of many imams' voices suddenly crackled from loudspeakers throughout neighborhood mosques, calling the faithful to prayer and marking the end of the first day of Ramadan that year. One or two voices sounded at first, rising to a crescendo in a sea of chanting, all at their own pace and tune yet somehow synchronized. The chorus died down as quickly as it had started and was followed by several flashes of light and booms—fireworks! Dogs barked, and I felt electric, having found some comfort in the land of Muslim saints after all. We took a water taxi back across the Golden Horn. I stood on the upper deck and watched as we approached the lights of European Istanbul, sparkling across the Bosporus. A crescent moon slit the dark tapestry of sky.

One last ritual was in order before we returned to Scotland: a Turkish bath. A few hours in a hamam would surely loosen up my muscles, which had become as pliable as kiln-fired clay from the cold. After hearing stories about scrubbing brushes like floor waxers and masseuses who pummeled you like professional wrestlers, my three companions and I asked our non-English-speaking taxi driver the Turkish word for "gentle." Lots of sign language got our point across, and the driver finally understood our aim, laughed, and delivered a phrase that we speculated meant "ease up, we're wimpy tourists." Unfortunately, the words escaped me when I needed them most.

At the three-hundred-year-old Cagaloglu Hamami, we each chose the assisted scrub from a list of options. The bath area was more like a humid, steamy church; a thirty-foot-high domed ceiling capped a large room and four alcoves, with floor-to-ceiling marble in swirling colors of gray and white. Scalloped marble basins protruded from the walls, each with hot and cold running water. In the center, a monstrous hexagonal slab of marble stood like a sacrificial altar.

The matron motioned for us to remove our towels and rinse our naked bodies. Using shallow copper bowls, we anointed ourselves with water that issued from basins along a wall. The scent of sweet almond soap only slightly masked the dank eau de locker room smell. One by one, at ten minute intervals, our personal scrubbing ladies would enter the room, slip out of their robes, scrub themselves, and then splash a bucket of soapy water on the slab. Each would motion for one of us to come lie down. Karen was first, then Linda, then Lucy. Each successive scrubbing lady seemed to grow in body mass by half-again as much. As I waited my turn, I watched the others. It had the all appearance of furniture being sanded rather than taking care with live bodies. Karen began uttering faint cries of distress.

Then my scrubbing lady entered the room. To say she was large would be like saying the Hagia Sophia was a nice bit of masonry. Accurate, but a tad understated. She had to weigh close to three hundred pounds and wore only a G-string. Linda, who had already reached her first rinse cycle and was sitting next to me by the basins commented.

"This should be interesting for you," she said.

The scrubber's eyes glinted at me. She pointed her sausage-like finger.

"You," she grunted.

I stood and hesitantly approached her and the

sacrificial slab.

"Lie," she growled.

I laid myself on my stomach. Using a thirty-grit loofa sponge, she began scraping off the top three layers of my skin, hitting all the tender spots I could never reach.

"Roll over."

I obeyed, squeezing my eyes shut so I wouldn't have to look at her. After scrubbing my front side, she barked at me to sit. Then she grabbed my right arm and pulled it into her naked breasts, big as pumpkins. My hand was lost in the crevasse of her cleavage. I cringed as this whale of human flesh dragged the loofa up and down my arms.

"You rinse," she said, pointing to the basins.

I stumbled to the wall, fumbled with the copper bowl, and rinsed. Millions of tiny rolls of skin that once made up my epidermis washed down the marble floor into the drain. I took stock of my moles: three still intact, one hanging by a hair, and two gone, saving me the trouble of having them hygienically removed by a doctor.

Thinking that was it, I reveled in the sensation of pouring bowl after bowl of warm water over my head. Then came a chilling, high-pitched voice.

"Heeellllloooo."

My matron was eyeing me like a starving wolf.

"You come."

I reluctantly obeyed, lying down again for round two. When that was finished, she said:

"I rinse, you towel, you leave, I cry," without a hint of tenderness.

She waddled over to one of the basins, her buttocks like Sumo wrestler Siamese twins cleaved by a thong. She commanded me to sit at her feet between her legs. But before I could decline, she grabbed my wrist and pulled me down. She began shampooing my head with all the gentleness of kneading ekmek (Turkish bread) taking care to run her hands over my ears and forcing soap deep into the canals. She wrenched my head backward into her breasts and stroked my face as if rubbing a nasty stain from a carpet.

"Face massage. Good?" she asked.

As I was about to turn as blue as Iznik tile, she stopped and poured enough buckets of hot water over me to drown a fish.

"Okay," she said.

Finally, it was over!

Our scrubbers waited in a line by the door to wave us goodbye and accept tips. The expression on my matron's face, though seemingly pleasant, was not tearful as she had claimed it would be. I shoved a few hundred lira in her hand, which I discovered later was considerably less than my companions' tips. God help her next victim, I thought. Outside, the December night air was strikingly cool. Re-baptized, my new skin tingled, free of the old layers, which were now trickling down the drain into the Bosporus on their way to the azure sea. A new me, a new beginning. If only I could have held onto that feeling.

CHAPTER 14

Celebrating

We Turkey pilgrims returned to the United Kingdom a few days before Christmas. At the airport, I handed over two kilos of olives to student Mike to take back to Braemar, having fulfilled my contribution as a culinary smuggling mule. Dozens of Braemarites would be in Scotland for the holidays, but Trevor and I would be spending Christmas with my friends Ruth and John in Kent. In keeping with our efforts to hide our romance, Trevor and I cordially greeted each other at the airport in front of the others, then waited until we were safely in his car to passionately kiss.

During the drive south, he updated me on the Braemar news:

1. The new Steading fuel tank had been installed.

2. One of the children had stuck some unknown object up her nose and had to be rushed to the doctor. He couldn't find anything and sent her home. The next morning, she found a red bean on her pillow.

3. Two of the staff had a shouting match in

the kitchen one night after supper, subject unknown.

4. The cook had quit without notice but was persuaded to come back the next day.

The Soays had escaped when a gale blew open the chicken field gate, but Trevor had coaxed them back with a bucket of food pellets.

"I hope the Soays behave for Derrick," I said to Trevor on our drive to Kent.

Derrick, one of the staff, would be looking after them while Trevor and I were gone. Trevor patted my knee, assuring me that everything would be fine, that the students would muck out the chicken coops and waterfowl pens, and that I had nothing to worry about.

"Let's just enjoy the holidays and forget about Braemar," he said.

Christmas was blissfully quiet. Since I had been in Turkey during the run-up to the holiday, I had avoided the bombardment of commercialism and the pressure to buy gifts. The experience in Turkey helped me focus on the spirit of Christmas, the real gifts of kindness, love, and forgiveness. The simpleness of spending time with good friends was enough. Ruth and John quizzed Trevor about his intentions toward me before moving on to more important topics, like why England always lost at cricket even though they invented the game. We took walks by the river and enjoyed a few evenings in the pub. I even had my first taste of Christmas pudding—a dense fruit cake doused in brandy and set on fire. Only ours didn't light, so John dumped half a bottle of vodka on it. That lit, and we toasted Russia.

Two days after Christmas, Trevor and I headed back to Scotland. The temperature dropped noticeably as we headed north. When we reached the Scottish Borders five hours later, a layer of wet snow greeted us. While we were away, a Boxing Day gale had blown through Scotland, knocking down power lines and trees. Braemar lost a few large spruces in the surrounding forest, as well as a large chunk off the sawmill roof. The corrugated iron sheets lay scattered among the surrounding trees. Several large tree branches came down near the big house, including one half of a massive ash tree on the edge of the front hill pasture. There was a lot of clearing up to do. But that wasn't all. Most of the students were down with the flu, and many of the chores had never gotten done. Both the chicken coops and the waterfowl pens were a sodden mess of pooey, reeking straw. The new Steading fuel tank didn't seem to make any difference in warming my room, but at least the generators were working. I fished the hair dryer out of my dresser drawer and basked in its glow, half wishing I had stayed in England. Worst, however, was the news Trevor had withheld until the day after returning to Braemar.

"So you know how I said that while you were in Turkey, the Soays escaped into the adjacent field?"

We had intentionally tried to keep the sheep out of that area so they wouldn't eat the tree saplings that had been planted there a few years earlier by another estate manager.

"Yes," I replied, not so eagerly awaiting the rest of the story.

"Well, they made a hole in the fence. And I made it a little bigger for them to get through," Trevor confessed.

"You said the wind blew open the gate."

"And then later they got through a hole," he said.

"Which basically you created," I finished his story.

By this time, everyone at the breakfast table was listening to our conversation.

"Everything's fine. The grass needs grazing down a bit,

and that'll take them months. If they start nibbling on the young trees we'll move them back," Trevor said.

"What if they escape from the tree field into the farmer's pasture?"

"His fence is impenetrable," Trevor said.

One of the students politely interrupted us. "If you're talking about the sheep, Derrick had to put them in the duck pen a few days ago. They kept getting into the farmer's pasture."

At that moment, Derrick was lying in bed with the flu, probably contracted from chasing the sheep in the wind and rain. I glared at Mr. His Fence Is Impenetrable.

"I'll just give the farmer a ring," Trevor said, getting up from the table.

I headed for the lake to say hello to, and scold, my hoofed Houdini headaches. More time mending fences would be in order before tackling the horned beasts—again!—and moving them back to the chicken field.

Later, Trevor relayed the farmer's story of the Great Soay Caper, which involved the Soays' three-day romp through the farmer's pasture and dozens of attempts at rounding them up with his sheep dogs, which at one point had quit chasing the Soays and looked at him in exasperation. Eventually, Farmer John caught the sheep, and he and his son bunged them in the back of a covered pickup truck and drove them back to Braemar.

For the next two days—by myself—I pounded in more fence posts, patched chicken wire, and added two more strands of barbed wire to the lame fence surrounding the chicken field. On day three, I tackled the Soays in the duck pens, struggling to hand each wriggling mass of wool to the students, who carried them a third of a mile to the chicken field. The farm vehicle we used the first time had broken down, and using the Land Rover was out of the question. Surely, the fence was strong enough to hold them now.

So much for the peace of Christmas. Maybe the New Year would bring better days?

Braemar's New Year's Eve feast was nothing short of spectacular. A dedicated group of guests and residents prepared mountains of food. Additional guests swelled our ranks to around seventy, stretching the generators to their limits and costing poor Rafi his peace of mind for the week. The guests uplifted the rapidly fraying attitudes of us staff, and following supper, we celebrated with a traditional Hogmanay (Scottish for "party till your kilt drops"). Braemar's annual talent show took place in the Mead Hall, though talent was clearly optional. People who wanted to could stand in front of the crowd and make a total fool of themselves. I jumped at the chance, reciting a poem I had composed that day in a flash of creativity. It was a light-hearted take on my experience thus far, and was well received with laughter and applause.

For the countdown to midnight, staffer Adam marched into the Mead Hall, followed by four others, who all pounded on copper pots from the kitchen and a couple of hand drums. On their heads they wore the shells of pumpkins. (Some call it performance art.) One guest, a professional musician and DJ, spun some tunes, and we danced until the midnight bell chimed on the mantle clock. Then we gathered in a circle and sang "Auld Lang Syne," followed by more dancing until the early hours of the morning when the steam ran out and the rickety Mead Hall floor began to give just a little too much for comfort.

The evening was a much-needed excuse to forget about gripes and enjoy ourselves. Even Trevor and I agreed to bury the fencing pliers and forget about the sheep for once. I looked forward to more peaceful and cooperative months ahead. Ah, if wishes were sheep, fools would think they could keep them confined.

CHAPTER 15

Getting Fleeced

December had been warmish with more rain than usual. Although the swamp outside the walled garden had lost some of its oomph after we dug a French drain, it continued to feed on Wellington boots, wheelbarrows, and the tractor whenever we forgot to walk or drive around it. The contractor we had hired to fix the problem never returned to finish the job, which became yet another unfulfilled item on the wish list of estate projects. A leak in the garden shed had grown worse, too, so when it rained—eight days out of seven—water coursed down the walls, nourishing a colony of mold while simultaneously eroding our tools.

January brought a reprieve from all the rain, drying things up a bit and freezing most of the ground solid, with the help of persistent, psychoses-inducing winds. In some ways frozen ground was better than boot-sucking mud. We could drive the tractor into more places without it tearing up the ground. In other ways frozen wasn't so good. I began carrying a hand-size sledgehammer to smash the ice in the birds' and Soays' water containers. The garden spigots froze shut, which meant having to stomp through the ice on the lake (in leaky wellies) to fill buckets of water, which I then schlepped to the waterfowl pens to fill their water containers. Though tough, these were jobs I didn't mind because I did it for the animals. Freezing temperatures also didn't favor the already trampled short grass in the chicken field, prompting the Soays to search out more succulent fare in the forbidden neighboring tree patch. Daily. Thus, the opening weeks of the New Year began to feel like the film "Groundhog Day."

Every day, I had to coax the fleecy monsters back to the chicken field with a bucket of food pellets. But I couldn't figure out how they kept escaping. We had patched all the holes. In case they were leaping over the fence, we added another strand of barbed wire at the top. Surely they couldn't jump six feet high. I was right. No sooner had we finished installing the extra line of barbed wire than Mo shamelessly led her followers *under* the fence by pulling at the chicken wire with their hooves to break it. Again, Trevor lobbied for letting them in the tree field to graze down the grass so it wouldn't invade the struggling saplings. When the grass was short enough, and before the Soays started eating the saplings, we'd find a way to properly mend the fence and move them back to the chicken field. He persuaded me, and the arrangement worked, until two weeks later when Walid came to visit Braemar. A former estate manager, he periodically dropped in for a time to help on the estate. It was he who had planted the saplings where the sheep now grazed.

"I don't think it's a good idea to let your sheep in that field," Walid said to me at supper one night. "They're eating my trees."

Actually, they hadn't touched his trees because the grass was so high and succulent. Besides, sheep were primarily grazers and much more interested in more palatable grass than leafless twigs. I told Walid as much.

"You can't let them in that field."

"It was Trevor's idea," I said, trying to shift the blame

on, well, the person whose idea it was.

Surly and blunt, Walid wasn't easy to argue with.

"You're responsible for the sheep, aren't you?"

"Only by default."

"Then you must move them. They can't be in that field."

Trevor wasn't at supper that night to defend me. I thought about the six thousand trees we'd be planting in April and how upset I'd be if sheep ate them.

At breakfast the next morning, I told Trevor about Walid's comments and my plan to really, really, *really* fix the fence this time. We would have to use new materials that Trevor had been saving to fix other fences around the estate and ask Latif for permission to buy more materials. Trevor didn't respond. Communal meals weren't the best times to strike up an argument with your boyfriend, so I waited until we had a chance to talk outside.

Trevor was in the garden digging over one of the plots when I repeated my plan. He moved a few feet away from me then jammed his spade into the wet clay.

"I took Walid's heat for your letting the sheep in his tree field, you know," I said.

Trevor grabbed a wheelbarrow full of muck and pushed it to the other end of the garden plot. He dumped the manure, which splat on the ground. He stuck a pitchfork into the soggy pile of horse crap and began spreading it.

"We're spending too much time on these nuisance Soays and the bleedin' fence," he said.

He pushed the wheelbarrow toward the manure pile outside the garden wall. I hurried to catch up with his long strides.

"WE?" I raised my voice.

He loaded the wheelbarrow with more horse apples. Eventually, he spoke.

"I've washed my hands of it."

"Well that's funny, because so have I. But obviously it needs more work, so why don't we solve the problem together instead of huffing around like a couple of angst-ridden Pontius Pilates?"

"I have other problems to worry about," he said.

"This isn't a problem?"

"They're your sheep."

Had I been wielding the pitchfork at the moment, Trevor would have found it lodged in his belly. I reminded him whose idea it was to buy them. He didn't respond. After a long pause, I spoke.

"What are these other problems?"

"Well for one, the farmer's sheep are still getting into our patch and eating living trees. We need to find those spots and fix them."

"So, I'm supposed to help you fix another fence to keep someone else's sheep out, but you won't help me fix a fence to keep our sheep in?"

"Look," he said, resting an elbow on the pitchfork handle, "we can't spend all of our time on these Soays. I need you and the students in the garden and greenhouse."

Reluctantly, I agreed to help him with his fencing project. For two days we put up what seemed like eight thousand miles of wire. Our anger at each other enabled us to pound staples with fierce precision. The only sound was the knocking of hammers and the swish-swish of waterproof outerwear as we moved along the row of posts, not speaking.

For the next couple of days, I thought about how to approach my latest fencing plan to confine the Soays, waiting for Trevor's offer of help. In the meantime, mole hills continued to crop up on the billiard table front lawn, giving him another war to fight. His offer to help with my sheep fence never came, so I went to Principal Latif instead.

After explaining the problem, Latif granted permission to use Trevor's new fence materials to fix the Soay fence. He told me not to worry about the money, that Braemar would find the funds to buy whatever materials we needed. He asked how I was getting along and how living at Braemar suited me. I lied and said everything was great. He also informed me that a woman from Spain would be arriving soon to work on the estate. He didn't know any other details about her, like whether she spoke English or knew anything about moles and sheep.

The next day, students Mike and David, and I began the fencing-project-to-end-all-fencing-projects. It wasn't long before Trevor stomped up the chicken field, asserted his managerial self, and ordered me to stop. I asserted my insubordinate assistant self and told him Latif had approved everything. Trevor scowled and walked away. What was a fed-up reluctant-shepherdess girlfriend to do? That evening after supper I went to Hadiyya's room to ask for advice. As the person who worked in the office, she was in touch with the heartbeat of the place, knew all the gossip, and also served as a good shoulder to cry on.

"You're looking for God in a man. You expect perfection," she said.

I tried defending myself.

"Trevor's disorganized, jumbled priorities drive me bonkers. I want to work efficiently, to do things the right way, but he just crashes along, quick and dirty, consequences be damned. We're forever chasing after miscellaneous projects that we never finish, and he doesn't want to finish the ones that are important."

"And who decides what's important?" she said.

"It appears he does, but we're supposed to be a team," I said.

"No, I mean how do either of you know what's *really*

important?"

"What do you mean?"

"You expect things to be the way you see them. His methods might not seem practical to you, but they make sense to him."

"Nothing about him makes sense to me," I said.

She got up from her chair and plucked a book from the shelf. It was a thin copy of Ibn Arabi translations called "Kernel of the Kernel." She thumbed through the pages for a particular passage and began reading.

"The power of God is constantly and permanently in a state of perfection. Because of this perfection, He does not reveal himself twice to the same person in the same manner. He is constantly in new revelations, and just as it has not happened up to now, so the same revelation may not ever happen to two different people."

She closed the book and handed it to me.

"So you see, how can God, who's constantly changing within each person in a unique way, manifest the same way in two different people? What's revealed to him as important, his approach to work or life, is different than what God reveals to you as important, as the right way, as you put it."

She added that my nafs (my ego) was the real problem.

"When you change your opinion of and reaction to how things are, you begin to see perfection in things *as* they are, not as how you *want* them to be," she said.

Agreed, but how would accepting that there were multiple "perfect" ways to do things lessen my workload, which was killing me? Trevor's approach perfectly—inevitably—increased my work.

"What is the real work? Building fences? Chopping wood? Or is it something altogether different?" Hadiyya asked.

I began to see where she was going with this, but

before I could respond, she continued.

"The point of work at Braemar is not to get a job done, although that can be the goal. The real objective is to pay attention to where your mind and heart are while you're doing your work. And even after you've figured that out, there's still this thing called life."

Essentially, she was describing a Zen Buddhist saying I had heard years earlier:

Before enlightenment, chop wood, carry water.
After enlightenment, chop wood, carry water.

In other words, regardless of whether we reach some greater understanding of ourselves and the world, we still have human needs to fulfill. And that means work in all senses of the word.

"How can you truly be of service to anyone, let alone yourself, if you're filled with anger while mending fences? And angry at the person who burdened you with sheep?"

Hadiyya prompted me to think more deeply. The real work is in the details of the mind. How do we choose to approach the work of life? With resentment, joy, drudgery, anger, fun? Lightness, heaviness, excitement, fear, boredom, annoyance? The awareness and thoughts we bring to our work is the hub on which personal experience turns. I was only just beginning to explore this.

Hadiyya hit on something else, too. It wasn't about getting the work done "right" or "efficiently." These were relative terms and could mean different things to different people. For example, if I needed to learn patience (ahem) maybe the most efficient way would be to experience situations that tested my patience. If I wasn't paying attention, Trevor's approach would seem inefficient to me. If instead I approached my work with him in a more mindful way, my experience would become an opportunity to learn patience. For his part, Trevor might need to learn how to wisely use time (in my humble opinion). So a mindful experience for him might result in the realization that I wasn't so much a nitpicking nag as a lesson in wise use of time. Yes, in an ideal world of personal illumination and paying attention. But that wasn't our chosen reality.

When Trevor and I finally did speak to each other three days later, it was to break up. Though we agreed it would be better for our working relationship, I was gutted. He seemed more at ease about it. I was headed to my room in the Steading for a good cry when I took a detour to Wakil's room. He was lying in bed with a cup of tea after spending the morning baking bread and helping prepare lunch.

"Oh hiya, come sit down," he patted the bed, and I rushed to curl up in a fetal position next to him.

"I hear there's trouble at mill," he said. His vernacular always made me smile, despite the circumstances.

"We broke up."

"Yeah, he told me he was thinking 'bout chuckin' ya. Says he's tired of your whingeing. You're better off without him." Wakil said casually.

"Do you have any idea why I whinge?" I said.

"Yeah, he's a bugger to work with," Wakil said. "And from what he tells me, so are you."

He might not have been able to charm the pants off a girl, but you couldn't fault Wakil for his honesty. So much for my newfound wisdom of taking a different approach to my expectation of others.

"Cheer up. It'll all work out in the end," Wakil said.

That evening I doodled in my journal a fake ad for the local paper:

> *For Sale: Seven darling Soay sheep to a good*
> *any home; must be able to remain calm in*
> *a crisis, have oodles of patience, and access*
> *to an ample supply of Valium or similar*
> *drug; experience with delinquent teenagers*

helpful, as is exceptional relationship with significant other who can provide undying support and ability to admit defeat; must have understanding neighbors and a large field with an impenetrable fence (6-foot-high, 4-inch-thick, electrified steel sheeting is best). Enquiries to the former shepherd-ess, Braemar House, Creston valley.

In my next life I wanted to return as a Soay sheep and spend my days eating grass where I pleased.

Chapter 16

Stumbling Along the Way

During some days it seemed that January would never end. In addition to the cold, the relentless rain seeped into our souls. The few moments when the sun did make brief appearances were limited to between ten in the morning and two in the afternoon. Three days of nonstop rain draped us in absolute sheets of water, pretty much halting any estate work, save one: digging trenches to help carry away the water.

The local health department made a surprise visit to test Braemar's water and discovered too much *E. coli*. Until we could install a filtration system, we were ordered to boil water for all consumptive use. Our water system consisted of a natural spring up on the moors, which was piped above ground into an honest-to-god ceramic kitchen sink buried up to its rim at the bottom of a hill. From the sink, the water drained into a buried pipe, which led to a huge underground storage reservoir. It then flowed across the moors and down to Braemar through more than a half-mile of Victorian-era iron pipes. Because of heavy rains that winter, the water had been streaming directly off the hill into the kitchen sink, mixing with the fresh spring water. The hill was covered in sheep poop, the source of the *E. coli*. As a temporary solution, three of us battled forty-mile-an-hour winds and horizontal rain to dig a foot-deep trench around the sink, plus another ten-foot-length of trench in the rocky ground to take the runoff from the hill far away from the sink.

In addition, other estate problems continued. Rafi's battle with the generators had been made worse by visiting Braemar board members, and my room was even more desperately chilly. Having discovered Rafi's hiding place for the banned electric heaters a couple of months ago, I decided to liberate one. When Rafi discovered it in my room during his Thursday rounds to empty trash bins, he confiscated it. We argued about my need for heat, until he finally relented, and brought back the old propane heater for me, which he had to take from the other person he had given it to. After trying it out—and realizing that it wasn't going to kill me in my sleep—I regretted having made all the fuss back in October. Every night, I would turn it on before heading for the big house for supper. My room would be so toasty when I returned that I had to change into a T-shirt and shorts.

A warmer room began to improve my life somewhat; however, Trevor actively avoided me, and I was given to bouts of crying because of it. I wanted to talk, but he was as cold as a dead Soay, and as distant as my dreams of a sheep-proof fence. For several days I gave up completing my latest idea for the fencing project, and the sheep just escaped daily. Walid had left, which meant no more pestering me about his precious patch of saplings. So who cared? The sheep were happy, and I didn't have to deal with them, although I knew the wooly home-wreckers would shake me down eventually.

To give Trevor time away from me, I started working in the office a few days a week, preparing for the spring tree planting. Hadiyya was good company, and she helped me design the volunteer invitations to send to a select group of 350 people on Braemar's mailing list. What was the best way to appeal to volunteers to bust their butts in the freezing rain in exchange for a hot meal and a dormitory room? Hadiyya assured me they would come; they had before. Who wouldn't want to slog in the mud and sleet putting leafless twigs in a waterlogged hole so that their grandchildren could appreciate the someday forest?

Former estate manager William's meticulous notes from the previous year described the preparations needed: buying the tree tubes and stakes to tie them to; ordering the seedlings from local nurseries; reserving the army tent, tables, and chairs from the local Boy Scouts as a mess hall for volunteers; and hiring a backhoe contractor to dig starter-holes in the areas where we would plant. Per the Braemar board of directors, we would also have to do something about the now precariously leaning sawmill. They didn't want inquisitive tree planters tempted to go inside and potentially get hurt. Trevor and I would have to fence it off or tear it down. The latter seemed extreme, and sad. One more job to add to the list.

While working in the office one day, I had come across the to-do list that Trevor and I had created a few months earlier. Unceremoniously, I scratched off a couple of projects we had actually managed to finish: build a new goose pen, clean and organize the garden shed and lean-to, and move the chicken coops to a different part of the chicken field. At least thirty other items remained unfinished or not started. I began to feel sentimental about the "good old days" of never-ending chores, Trevor and I working side by side, and arguing about the best way to do something.

The students, too, were being put through their soul-searching paces. They began developing skin rashes from the constant dishwashing and the four-times-daily personal abluting. Their studies grew more intense as they grappled with more challenging topics about God's will and intentions toward mankind. And the staff returned to feeling as gloomy as the weather.

What Braemar needed was fresh blood; visitors always seemed to perk us up. Ahava was just what the psychologist ordered. A twenty-something lady from Israel, Ahava had taken the Nine Day Course the previous summer and would now join the Six Month Course, even though it was halfway finished. Her cheery disposition was more welcomed than a spring flower, and jeez, could that woman work! She inspired us all with her strength, enthusiasm, and joie de vivre.

Another visitor arrived as well, the woman from Spain, whom Latif had told me about several weeks earlier. She would work on the estate with Trevor and me full time. Finally, the end of January began looking brighter. When Latif first told me about Louisa, he had no idea whether she spoke English. Since Trevor was still avoiding me as much as possible, as long as one of my coworkers would talk to me, whatever language she spoke didn't matter.

I fetched Louisa in the Land Rover at the bus station in Eltondean, quickly discovering the answer to our question about her English skills: nada. No one else spoke Spanish except for me, and by "speak," I mean I could say "please," "thank you," and "Where are the boys?" That last phrase a college friend had taught me just in case it came in handy one day. The day I met Louisa wasn't that day, but for lack of anything else to dazzle her with, I tried "Dónde están los muchachos" anyway. She responded with knitted brow, probably thinking I was disappointed that she wasn't a guy. I quickly changed the subject.

Luckily, I had primed myself for Louisa's arrival by buying a Spanish phrasebook and dictionary at the local W.H. Smith store and cramming all week for my debut conversation. The problem with learning a few foreign phrases and pronouncing them well is that your conversational partner thinks you're fluent and starts carrying on as if you understand the language. Only after she asks where you're from, and you respond in her language with "I have a sheep's head with much beer," does she realize she's misjudged your comprehension skills.

Still not fully grasping Spanish by dinnertime, I introduced Louisa to some of the others by saying, "Su nombre es huevos"—her name is eggs. In my defense, Rashid had made omelets for supper. I tried to correct myself. "Te amo"—meaning I love you—which Louisa probably thought a bit forward on our first date. She looked at me and giggled.

"Louisa, Louisa!" I finally said. "Her name is Louisa!"

"Me llamo Louisa," she corrected politely, grinning.

Now that I wasn't spending my evenings at the Gate Lodge, I would have ample time to learn a new language.

Like Ahava, Louisa was an eager worker, jumping right in on her first day to help us finish the Soay Prison Project, which I had recently found new enthusiasm for. In no time she was chortling with students Mike and David, all of us taking a crash course in Spanish (she in English), and communicating effectively with sign language and sound effects. By teatime, we finished the fence and prepared to introduce the wooly parolees into their expanded pasture. The idea was to keep them happy in a grassier part of the chicken field so they wouldn't be tempted to escape into the forbidden tree field. As soon as we peeled back the one side of their old boundary fence, the sheep bounded into greener pastures and began nibbling their way through fresh grass. Success at last!

But for every Braemar arrival, another inevitably would depart. Late one night a knock sounded on my door. For a moment, I thought it might be Trevor coming to apologize for even thinking of getting those blasted sheep, agreeing to send them to the butcher's, and wanting to have hot make-up sex. Who else would it be after 10:00 p.m.?

It was one of the older students, Jill, just returned from the evening zikr. She and I often sat next to each other at meals and talked about our love of the Scottish countryside, the Borders Abbeys, and the many fantastic hill-walking opportunities around. I felt a kinship with her ever since she had hugged me at Mary's House in Turkey. I invited her in, and she sat on my bed, forcing a smile.

"I hope you don't think this an imposition. It's just that a lot of issues have been coming up for me in the Course. I'm not sure how to handle them. I also don't feel comfortable talking to anyone else."

She felt that some of the students and facilitators took offense at her questioning of the Course's teachings. She felt put down in her contribution to discussions. She was deeply saddened by what she experienced as a lack of support.

Spiritual retreats can attract those judgmental types, the proudly pious who presume to set the standard for right thought and action. Thankfully, they were few, and I knew better than to judge all of Braemardom based on those rare attitudes. But Jill couldn't see her way through. She craved affirmation, acknowledgment for her differing viewpoint. Even if God had in mind that she needed rebuke in order to grow, for Jill, the Braemar Order simply was not working.

"I'm thinking about leaving," she said.

I got up from my chair and dug through a pile of books on the floor by my bed, finding the copy of "Conversations with God." Trevor had given me his copy when I had lain ill in Fairy Cottage. I found Neal Donald Walsh's take on the Divine and spiritual matters refreshing and intellectually accessible. I handed the book to Jill.

"It's helped, even though I often backslide into false and damaging beliefs about myself and others," I said.

"One thing it's good at is encouraging you to follow your own path and not worry about what others think it should be. Much of the book is about exactly what you told me in Turkey—finding what the true essence of God means for you personally."

Here I was dispensing spiritual advice that I struggled to practice myself. Jill stood and hugged me again. A week later, she and I shared lunch at a two-person side table in the dining room, her last meal before quitting the Course and going home. I told her I was sorry that Braemar couldn't offer her the support she needed, but that maybe it was meant to be. At least she and I had been brought together.

"You're on the verge of change. You're shedding old skin, but the new skin doesn't quite fit yet, so things feel scary and uncomfortable," I said.

"Die before you die," she said, wiping her eyes.

"What?"

"It's a spiritual concept in just about every religion. You've just rephrased it. We've talked about it during the Course."

The breakup with Trevor, issues of control, and Jill's departure opened me up more to the teachings of Braemar. I needed to turn more to God for comfort and guidance. In particular, I began contemplating this business of die before you die. I picked up another book of Ibn Arabi translations from a shelf in the house library titled "Whoso Knoweth Himself . . .", and began deepening my interest in Ibn Arabi. To die before you die is to know yourself, your true nature, before the time of your physical death. The Christian version is found in the Gospel of John and says something about no one entering heaven until being born twice. Voluntary—and presumably figurative— death of the unenlightened self was a Sufi quest, leading to a "lifting of the veil" to see God more clearly. As the mystics see it, Truth lies in knowing your existence to be God's existence; to stop living an ego-centered life in favor of a spirit-centered life. It all tied into paying attention. Attention to your thoughts, to your deeds, to the experience of now. And, to know that you are God manifest in human form on Earth.

It was deep stuff, and I began wondering what it could teach me about my current experience and how I could use it to be happier. My experience in Turkey at Mary's House had opened me up a crack. Now I was being cracked open further.

In a mix of Spanish and English, Louisa began asking me about Braemar's practices. When faced with trying to explain them, I realized there was still a lot I didn't understand either. What I was starting to grasp was too complicated to explain in English, let alone Spanish. I called Eltondean High School to invite the Spanish teacher to come translate. Penny interpreted while I told Louisa about basic house rules, how we run the estate, and what I had gleaned so far about the Sufi-based spiritual practices. Louisa wondered whether her Catholic background conflicted with her being there. I assured her that we all came from a variety of religious backgrounds, so it didn't matter. The focus was on Dios.

In the garden, I explained to Louisa while the translator translated, how Trevor approached work versus how I did: leaving the tools strewn about versus putting them away; killing moles versus not; hanging onto no-good sheep versus admitting they were a mistake. I warned her that Trevor would eventually make her drive the tractor. We also reviewed the bird and sheep feeding routine. I happily handed over the barley bucket, recognizing I needed a break even from my beloved chickens, ducks, and geese. I didn't discuss the situation between Trevor and me, though Louisa was likely to figure it out eventually.

Nearly a month had passed since our breakup, and Trevor and I still weren't saying much to each other except to briefly discuss estate matters. I assumed a more submissive role, following his instructions on days when I wasn't working inside on tree planting preparations. Trevor spoke coolly when relaying work orders, and I pretended to go along happily, not letting him know that I was sad and missed his company. He seemed to despise me more than mole hills.

When one day I couldn't bear it anymore, I skipped lunch to lie in bed and sob. Wakil came to my room to check on me. He climbed into bed next to me and put an arm around my shoulder, listening to my sorrow about missing the old Trevor I knew.

"Hey, I just thought of summat," Wakil burst out enthusiastically. "We could commit suicide together!"

"You really know how to cheer a person up," I sobbed in reply.

"We could gas ourselves to death with your fire!" (He meant the propane heater.)

"Charming, Wakil."

"Just think what everyone would say if they found us lying dead next to each other in your bed. That would really get tongues wagging!"

Then he laughed, which made me laugh and cry simultaneously.

"I'm depressed to tears, and you're talking about a suicide pact."

He gave me a big hug. "Aw, I'm sorry. Now get up, ya big baby, and stop feeling sorry for yourself."

Wakil got out of my bed, winked at me, and walked out the door.

I followed his advice and took a walk around the estate track through Braemar's varied landscape. I thought about what had brought me here in the first place: boredom, feelings of lack, emptiness. Had I found relief or simply plugged the gaps? Should I pack up and go home? What would I be running away from? Another failed relationship? *Been there; move on.* The hardships? *Welcome to life.* The cold, the rain? *Accept what you can't change.* I stopped at the Knowe Hill clearcut to look across the Creston valley and last year's sea of tree tubes. Below, the Stanwick River flowed through sheep pastures, still green in winter. A voice popped into my head: *You'd be running from yourself.*

On some level, I had asked to be brought to Braemar. I realized that no matter where in the world I found myself, no matter what I did, no matter the lifestyle, the hardships or easy times, the conditions, the job, the people, whether anybody accepted me or even liked me, it was up to me to find some measure of satisfaction for myself. So the only escape from whatever I perceived as against me was to work on my perception of things, to see things as they are, not as I am. Braemarites called this "surrender," a word I never liked because it sounded like defeat, vulnerability. What might this "defeat" feel like? Allowing myself to be wrong and wronged? I could at least start by learning how to say "no" when I felt overburdened, to excuse myself from washing dishes or mopping floors or chasing sheep. It wouldn't be easy, but I hadn't come six thousand miles to be miserable. Braemar was meant to be an opportunity of a lifetime, even in all its imperfection. After all, imperfection was just an alternative choice to experience what was perfect in its own right. The choice was mine: self-sabotage or freedom.

I continued along the track and saw Principal Latif approaching from the opposite direction with his dog.

"Hello," he said, as we met.

"Hiya. How are you?" I tried sounding casual to hide my melancholy.

"Is anything wrong?" he asked in his inimitable way of knowing.

Without thinking, I launched into a condensed version of my woes with Trevor. Latif's eyes focused intently on mine. When I finished, he continued staring at me for a moment.

"Who broke up with whom?" he asked.

"It was mutual." At least, I thought it was. I wasn't sure anymore.

"Hmm." He thought for another moment, his eyes drawn away now across the valley. "Would you like me to have a word with him?"

His offer shocked me. Really, he'd do that? I looked away so he wouldn't notice my tears.

"Thanks, but I'd rather just leave it for now."

"As you wish. But I shouldn't worry. He'll come round eventually. Just give him some time."

I smiled, barely managing an audible, "Thanks." He smiled back, nodded, and called to his dog as he walked on.

I had seriously misjudged Latif, who now seemed more human, less demi-god. I remembered something we had discussed a few times in the morning meetings, something from the Qur'an: *Everything is perishing but His face.* All my preconceived notions about Latif as unapproachable, intimidating, clinging to spiritual hubris, had perished, leaving nothing but the face of God, the true essence of a fellow being. The experience was fleeting, but I caught it just long enough to feel—not know but *feel*—that we were all the Face of God.

On the last day of January, I went for a five-mile walk, heading down the end of our road, across Glebe Farm, over the moors, down the big hill, across the bridge by the church in Creston, and back up the road to Braemar. As the wind blew in my face, I imagined it sweeping my soul clean. God had given me every second of every day to create a world of my choosing; not a sanitized environment free of troubles, difficult people, and hard decisions. What fun would that be? I got back to the Steading and abluted every inch of my odd-angled, cubby-holed room.

"Ablution extends to our bodies as well as to our minds," Latif intoned at most Thursday morning meetings, encouraging us to look at those thoughts that failed to reflect who we were as Divine creations.

For the first time, I really understood the significance of his words.

Louisa's English and my Spanish seemed to improve, too, thankfully, since it had become tiring using sign language, playing charades, and bahing and crowing whenever we needed to discuss the sheep and chickens. What better way to improve our skills than by discussing former boyfriends and shoveling chicken crap? We made up vocabulary and phrase lists to help. Instead of "sheep's head with much beer," I could say, "hammer," "shovel," "chicken food," "Trevor is killing moles today," and "sheep fence sucks, we need to fix it."

In my broken Spanish, I told Louisa about mine and Trevor's breakup, flipping through my Spanish-English dictionary for key words to describe "one who can't admit he never should have gotten the sheep." I told her I still had feelings for him but that it was difficult to be with him sometimes.

"El quiera la mujer perfecta," Louisa said. *He wants the perfect woman.*

"Es verdad!" I laughed. *It's true!*

"Y qué quieres?" she asked me. *What do you want?*

I thought about it for a second. Then we looked at each other and spoke in unison:

"El hombre perfecto!"

We both giggled about that for the rest of the day.

CHAPTER 17
Shoveling Shit

February brought more heavy rains. (Come to think of it, just about every winter month had.) In a wide, flat river, water flowed off the hillside pasture, forming a large pond outside the garden shed. I was inside the shed when the levee burst. Water rushed in under the door, and soon I was shin deep in its roiling, muddy midst, plastic pots and plant tags swirling around my legs. I opened the door on the other side of the shed to let the torrent out, and the river then flowed from the hill through the shed and into the garden. I cleared away three bags of sodden garden clothes that had been stored under the work benches, and hung tools left leaning against the wall, the rust now growing faster.

More of a worry than rotting tools and work clothes were the birds. Instead of taking shelter in their coops on drenching days, the chickens just stood around in the downpour. Some would shelter under the shrubs, but we sometimes found one or two dead chickens after an exceptionally heavy rain. We never knew why. Oddly, we would also sometimes discover a couple of chickens with their feet tangled in fishing line. The origin of the fishing line remained a mystery. It would tangle and tighten around the chickens' feet and legs, making them swell and bleed.

We would catch them, carefully cut off the tangled mess, and dunk their feet in warm salt water to aid healing.

The rain made people act funny sometimes too. One evening, someone made off with Rafi's sculpture, a gold-painted cast of a nude woman. He had moved it from the front porch of his caravan to the hay barn, in full view of everyone passing by along the drive (Braemarites, Glebe Farm residents, and delivery persons to Glebe Farm). The police must have found the report amusing, while the rest of us kept an eye out for delivery trucks with unusual hood ornaments. Rafi was flattered that someone had gone to the trouble to steal it. Maybe they mistook Our Lady of the Hay Barn for a real bronze? A month later, the police found her head in a rundown housing project in Eltondean. Rafi displayed it on the steps of his caravan. Her body was never recovered.

While we waited for the rains to subside, Trevor showed Louisa and me how to lay a hedge, using the hawthorn hedge that separated the forbidden tree field from the neighboring sheep pasture. It was so thick and gnarly not even the Soays could penetrate it. After having spent several weeks on that part of the estate—the coldest, windiest part—fixing sheep fencing in previous weeks, I wasn't looking forward to spending more time there. Yet, the hedge was becoming overgrown and needed rejuvenating. Hedge laying was another of Trevor's many skills, and he had won a few contests at agricultural shows. Like sheep dog trials, hedge laying has its own special event category.

The technique was simple, but actually doing it took more skill than one would think. The purpose was to rein in the branches, which wanted to grow tree-like, and force them to grow more horizontally to create a thick mass of thorny branches. After a decade or so, the innermost growth of a hawthorn hedge begins to die for lack of light, which calls for occasional refreshing. The job involved partially slicing the base stems of the individual plants vertically, pulling them down, and then tying them with twine to the next plant down the line. Imagine a row of people all bending forward to grab the waist of the person in front of them so that everyone's backs formed a level row. Everyone's legs would sprout new growth and eventually fill the gaps. It reminded me of how we all relied on one another for our own growth.

Laying a hawthorn hedge wasn't much different than working with jumbled barbed wire, with which we had plenty of experience. The only difference was that, with hawthorn, the thorns worked under your skin, becoming sore until they worked their way out again. Or until you couldn't stand it anymore and dug them out with a kitchen knife. Gloves were useless because you couldn't manipulate the finer details of the work (like trying to milk a cow wearing a catcher's mitt). After six hours on our first day, Louisa and I had laid two yards of the one-hundred-yard-long hedge. The job would keep us occupied off and on for the next three months.

When Louisa and I weren't hacking the hawthorn hedge to within a sliver of its dormancy, we were hauling trailer load after trailer load of horse dung for fertilizer. Trevor had developed a bad case of garden fever in early February, which included plowing a half-acre of ground near the lake for a potato field and building two polytunnels near the garden shed. When seven visitors arrived to take the Nine Day Course, we took advantage of the extra hands for a polytunnel raising.

Essentially plastic-covered greenhouses supported by aluminum half-hoops, the polytunnels were harder to put together than they looked. Fitting together all the pieces of this giant Erector set was like trying to build a house out of drinking straws on a flowing stream. Within a few days, the temperature inside our makeshift greenhouses had reached a balmy seventy degrees. Some suggested using one for a Turkish bath.

All of this new garden space called for lots of horse dung fertilizer. The riding stables were ten miles away across the valley and over the moors. Louisa and I drove back and forth between Braemar and the stables, shoveling manure by hand onto the flatbed trailer, hauling it with the Land Rover back to Braemar, and shoveling the load onto a pile outside the garden wall. During two weeks, we made four trips a day, at an estimated four-hundred pounds per load. Every night we went to bed aching, and every morning we woke aching. I was just about to tell Trevor we had had enough, when the bushings on the trailer gave out, putting an end to our manure hauling days. Trevor was perturbed because he thought we needed at least another week's load of crap. No one seemed to care about Louisa's and my backs.

For the next two weeks the students helped us spread our mountain of horse apples, shifting endless wheelbarrow loads of it to the garden and polytunnels. After five days, the mountain didn't appear to be shrinking, and Trevor announced more would be delivered from the stables. I had already been to the chiropractor three times. So one day, while shifting what seemed like my fiftieth ton of crap, I rammed my pitchfork into the mountain and yelled, "I'm sick of this shit!"

The students stopped and stared at me, pausing before breaking into laughter. I had been half-serious, but for the next half hour, as we shoveled, loaded, and unloaded, we ran through every conceivable related phrase: "Don't give me your shit"; "What is this shit?"; "I can't take this shit anymore"; and on and on, until we finally settled on "This is good shit."

"Are you having fun?" Trevor burst in eventually, somewhat sarcastically.

"Shit, yeah!" we all cried.

It was the first good guffaw most of us had had in weeks. Trevor's seemingly playful response to it gave me hope that maybe he was softening.

The shit metaphor hadn't been lost on me either; a lot of my inner work at Braemar could be likened to shoveling crap, or even just shifting it from one place to another without really dealing with it. I had been paying much more attention to my thoughts while engaging in everyday Braemar life, and feeling better for it. The work didn't seem so onerous now, despite its physical toll. I still missed Trevor and me, so my days had a veneer of sadness but I would have to squeeze joy out of whatever I could. It began to sink in that "getting it done" wasn't the point. The simple act of being present while doing the work could bring its own satisfaction.

As the tree planting project grew near, I spent more time at the sawmill, tidying the heaps of junk to make room for the delivery of tree tubes and stakes. We also needed to clear an area for the M*A*S*H tent, where we would serve lunches. Though the sawmill was now a deathtrap, I had persuaded the Braemar board of directors to give it a stay of execution. I put up duck wire around the building to keep people out. I wondered whether one day the listing mill would collapse with me inside (because I still liked to go in the small building). I could be trapped for days before someone finally noticed I hadn't shown up for meals.

I found peace, and some pleasure, working around the sawmill. It was far enough away from the main seat of activity to not be bothered by the demands of others, yet near enough to the garden shed to—inevitably—trudge back to fetch a much-needed tool. The pungent, musty aroma of forever-wet soil and the neighbor's bleating sheep in the surrounding pastures soothed the soul. Gray clouds often raced through the sky, creating alternating patches of sunlight and shadow over the land, reminding me that all conditions were fleeting, that dark shadows eventually gave way to the light.

At the end of a day working around the mill, I usually walked back to the big house along my favorite shortcut: a grassy path beneath a canopy of beech trees. The path emerged at the far end of the lake before curving toward the garden. The ducks and geese, always out for a paddle, would head for the bank when they saw me and gather around my legs while I filled a bucket with grain. These were cherished moments that kept me tethered to Braemar. They were also reflective opportunities that spurred me toward trying to understand more about the Sufi wisdom the students were studying. In another of Braemar's short publications, titled "The Twenty-Nine Pages," was a discussion of Ibn Arabi's interpretation of Adam, whom Muslims revere as the first Perfect Man. In the Qur'an is this phrase, attributed to God (Allah):

> I was a hidden treasure and I loved to be known. So I created the world that I might be known.

Perfect Man (the hidden treasure) contains all of God's attributes and perfections. But until a person realizes unity with God, Ibn Arabi said, he cannot manifest those perfections. In other words, we all have the potential to manifest God's greatest attributes, but unless we realize our Unity, we are just potential, a coiled spring waiting to be sprung, waiting to be known. Ibn Arabi wrote that in us lies the power of knowing God absolutely, for we are the manifested consciousness of God.

So what did it mean to know God absolutely? Or to contemplate God perfectly, something else this little book instructed. Given the array of personalities with whom I lived, attempting to contemplate anyone usually left me with more questions than answers. In contemplating Trevor, I could see that we were absolutely unified in sadness and blaming each other for our respective miseries. Sometimes my attempts to follow his work instructions were met with his harsh orders. Feeling guilty, he would be kind the next day, which was my cue to snap at him in retaliation. Back and forth went the olive branch, as we took turns extending and retracting it.

One day I was watching him from the office window in the big house as he slung dirt from mole hills across the front lawn. I got the impression it wasn't just the mole hills he was attacking. Every shovelful of soil seemed to contain hurt; an ended marriage, lingering pain from childhood, an unkind word never let go of, or whatever else gnawed at his soul. Compassion overtook me, and gradually my own hurt and frustration softened into realizing none of his behavior toward me was about me. Time to focus on my impending nascent forest and leave Trevor to tend to his own garden.

That winter was an introspective time for everyone, and during the morning meetings, Latif tried endlessly to draw us out of our funk. We talked about the nafs, the ego. Someone remarked that it was hard to focus on God when the nafs got in the way. I envisioned them as little devils on our shoulders giving bad advice. We couldn't discount our nafs, Latif said, but we could learn to shape them, shape ourselves, by more consciously recreating ourselves with the daily choices we make. We didn't have to get stuck in behavior that veiled us from God, that kept us distant from God, he said.

As I listened to Latif one morning, I watched smoke from the wood stove curling out of the cracks of the black iron door. I imagined the smoke as nafs wrapping their sinuous, ephemeral tendrils around our heads while seducing us with the heady scent of wood smoldering in a cool fire.

It was easy to see how choosing anger or resentment could veil us from God. As long as our fires were cool, the nafs—the smoke—would veil us from the heat of true fire, that burning desire for closeness with God, which necessarily meant loving our fellow housemates.

One morning, Latif began the meeting with this gem: "Live every moment as if you were going to die today."

It wasn't exactly the uplifting thought I wanted floundering in my head, but I tried to accept the challenge, and wondered, if I died that day, what would my regrets be? For one thing, I wouldn't have had Soay sheep twice in the same lifetime. I lost track of whatever else Latif said and sank into the overstuffed chair. I closed my eyes and let the sun warm my face, thanking God over and over again for the big ball of fire in the sky. This simultaneously small yet immense gift was enough to be grateful for in one day.

The next day, a blanket of fog rolled in, wrapping us all in a gray, heavy bolt of cotton batting. For several days afterward, I became hypersensitive to my own thoughts. "Intention" became my new buzzword. How might life improve if the intention behind my actions and thoughts were different? What if mucking out the chickens were an act of love for the birds rather than a never-ending chore? What if every action was one of love in service to others? What if, rather than feeling overwhelmed by the chores, I cherished the opportunity to live in Scotland and work outside in a beautiful place? That was, after all, my original intention.

Complaint had become a crutch, a mind-numbing loop playing repeatedly. It kept me from realizing my potential, veiled me from God and from compassion for the one person I had neglected to care for all my life: myself.

I took a lot of walks that winter, sometimes two a day, often reminiscing about happier times with Trevor. Despite what I was learning intellectually about surrender and love and accepting everything as perfect in its own right, I still had bouts of depression and doubt. I still, occasionally, thought about leaving. I even asked Latif for his advice.

"Unless you hear the call three times, I think you should stay," he said.

I never asked what the significance of three was, but for a second opinion, I ambled up the front hill to the Monument, where Braemar's founder, Iskandar, was buried. I sat on the concrete steps and confessed my frustrations, wondering aloud how, if we know something has the potential for a good outcome—like changing your intention—why is it so hard to practice? *What was Braemar like when you were alive?* I asked him. I cried, waved my arms furiously, and told him everything, including about Trevor. Trying to forgive or ignore Trevor wasn't working.

Two blackface sheep stared at me through the fence. I had always seen domestic animals as vulnerable, dependent on people for their survival. Possibly true to an extent, but they also just got on with it. Whatever was thrown their way, they coped, without judgement, or trying to make what simply is into something complex. I took it as a sign from God that Iskandar had spoken. The urge to flee Braemar had vanished.

I continued my walk down the front hill pasture and trekked over to the rise into part of the estate called Hoscote, just as the sun was setting over Glenmeade Forest in the distance. The fierce orange glow resembled a forest ablaze. I headed back and stopped by the chicken field to say goodnight to my cluckers and thank the wooly wonders for having stayed in the chicken field for the past several weeks without escaping once. Inside the big house I poked my head in the meditation room and studied the large framed picture of the Qur'an in micro print. The swirly greens, reds, and golds caressing the black calligraphy of Arabic script had been created with such love. Their similarity to illuminated manuscripts in the Christian tradition was interesting. Muslims, too, were moved to bring the living word of God to light. How could we not fall to our knees in the face of such mercy and love?

I returned to my room and sobbed.

CHAPTER 18

Gaining Ground

Sometimes Braemar could be a miserable hell hole of frustration and unfulfilled desire to be closer to God; drenched by the relentless rain, never-ending work, and the subtle reminder that we were all no more than a bag of skin containing useless thoughts that have suppressed the true nature of our souls since the day we were conceived. Other times Braemar was all the heavens combined into one; a phantasmagorical silken carpet ride through the infinitely faceted expressions of the Divine, everything a testament to the glory of God, where even a few errant Soay sheep could make you thankful to be their guardian. (Okay, God really would have to be working in magical ways to make the latter true!) In other words, sometimes Braemar really sucked, and other times I didn't want to be anywhere else. And sometimes both those strong feelings occurred within the same day—simultaneously, even.

One morning, following a particularly dreary week, Latif called everyone into the Mead Hall after breakfast, including the students. This was a first! Were we about to be scolded for something? All eyes darted nervously around the room at one another. Latif sat in his usual chair by the windows at the front of the room. He smiled widely.

"Good morning!" he greeted us heartily.

He raised his hand to the windows.

"Just look at this beautiful day. We give thanks to He who brought us the sun!"

Everyone nodded, waiting for the other Wellington boot to drop.

"I would like us all to join together and ablute both inside and out. Let's clear the cobwebs and celebrate God's love and mercy."

Everyone in the room suddenly exhaled. I took Latif's command with unguarded pleasure and was the first one out of my chair and running for the dust rag. Trevor followed, catching me in the foyer.

"I haven't been very nice lately," he said, sheepishly. "I'll try to be better at communicating."

"I've been meaning to talk to you about that," I said.

"Go on then. Say whatever you have to."

He forced himself to look at me, though it was obviously difficult. His eyes darted to the ground and back to meet mine. He was extending the hawthorn branch. Why not just grab it?

"I look forward to our new and improved communicating relationship," I said.

His shoulders dropped in relief. His eyes met mine.

"Me too. I wanted to say you did a great job on the tree planting invitations. Everyone's saying how hard you've been working in the office. I'm sure we'll get lots of punters for the April planting."

I felt a tinge of hopefulness. Was this a door opening to giving romance another try? Coupled with properly behaving sheep, Trevor's compliment made me wonder whether I'd been transported to a parallel universe. Why not follow his lead and try a new practice myself? I decided to give zikr a go.

The ritual required full ablution—showering and

washing everything, including your hair (not communal showering, as I had wondered upon first arrival back in September). Clean clothes were mandatory, not to mention challenging for those of us who worked outside all day. House shoes were left outside the Mead Hall door, and upon entering the room, silence was required. When I walked in, ten people were kneeling on the floor in a circle in the middle of the room, heads bowed, eyes closed. Three of the students opened their eyes when I walked in and slipped me a wry smile.

A few people sat in the Mead Hall chairs, which had been pushed up against the walls. Not knowing the procedure, I decided to sit and watch. When everyone had gathered, Latif recited a short passage in Arabic from memory. After a pause, the group began chanting Arabic phrases. I recognized some words—the attributes of God—which in Islam represent the qualities of God manifested in people (merciful, powerful, gentle, etc.).

"Hu Allah, Hai Allah," they chanted on their knees. After several minutes, their voices hit a crescendo, ringing in rhythmic, robust unison. Their affirmation of God exuded from their brows in beads of sweat and coursed through their bodies in a gentle, swaying side-to-side motion. Several minutes later, the pace of the chanting diminished; the voices quieted and then stopped. Everyone stood and locked arms at the elbows.

"Hu Allah, Hai Allah," their voices sang out again, rising in unison before softly tapering off. Getting the hang of the chant, I joined in from the sidelines, while the group walked in a circle around the room. They took a short silent break, passing around glasses of water and Turkish cologne, which they slapped on their faces. The room filled with the fragrance of lemons. They started again.

"Zul Jelal-a-wa'l ikram," they repeated, locking arms and moving forward and backward in two lines. They knelt again. "Zul Jemal-a-wa'l ihsan," invoking the beauty and glory of God.

After about an hour, the zikr was drawing to a close. Everyone moved around the gathered circle, wishing each person salaam, peace. For a final time, they knelt again, and Latif recited another Arabic passage. They slowly rose to their feet in silence and sat on the sofas and chairs. After a few minutes, quiet conversation began. Some people served special chocolates, dates, and other fruit, along with coffee and tea, transforming the whole affair into a chatty but subdued tea party. I felt alert, exhilarated even. More importantly, I learned that zikr wasn't some weird cult ritual. It was an affirmation of God, a remembrance of the spirit of Love from which we all come.

"It's brilliant you're here," Wakil said, extending a plate of sliced oranges.

I took a wedge. "Thanks, Wakky."

"Did ya like it?"

"It was good."

"Aw, I'm chuffed you came."

Wakil flashed one of his big smiles and continued around the room with the fruit plate. Rafi sat down next to me.

"So, to what do we owe the pleasure?" he said, somewhat smugly.

I bit into my orange slice, sending a mist of citrus toward his face. He grimaced.

"Thought I'd see what all the fuss was about," I said.

"And?"

"It was interesting."

"Will we be seeing more of you then?"

"Maybe."

Rafi had been goading me for months to come to zikr, and I had stubbornly refused on the grounds that I didn't want to practice a religious thing I knew nothing about.

Now I didn't want to give him the satisfaction of knowing that I had misjudged it. I loved Rafi—and sometimes I loved getting under his skin. He harrumphed, and our conversation turned to other things.

The next day, Trevor lent me his car so that Wakil and I could have an afternoon outing. We headed for town on a teaser of a spring-like day, nosing through a few thrift shops—Wakil's favorite pastime, after drinking Guinness. I bought a dress, a strictly therapeutic purchase since I had no need for such clothing on the estate and didn't know of any upcoming art openings. We drove to the charming town of Melrose to stroll through the abbey ruins and graveyard. Many of the headstones had a skull and crossbones carved at the top. Wakil explained that they warded off evil spirits. And here I had thought Scotland just had a lot of dead pirates.

"I used to do this sort of thing with Trevor," I lamented to Wakil.

"You're not still thinking 'bout him, are you?"

I didn't respond. Obviously I was, and Trevor's having reached out to me sparked hope for a more complete reconciliation.

"Forget about him. Besides, you have me, haven't ya? Come on, I'll buy you lunch at pub."

Why couldn't I view life so simply, like Wakil? While waiting for our lamb stew, he rolled a cigarette and chugged down a pint of Guinness. I knew he wasn't supposed to drink because of the medication he was taking, but there was not much I or anyone could do to stop him.

"Do you ever notice how time is so compressed at Braemar?" I asked.

"Oh yeah, all the time."

I laughed at his joke.

"It's like major personal revelations seem to happen within just a few weeks, or even days. In the outside world, that would take years."

"Scary in'it? Like Star Trek," he said.

It was funny he should mention that, given that my first impression of Braemar was that it reminded me of Star Trek.

"Last week I was weeding the border plots in the walled garden, and getting angrier with each weed I pulled, imagining it was Trevor I was ripping out of the ground."

Wakil exhaled his smoke with a choking snortle.

"After my anger subsided, it occurred to me that I had been pulling out perennials instead of weeds."

"Isn't that what they call a metaphysical, or summat?" Wakil said.

I laughed at his muddle. "A metaphor. And no, not exactly. I'd been judging things for weeds that weren't weeds after all."

Wakil nodded.

"So do you think you'll come to zikr again?" he asked.

"I'm thinking about it."

"Do you like zikr?" I asked him.

"It's brilliant! Well, most times. Sometimes I can't be bothered, you know, if I just wanna lay in me bed or summat. Then Hamida complains to Latif, the bossy old cow, and he makes me start going again."

"So I see fifteen years of zikr has helped you to love your fellow Braemarites," I said.

His harsh honesty and demonstrable devotion to God—in his own Wakil way—might have appeared at odds to the outsider. But strangely, these seemingly incongruous thoughts and behaviors perfectly characterized Wakil.

When we returned to Braemar, Trevor's children were there and eager to play with me. I agreed to watch them for a while, and we walked from the Gate Lodge to the nursery in the Steading.

"Do you still love Dad?" Daisy asked.

The question from this soon-to-be-six-year-old came as a surprise. All I could think to say was that we weren't girlfriend and boyfriend anymore.

"He still loves you," Daisy said.

"How do you know?"

"He told me."

"Did he tell you to tell me?"

"No, he just said he still loves you."

"Oh."

Love seemed a strong word, given that we'd known each other only five months. But Daisy had planted a seed. Not that anyone would have known, least of all me. He had reached out with a promise to improve communications, but then things suddenly cooled again. Trevor's goodwill toward me lasted only a weekend.

About a week after Daisy's pronouncement, I was working in the rain by myself for most of the day, shifting huge planks of wood at the sawmill. My sopping jacket, which was supposed to be waterproof, had plastered itself to my wool sweater underneath and was just as wet inside as out. At last, day's end rolled around with teatime. Back at the big house, fresh-baked delights were waiting to be washed down with pots of hot tea. I trudged along the gravel drive, warmed by thoughts of the nectar awaiting me, caramel-colored from a dash of milk. As I approached the big house, Louisa emerged from the grain shed, her nose scrunched between her pursed lips and furrowed brow.

"They have got out," she said, clutching a bucket of barley in her arms.

She had gone to fill the Soays' water trough when she noticed them in the forbidden tree field. After several weeks of success, the fence had finally failed to keep our Houdinis contained. I wanted to attribute their confinement to my superior fencing job. The reality, how-ever, was that the Soays had eaten all the tall grass in their own field and were ready to move to greener pastures. Louisa and I walked the fence line, scrutinizing every strand for their escape route. Then Trevor appeared. He strode up the chicken field, sending splatters of mud in his wake. The relief map of Wellington boot prints, leading from the gate and across the muddy field, showed indis-putable purpose and headed in my direction. He had to raise his soft voice above the wind from the gathering storm across the moors.

"Will you come with me, please?"

He didn't sound happy. Now what? I thought, eager to go inside and tuck into warm scones slathered with strawberry jam. Derrick had made them especially for me that day.

"See if you can find where they're getting out and try to get them back in," I told Louisa about the Soays.

Then I followed Trevor to the Land Rover. He drove us up the slope along the woodland track, then through the spruce plantation across from the Gate Lodge. The vehicle straddled the foot-deep ruts, and he rammed it into low four-wheel-drive when it slid. We emerged near the top of the hill pasture and got out. Trevor pointed sharply to the fence that separated the pasture from the dense trees.

"I want the whole length reinforced beginning tomor-row morning. You and the students can start in this corner and work all the way down to the dyke along the moor."

His attitude was uncharacteristically aggressive.

"It should only take a day or two, and when that's done, you can carry on along the fence by the far wood-land. Simple enough instructions for you?"

He emphasized the last statement as if I had already messed something up badly.

"Sure, no problem." I shrugged, pretending to be fine

with it.

We headed back down to the big house, where afternoon tea was just wrapping up. Not a crumb left to sate the soul. Not a drop of tea to thaw the harsh day. I hurried to my room and promptly collapsed into tears. Where had his attitude come from? Why had he verbally attacked me?

The next morning, still upset about the previous afternoon, I found Hadiyya, the ever strong office manager, and told her I could no longer bear Trevor's blowing hot and cold, his unpredictable mood, love turned to bitterness. She persuaded me to tell Principal Latif everything, right away. But Latif wasn't available. Not wanting to lose momentum, I bent Rahman's ear instead, the second in command after Latif. Afterward, I certainly wasn't up to the fencing project Trevor had demanded the day before. Instead, the students and I worked on the hedge. About an hour later, Trevor strode up the field toward us.

"Can I have a word?" he said to me, sternly.

We walked several yards away out of earshot of the students.

"I thought I told you to start on that fence."

"Did you, now?" I fronted up to him.

There's nothing like a good cry to empower a person. It was time to grab the chicken by the spurs, throw the chainsaw out with the dishwater, take off my wellies and run in the mire with the sheep. I told him I had had it with his mood swings, his attitude, his BS. I wasn't his whipping post, and if he didn't like it, he could take it up with Latif. My diatribe got Trevor's attention, and he trudged off to find the principal. Later, I met with Latif on my own.

"I suppose our stories differ vastly," I said.

"Of course, but that's irrelevant. I want you to know that things will change straight away," he said.

"How?"

"The two of you must work toward a compromise."

"I've tried that."

"Compromise means both parties discuss things until both are clear and satisfied. It also implies surrender," he said.

How I hated that word. Surrender.

Surrender forced me to my bed the following day, with a migraine and full-body ache. Then lo and behold, Mr. Estate Manager, himself, came to my room to apologize. He knelt by my bed and took my hand in his.

"I've been horrible. I'm sorry."

Trevor's sincerity was clear. It was all I had wanted.

"Apology accepted, but you've really hurt me these past couple of months."

"I know."

He said more, but I missed most of it because my head was so stuffed up, and his voice was so soft. I just nodded as he spoke.

The good thing about being sick at Braemar was that meals were brought to your room. I had one of the best Sunday lunches ever. Alone. No kids begging for my attention, and no sulking Trevor sitting as far away as possible from me. I should have been sick more often.

CHAPTER 19

Growing

After our fallout, Trevor and I met with Latif to discuss how we were going to play together nicely. Not much came of it except an ambiguous promise to behave better toward each other. It seemed we both wanted another try at romance, but both of us were afraid to make the first move for fear of rejection. Though I still reminisced about evenings past, stumbling in the dark to the Gate Lodge after supper and falling asleep in his arms while listening to the tawny owl outside the window, I slowly began letting go of hope of a reconciliation. At least we were more civil toward each other now. Considering that a few weeks earlier I had contemplated gassing myself with Wakil in my bed, it was a start.

March brought the promise of spring and more rain. The birds had begun laying dozens and dozens of eggs, dropping them everywhere. My egg-gathering rounds expanded from the nest boxes in the chicken coops to beyond the outbuildings, under the front porch of the big house, and throughout the border gardens and gnarled rhododendrons near the big house, a favorite laying spot for the turkey hens. The ducks somehow squeezed themselves into the narrow gap between the pen fencing and the wooden shelters that backed up against the fence. I had to use a broom handle to carefully draw their eggs to within reach.

Trevor handed me a stack of books about rearing poultry. Every one of them proposed a different method for incubating eggs.

"Just pick a method and see if it works," he instructed.

I learned that birds lay one or two eggs a day but don't sit on them until they have laid a clutch of eight to twelve. Once the hens do start sitting, all the eggs begin to incubate at the same time, regardless of when they were laid. I kept the egg collection in a cardboard box in the dry food storage room at the back of the house. The kitchen crew kept snitching them until I put up a sign that read: DON'T MURDER US; WE'RE GOING TO BE INCUBATED.

My foray into incubation began with a set of seven goose eggs. Collecting goose eggs involves tricking smart and protective geese to leave their nest, then trying to escape from their pen unharmed after the geese realize you have tricked them and they corner you on the attack. A few weeks earlier, the geese had pecked to death one of our Muscovy ducks because the drake had wandered into the goose pen accidentally during the evening roundup. I feared becoming a similar casualty. I managed to get the eggs while Louisa kept the geese occupied at the lake with a bucket of grain. Several weeks later, one goose started sitting permanently on her clutch and would not budge. We left her to it.

With a bit of careful configuring, the goose eggs I collected only just fit in our single-rack incubator, which was meant for a dozen chicken eggs. The contraption was supposed to turn the eggs automatically every twenty-four hours. But because the goose eggs were too heavy, the mechanism didn't work. Instead, I had to turn the eggs by hand every day. The eggs also had to be misted with water, "not too warm and not too cool," according to one of the books, which wasn't helpful. God forbid the generators would quit working during the next twenty-eight days. The incubator sat on the floor of my room near the radiator, humming away all day and all night.

I continued to collect more turkey, chicken, and duck eggs to hatch later, but I left a nesting turkey to her own devices, protected in the rhododendrons. A few other duck and chicken hens went missing. We would have to wait and see whether they had gone off to hatch eggs or been taken by a fox.

After a while I was forced to give up my growing egg collection when I read that eggs should be incubated within one week of collecting. I had been collecting them for at least fifteen days and could not bear to throw them away. So, I put them all in the kitchen and started over. (I never did hear complaints from the cook about bad eggs.)

Other creatures responded to the stirrings of spring, as well. The troublemaker Soays escaped daily into the forbidden tree field to munch the beautiful grass. Every evening they were easily coaxed back with a bucket of food pellets. I couldn't be bothered to care anymore that they spent the day in the tree field. So far, they were still only just eating the grass.

Determined to revive the walled garden back to its Victorian splendor, Trevor spent most days there turning over the soil and planting seedlings we had started in the greenhouse back in early February. In the new polytunnels, Trevor had planned for lettuces, tomatoes, runner beans, and flowers. Outside in the main garden, cabbages, carrots, onions, and parsnips would grow to fill our plates in months to come. Louisa and Ahava labored alongside Trevor while I spent more days preparing for the tree planting. Ahava agreed to help the kids with their own little garden. Trevor had graciously donated a small plot next to the garden shed for them. Esmé and Matea made a list of the things they wanted to plant: tomatoes, carrots, peas, daisies, oranges, lemons, coconuts, and flour for making biscuits. I said they could plant whatever they wanted as long as they didn't expect me to weed.

As the Course drew near its end, the students had begun to practice another form of zikr that involved repeating Allah, God's most exalted name in the Muslim faith, a specific number of times. At the end of three weeks, they worked up to chanting Allah 21,000 times in one go, which took several hours. The practice was intended to invoke love, and leave the students both profoundly refreshed and exhausted. The effect seemed to work.

"Remembering with the tongue leads to remembering with the heart," Latif said many times during March's morning staff meetings. "In remembering God, we acknowledge what we already know. There is no God but God, and from Him we draw our strength."

I seemed to find a little of my own, as did the students. Their rashes cleared up, their bloodshot eyes turned bright, and they joyfully tackled any job at hand. I envied their vitality, the peace they had found after the long, challenging winter. Trevor and I got along for the most part, though cordial at arm's length. Sometimes I'd stop work and watch him for a few minutes, enamored by his obvious love for the garden—not to mention by his strong, lanky body. I watched as he meticulously edged the garden plots, measuring them in perfect straight lines with the string; the gentle way he handled the vegetable seedlings when planting them in tidy rows; his endless hours of building the soil by digging in manure and compost. His quest to grow food and flowers for our little community endeared me to him more. I had always been attracted to men who could create with their hands, and this particular man's devotion to creating nourishment and beauty was his gift of service. It was love. I could see that more clearly now.

One day, we were sorting out seed packets in the garden shed, standing closer to each other than we had in months. He asked which flowers and vegetables I thought we should plant more of.

"Do you like cornflowers?" he asked.

This had been one of the last remaining flower species in the garden when I had first arrived at Braemar, and Trevor had brought me a small bouquet of them a couple of times just before we had had our first kiss.

"Love them," I said.

"But not nasturtiums," he said.

We chuckled, remembering our battle with clearing the garden that previous autumn of the nasturtium jungle that the previous estate manager had left behind.

"Do you like runner beans?" Trevor asked.

"I don't think I've ever had them. What are they like?"

"Lovely with a bit of butter, lightly steamed but not too soft. Look here." He pointed to the picture on the seed packet.

I reached for the packet to have a closer look, intentionally touching his hand lightly with mine. Out of the corner of my eye, I saw him staring down at the side of my face. When I looked up, he quickly turned his head away and began thumbing through the other packets on the work bench. He took a step to the side, farther away from me.

Over the next couple of days his attitude grew a little cooler again; I was used to it by now. He chided me for planting crooked rows of beans, or for not digging the compost in thoroughly enough. During one particularly tiresome day of helping the students fix the door frame for one of the polytunnels, he criticized me for not asking for his help to make it square. Rather than argue, I set down my hammer and walked away without a word—terribly uncharacteristic for me.

I headed across the garden to Braemar's oldest section

of forest, White Wood, following my usual route along the estate path. Trevor had once told me he was still stinging from a betrayal in his former marriage. He used to sometimes talk about it, not with anger but with obvious hurt. His blowing hot and cold with me was an inability to trust in love. Getting too close to someone risked being hurt again, the age-old problem with romance.

I stopped to examine some of the previous year's trees, which had started to form buds. They were hard, brown messengers of hope and promise. Cuckoo birds serenaded me from high in the oaks, and I came face to face with a tawny owl behind the sawmill, sitting on a branch at eye level. We stared at each other for several minutes. I asked whether she had any messages from the Divine. She turned her head away.

In The Brae section of the estate overlooking the Creston valley I found a cozy spot by the stream under a tree and lay down on my back. Through the branches I watched the clouds wheel across the sky. I had fallen in love with Trevor despite our differences—or maybe because of them. But until he could find trust again, we weren't going to work as a couple.

Recently, the people who had been living in my house in Montana had emailed to say they were moving out in May. I didn't want to be a long-distance landlord anymore, and I also didn't want to go back to the States. Selling my house could finance more travel. Whatever the future held, I feared it was no longer at Braemar, if only because I couldn't hang around in hope, feeling encouraged by an ex-lover one day and gutted the next.

I returned to the garden, where Trevor was spreading fertilizer by hand. I apologized for not asking for his help in framing the door and for being argumentative, bossy, and complaining in general. So this was what surrender felt like. It didn't matter who or what was "right" or "wrong." Without a word, Trevor carried on tossing the gray, pungent granules across the freshly-turned earth.

"I know all you've ever wanted was to work in your own way, in your own time, in a quiet, peaceful setting and not have people bother you," I continued.

"It's okay," he said.

We stood there for a minute longer in silence before I announced my intention to leave Braemar after the tree planting in April. His hand hesitated mid-sprinkle. I wanted him to believe that my reason for leaving was more about his need for peace than my inability to endure the emotional pain of hoping for love that might never flourish. I wanted him to talk me out of it, to put down the fertilizer bucket and take me in his arms, kissing me passionately and begging me to stay. But instead he resumed sprinkling the fertilizer.

I turned and headed for the big house in search of leftover goodies from afternoon tea, a little sadder yet feeling I had made the right decision. Wakil was in the kitchen chopping vegetables for supper.

"Hello, love. All right?"

I shrugged. We chatted for a few minutes, and then Latif walked into the kitchen and asked to speak with me. We took our conversation into the empty dining room.

"How are things going?" he asked.

"Okay."

He looked at me, waiting for more. But I was so stunned by his interest in my well-being out of the blue that I didn't know what to say.

"What are your plans for the summer?" he asked.

"I'd like to stay but . . .," I didn't know how to finish the sentence.

"Have things not improved?" he asked.

I assumed he meant between Trevor and me.

"Uh, somewhat. It's just—I need to leave for a while."

"Hmm. I don't think your work here is done yet."

I took this to mean the esoteric aspect of my inner work rather than something more mundane, like I hadn't finished cleaning out the barn.

"I have to go home in May to sort out my house. Plus, I really need a break. I'm sure you understand."

"Absolutely. But do think about coming back."

Did this odd time to probe me about summer have something to do with my announcement to Trevor just twenty minutes earlier? Nevertheless, Latif's encouragement made me feel better. Maybe Braemar wasn't finished with me.

Later, not only had I made up my mind to sell my house, after some serious thought—some 30 seconds' worth—I had also decided that the renegade Soays had to go. The next day, I shared my decision with Trevor.

"That's probably a good idea. They were a mistake to begin with," he said.

You could have knocked me down with a strand of wool! My mouth dropped open. I stumbled backward, tripping over a hoe in the garden, where Trevor had been planting onion bulbs. His admission did little to salve the wounds, however, after all the trouble They of Fleece had been.

"I'm glad you agree, because I've already called Tom and Cecily. They said they'd take them back if we caught them first."

Trevor raised his eyebrows.

"I know, I know. I'll figure out a way to catch them," I said.

"Right, well let me know what I can do to help," he said.

I watched as he continued plunking onion starts into the gloppy, manure-strewn earth.

Two days later, a backhoe contractor arrived to turn

over earth mounds for the tree planting. He also smoothed out the piles of dirt Trevor and I had dumped in the tree nursery the previous November. Like an artist, Backhoe Man skillfully formed one giant block of dirt, two and a half feet deep by ten feet wide and twenty-five feet long. The block of earth would be a holding area for tree seedlings, to be planted on the estate at some later date, not part of our planting. Backhoe Man also finished building up the gravel track by the garden. Finally, the mud swamp was gone!

Trevor began sharing his garden plans with me. He'd sow wildflower seeds along the track outside the garden and plant daffodils along the driveway. We neatly edged each planting block to stop the grass creeping in. He outlined the plot edges with string, the ends wound around wooden stakes and carefully set to form the straightest lines possible from one end of each plot to the other. Trevor stood by me and watched every cut of the spade, adjusting and readjusting the string to get the line perfectly straight.

"Stand to the outside when you make the cut," he said, taking the spade from me. "Look, like this."

Slice, divide, and brush the sod layer away. He made it look easier than it was, and I struggled to do it precisely his way. Funny how he was not particular at all about the things I found important. Now I was learning about his particulars, which seemed totally not worth the effort to me! God was appearing to each of us in Her own way.

"I wouldn't make any rash decisions about leaving Braemar," Trevor offered.

"I try not to be rash about anything."

He gently put his hand on top of mine on the spade handle and guided the spade to the left, making sure the cut was perfectly vertical.

"Right, well that's a good rule of thumb to follow," he said.

What was I to make of that?

CHAPTER 20

Ex-Shepherding

As the end of March approached, the staff stopped grumbling and started sharing in the bliss the students had discovered throughout their months of self-reflection. The skies cleared, too, prompting people to take more frequent walks along the estate track. The birds of all species started laying so many eggs that omelets and soufflés became regular offerings at mealtimes. I had collected enough chicken eggs to begin incubation, and we borrowed a forty-egg incubator from a local Braemarite. Unfortunately, the incubated goose eggs never hatched. Ahava and I set up the large incubator in my room for the twenty-one-day process. The machine hummed twenty-four hours a day, and every twelve hours its metal plates shifted to gently roll the eggs over.

March 30 was the last big zikr with the students. Braemarites from around the UK came to participate and celebrate another Course ending. I joined in the zikr, feeling energetic afterward and emotionally lighter. The next morning, everyone abluted the house, Steading, and grounds to prepare for the end-of-Course banquet. While scrubbing away vestiges of shepherd's pie and lamb roast wedged in hidden crannies of the kitchen stoves and ovens, I began to have a change of heart about leaving—or more accurately, about returning. I was definitely going back home in May to sell my house, but now I thought about coming back to Braemar. Actually, I had never really wanted to leave. It was only this business with Trevor that had pushed me in that direction. I took Latif's and Trevor's recent encouragement as a sign that returning was in my best interest as part of some grander purpose.

On April 1, the Six Month Course officially ended. After morning coffee, we bade farewell to three of the students and some staff. In tears, I hugged student Mike and Rashid, our cook, who was going back to Edinburgh. Mike was going home to Australia; I would miss him the most. He had been a ray of light during the dark, lonely winter; every day a smile, a hug, and a good word. The three remaining students and the rest of the staff would stay to support the tree planting project, cooking, keeping house, and managing the flow of tree planting volunteers. Louisa would work in the garden and look after the birds while I kept busy with the tree planters.

Now that the Course was over, breakfast became a do-it-yourself affair. I had taken for granted the students' laying the table and setting out breakfast food for the past six months. When I showed up in the dining room at half-past seven on April 2, not another soul was there. I fried some fresh hen eggs then sat at the table to eat them, staring out the picture window. On the front hill pasture new lambs chased one another, leaping and bounding about. Trevor came into view, walking across his masterpiece of a front lawn, a billiard table of green in a zigzag pattern. And, finally, mole-free. I wondered how our relationship would play out. For now, I was content that at least we seemed to be friends again.

The end of the Six Month Course brought another new beginning: life without Soays. Tom and Cecily, the previous owners, would retrieve their band of "little darlings" as soon as I had rounded them up. They had even offered to return our twenty-five pounds. Now that the monsters had been given ample space in which to roam, however, capturing them wasn't going to be easy. After a few days thinking about it, I came up with a plan that was so ingenious it was bound to fail.

The plan was to lure the sheep into a small enclosure that had been built years earlier in the chicken field to keep young chickens safe from foxes until they grew into adults. The wooden frame was about four feet high by ten feet long by eight feet wide and was wrapped entirely in chicken-wire so that nothing could get in or out except through a little door. Back in February, I had seen one of the Soays wander through the enclosure's open door and have a sniff around. The other six ewes had followed her, checking it out. The Achilles heel for Soays is their inquisitiveness, and I tucked this bit of information away for future use. That future was now.

On the morning of their capture, I strolled up the chicken field with a bucket of barley, ignoring the sheep lapping at my heels for the grain. I crawled into the enclosure and dumped the grain on the ground, then crawled back out again and pretended to walk away. While the sheep were focused on the barley, I slipped behind a coop and peered around the corner to watch them. Within a minute, all the Soays, except Mo, were in the enclosure scarfing down the grain.

Come on! I silently urged Mo. She inched forward, nose to the ground, checking out her surroundings. I was afraid the others would sense her nervousness and exit before she went in. After a few minutes, Mo couldn't resist. As soon as she entered, I sprang to shut the door. The sheep sprang, too, and began frantically searching for a way out.

I motioned to Louisa, who had been waiting down the

field out of sight. She ran to fetch Trevor. When he arrived, I crawled inside the enclosure, and for the sixth time since buying this little flock, I had to catch them. The enclosure was too low for me to stand up, so on my knees, I lunged at the frightened Soays, grabbing a hind leg, a horn, a handful of wool, slipping and splatting in the mud. Then I half-dragged, half-carried each struggling bundle to the door and handed them to Trevor. He put them in one of the chicken coops. When all seven ewes were in the coop, I stripped off my muck-covered outerwear, ran to the house, and bounded up the stairs to call Tom and Cecily.

"Brilliant! But we won't be able to get out there until tomorrow, say about six o'clock in the evening. We're fully committed to breaking our horse today and tomorrow," Tom said.

It was only eight thirty in the morning. It was gearing up to be a warm couple of days, and Tom had booked the horse whisperer to come by, while the sheep would suffocate in a small chicken coop for nearly two days until the couple could fetch them.

"You might have told me. Last time we talked, you said you'd come out right away," I said.

"To be honest, I didn't think you'd ever catch the little buggers," Tom said.

I trudged back up the field with a bucket of water in one hand and a bucket of food in the other. I opened a small window in the coop for air circulation.

"Sorry, babies, but you're going to have to stay in here until tomorrow night," I said aloud to them, as they huddled nervously in the far corner.

Seven pairs of sorrowful brown eyes stared back from the darkened coop. I felt terrible. By mid-day, the sun had come out, raising the temperature in the coop to around eighty degrees. I opened the little trap door at the bottom of the big door—the one that the chickens used to enter their coops at night. Any amount of fresh air would surely help the Soays. The trap door opening was only one-foot square, not big enough for them get through.

A few hours later, I returned with a bucket of fresh, cool water. Standing in front of the coop, I dropped to my knees, put my head on my chest, and tugged at my hair from the roots. The big door was ajar; the sheep gone. Somehow, they had managed to spring the latch or kick open the door. To rub lanolin in my wounds, they had also made a new hole in the fence and were in the forbidden tree field gleefully dining on succulent spring grass. The sun was shining, it was a beautiful day, and the sheep were content. How could I be upset? Well for one, they would never fall for the grain-in-the-chicken-enclosure trick again.

To blow off steam, I headed for the office and typed a few Braemar House rules to hand out to the tree planters when they arrived in another week:

No smoking in any of the buildings.

No outside shoes in the big house or the Steading.

Everyone must take a sheep on their way home.

Rafi walked in and added one more caveat to my list:

If you use an electrical appliance during your stay, you will be dunked in porridge and feathers and turned out to pasture with the Soays.

The next day, I tried luring the sheep back into the chicken field three more times. They hadn't even bothered to come back to their rightful field at nightfall, which they had always done when escaping in times past. Tom and Cecily were coming that evening around six, and I hadn't been able to get a hold of them to tell them we had a no-go situation. I didn't feel bad about the thought of them driving more than an hour to Braemar only to turn around again when they learned the sheep were still romping in the fields. It would serve them right.

They arrived at six, greeting me as they emerged from their fancy new Land Rover. I enjoyed wiping the smiles from their faces when I told them of the Great Soay Escape. So they could share in my pain, I gave them the long version of the story.

"So, if you had come yesterday, like you said you would, you could have driven into the field, backed up that horse trailer, and loaded them in with no problem," I said.

"Why didn't you call us?" Tom asked.

"I did, several times. No one answered."

They looked at each other. "Shite. We turned the phone off so we could get some sleep. We were bloody exhausted from breaking our horse yesterday," Tom said.

"What a shame," I said, feigning empathy.

"Well, we're here. Let's try herding them into the horse trailer."

I laughed. "I'll just grab a lawn chair and a pitcher of piña coladas. I'm going to enjoy watching this."

"Oh, bugger all. I've forgotten we're dealing with Soays," Tom said.

It would have been nice to sit and watch with a pitcher of booze. Instead, however, I fetched David and Louisa and a roll of duck wire. Tom backed his horse trailer into the chicken field. We unrolled the wire into a funnel shape, hoping to drive the sheep into the trailer. David, Louisa, and Cecily spread themselves along the duck wire, while Tom and I ushered the sheep into the funnel. About ten yards from the trailer, the Soays stopped, turned, and rushed the makeshift fence—mowing down David, Louisa, and Cecily—and were away in less than a minute. We tried three other variations on a theme of this plan until it worked. The coup de grace included Tom and I diving on the sheep and grabbing them by their kicking legs.

We caught five straight away. Amid the frenzy, however, Mo sailed over the chicken field fence, followed by Isabel. Their chutzpah was stunning, as if they had wings. The sheer beauty of their clearing the five-and-a-half-foot fence, with two strands of barbed wire at the top, nearly brought tears to my eyes. Trevor's words of last November echoed through my head: *I know sheep, and there is no way they can get over this fence.* It was a shame he had missed it.

Mo and Isabel ran through the wood and easily squeezed through another boundary fence into the great, wide-open pasture, where the neighbor's sheep safely grazed.

"I almost forgot," Tom said, reaching into his pocket. "I said I'd refund your twenty-five quid."

He pulled a twenty-pound note out of his wallet and looked at it before thrusting it my way.

"Will this do? After all, two of them are missing now. Give us a call if you ever catch them."

I resisted the urge to slap him.

At teatime, I related the capture saga to Trevor.

"At least they're out of our hair now," he said.

"Not quite."

I described how Mo and Isabel had cleared the high fence with room to spare.

"Maybe we should have entered them in the steeple-chase," Trevor said.

He poured himself another cup of tea. The milk sloshed on the saucer and dripped from the bottom of his cup when he raised it to his lips.

"So what are you going to do about them?" he asked.

"Nothing. They're not my problem anymore. Besides, they could be in Glenmeade Forest by now."

"You can't just let them run wild," Trevor said.

"Why not?"

"Because the local farmers won't want them mingling with their flocks. What if they're infected with something?"

"We wormed them last fall."

"It's not just that. They won't want them interbreeding. We've got to catch them."

"So it's *we* now?" I said.

He smirked. "I'll call the neighbors and ask them to keep a watch out."

The next day we got a call that two brown sheep had been spotted in the pasture below the chicken field. We went to observe from a distance Isabel and Mo lounging contentedly with their cousins, who didn't seem bothered by the intruders. In fact, they looked rather sweet together. Farmer John disagreed. We had to come up with a capture plan. Again. We met John and his dad, Robert, with their dogs by the hay barn. Robert shouted a command, and his dogs took off down the hill toward his flock. Swiftly, the dogs gathered the entire bunch into a flowing sea of wool. Isabel and Mo were sucked into the group, confused but unable to break away.

With shouts and whistles, Robert controlled his dogs, who drove the mass toward the barn. Like one giant amoeba, the flock shifted shape while the dogs worked their flank, keeping the sheep in a tight bunch. Robert signaled to the dogs to push the flock into one corner of the fence near to where we stood.

"On my mark, lads. You'll have only one chance," Robert said.

The sheep nervously bunched up against the fence as the dogs corralled them. The Soays were in the center and as panicked as ever.

"Now," Robert said. "Go, go, go!"

John and Trevor burst into the moving bodies, jumping and tripping over the fleecy mob. They leapt onto the Soays with all the grace of two dads fighting for the last-in-stock of the latest prized children's toy. Score!

We put Mo and Isabel in the back of John's truck, tied their legs with twine to keep them from jumping out, and drove them to the chicken field. We locked and sealed them in a more secure coop, and then I called Tom. Within a couple of hours he came to collect them.

"What about the other five quid you owe us?" I asked him, after we loaded Mo and Isabel into the back seat of his Land Rover.

"How about we call it even? Petrol money and all that, you know."

The man had some gall.

"Just take them," I said.

Tom drove away, and I shouted after him, "I hope your fencing and your marriage are both in good shape!"

CHAPTER 21

Preparing

Now that the sheep were out of my hair, I could put my full attention into the tree planting, which was only three weeks away. The biggest project was finishing the tree nursery so that we had a place to hold any extra seedlings we couldn't plant. The massive pile of topsoil that Backhoe Man had carefully shaped into one massive block of topsoil had to be carved into smaller, more manageable, blocks—eight in all—to be easily accessible for moving around and planting seedlings. For three whole days I managed to dig only one pathway through the plateau of soil, creating a trench three feet deep by ten feet long by three feet wide. At this rate it would take twenty-one more days to dig the other seven paths, not to mention daily trips to the chiropractor. Why hadn't we asked Backhoe Man to shape the blocks? Before coming to Braemar I had always thought about things like that. I had been efficient. Seems I was now unwittingly following the Braemar Order: work for the sake of self-contemplation, not for the sake of getting something done.

Wakil offered the bath in the Bothy cottage so I could soak away the aches after three days of hard digging. Since Trevor and I had broken up a few months earlier, hot baths had, once again, been hard to come by. Even though we were on more friendly terms now, our relationship was still tentative enough that I didn't feel comfortable bathing in his cottage.

Just as I was sinking into steaming heaven in the Bothy, Jerusha knocked on the door. She wanted to use the bath, and she wanted it now. She shared the Bothy with Wakil, so I felt obligated to get out. I took my soggy self back to Room 5 and fished out my old friend the hair dryer from the bottom of my storage cubby. Basking under its warmth, I had to laugh. Another day at Braemar. Not long after, Wakil came to my room to apologize about bathus interuptus.

"It's not too late to gas ourselves, you know," he said.

"I can always count on you to brighten my day, Wakky."

"So what do you think?"

"Who'd organize planting six thousand trees?" I said.

"There's all those other people coming to do it. Anyway, you're not that important."

"You know how to make a girl feel special."

"Aw, that's alright," he said and kissed my cheek.

I was going to miss this place come May. How could I not come back?

Other tree prep work included fetching seedlings from the grower; gathering and making an inventory of the tools and communal waterproof outerwear for the volunteers; and staging tree tubes, stakes, fertilizer pellets, and seedlings around the various planting sites on the estate.

On the support side, we needed to plan menus and stock up on food; organize tea breaks and bake goodies; make beds and clean rooms; and organize shuttles to and from town for volunteers arriving by bus. The thought of managing this project, which would include a total of more than one hundred volunteers coming over the two-week period, sent me into a panic. Latif was away for a few weeks, so Rahman, his second, called an all-house meeting to discuss the needs and assign duties. Apparently, my faith had been lacking. As I read through my to-do list to the gathered staff of ten, heads nodded, faces smiled, and assurances were made: "We know what to do." "It's already taken care of." "Relax, no worries."

A superb cook, Adam would head the kitchen, with former student David as sous-chef. After all David's hard work on the estate during the Course, I had hoped for his muscle with the tree planting. But after all his hard work on the estate during the Course, David chose the kitchen. With great reluctance, and strong persuasion from many of us, Wakil agreed to help the kitchen crew and continue his duties baking the daily bread. He didn't do well under pressure; just the thought of "bloody hundreds of tree planters" forced him to his bed for a day. Much to his relief, a drifter had turned up on Braemar's doorstep the day after the Course ended. Gordon had arrived by cab and claimed to be a champion bread maker. His arrival was unexpected because nobody knew him nor where he had come from.

"He was in a right buggerin' state," Wakil said about him.

Apparently, he had been wandering around Eltondean for a few days before someone paid his cab fare to Braemar. (Some of the townies were under the impression that Braemar was a halfway house for wayward souls, which wasn't so far off the mark at times.) Gordon passed the baking test, debuting a selection of breads and cakes to great acclaim during one afternoon tea.

"Just be sure to have plenty of cakes, cookies, hot chocolate, coffee, and tea. And especially Kit Kats," Trevor told me.

Apparently, Kit Kats had had some magical motivating energy to keep the previous year's volunteers working.

I took his advice to heart, and we stocked up. But Adam made us ration them because of the expense.

As the volunteers began to trickle in a few days before the official tree planting started, the place was transformed from quiet retreat to an energetic hive of Old Home Week. Nearly everyone scheduled to come, Braemarites and friends alike, had volunteered the year before. People told stories about how it howled with sleet and snow on the previous year's opening day; how Trevor's predecessor, William, had driven around on a four-wheeler, overseeing the labor and "acting like laird of the manor" and pushing everyone to work; and how a group of beautiful teenage girls from Holland—the "Dutch girls"—had commanded quite an audience of lads, young and old. One of them, eighteen-year-old Brianna, was returning. Trevor (a little too enthusiastically) offered to pick her up from the bus depot in Eltondean.

To prepare for the big event, we distributed all the supplies around the estate where we would be planting, dumping piles of tree tubes and stakes, boxes of zip ties to lash the tubes to the stakes, and buckets of fertilizer pellets. Trevor directed us in setting up the M*A*S*H tent at the sawmill, where we'd eat our lunch. Inside the tent we arranged folding tables using rough-sawn boards from Braemar's own ash trees for benches supported on log rounds. Rafi set up an industrial-sized stainless steel sink and counter top, which had been lying around at the hay barn. He also brought in a ten-gallon water boiler, fired by bottled gas, for making tea and heating water for dish washing.

At the big house, Adam and crew would cook two lunches: one for the tree planters, which someone would drive out to the tent, and one for the support staff, who would eat in the house. Everyone would regroup for supper at the big house.

The day before the event, Trevor fetched our seedlings from the tree nursery, bags and bags containing thousands of oak, ash, pine, aspen, willow, hazel, rose, beech, and other native species. More volunteers arrived, ranging in age from five through seventy-five; whole families, couples, gaggles of friends, parent–child combos, and singles from all over Great Britain, Holland, Israel, Spain, Turkey, Germany, and the United States. They were students, executives, housewives, shop owners, librarians, counselors, professors, doctors and healers, artists, actors, and simply-looking-for-something-to-doers. Some would stay a few days, others a week, and a handful for the whole two weeks. Some would help the support staff, cooking meals and preparing beds for new arrivals, while most would help plant trees.

I could hardly sleep the night before, thinking about the responsibility of planting six thousand trees and wondering whether I had forgotten to prepare anything. The rest of me was excited to finally get started on the project that had initially brought me to Scotland.

CHAPTER 22

Planting

DAY 1

Braemar's second annual tree planting began under blotchy skies and fifty-four degrees. Founder Iskandar's widow, Roseanne, arrived from England to kick off the event with a special ceremony at the sawmill. In Iskandar's memory, she planted an oak seedling.

"What a wonderful gift to Braemar, and to the world, these trees will be," she proclaimed.

She carefully set the seedling into a hole, and I packed fresh earth around it. Trevor slipped a tree tube over the seedling and battened the tube to a stake with two plastic zip ties. The crowd of thirty or so clapped, then we unceremoniously dispersed to begin doing the same, thousands and thousands of times over.

Our gang of macho young bucks (the "Young People," I called them) comprised a half-dozen guys, and a couple of women, in their late teens and early twenties. I sent them ahead to dig the seedling holes and to pound the tree stakes into the ground. A second wave of volunteers dropped fertilizer pellets into each hole, and a third wave placed the seedlings into the holes and put the tubes over them. Everyone seemed to know what they were doing;

we planted nearly one thousand trees by day's end! Only five thousand more to go.

DAY 2

Thirty more tree planters arrived, so I decided to convene a daily briefing on the front steps of the big house. We reviewed how to properly plant a seedling and attach a tube to a stake, which species we would be planting, and where that day. I threw in a few safety notes, such as being careful on the steep hillsides and watching where you step in the boggy sections, where Wellington boots and small children had been known to disappear.

In the afternoon, a local television station came to interview me on the scene about the Millennium Forest for Scotland project. I talked about our endeavors and stressed that we were part of a larger vision to replant Scotland with native trees for future generations.

Volunteers planted another thousand trees, while I spent most of the day replenishing supplies to keep pace with the swift work. I also had to round up a few volunteers to prepare and deliver drinks and goodies to the field for our breaks and to help the kitchen staff set up lunch in the M*A*S*H tent. By suppertime I could barely lift a fork to my mouth.

DAY 3

Trevor returned to his garden, confident that I had everything in hand (at least someone had confidence in me). I was sorry to lose not only his help and expertise but his company too. Derrick was now my right-hand tree planter. He had spent the winter helping with the Course, but he really lived for the trees. He had also played a large role in past Braemar planting projects and was capable of single-handedly planting several hundred trees in a day.

The Young Peoples' collective testosterone was so

abundant, they had finished digging six thousand holes and pounding a stake next to each one by lunchtime. No doubt their motivation was partly attributable to Dutch Girl Brianna, who had been hanging out with them and was clearly demonstrating her own hard work.

I suspect that one particular volunteer, Brewster, had dug the largest share of holes and pounded the largest share of stakes, since he was an early riser, and most of the Young People didn't even get out of bed before eleven. A svelte, forty-something chap, and self-described do-it-yourselfer, Brewster was a return volunteer. No one seemed to know how he had discovered Braemar. He always asked for the most difficult jobs and complained only when the job wasn't challenging enough. However, he had one dislike.

"I'm all for the trees but not really keen on sticking them in the ground," he told me.

I sent him to the tree nursery to finish digging the remaining seven pathways through the massive block of topsoil that I had tried digging myself a few weeks earlier. Brewster was delighted with the assignment but disappointed when the Young People showed up to help. Regardless, they finished the job in two hours. Brewster went to help Trevor in the garden, digging large rocks out of the polytunnel beds, digging additional drainage ditches, and shifting tons of muck from the compost bins to the garden beds. Trevor loved it. A bromance made in heaven.

Unfortunately, we had fallen short on house support staff. David and Jerusha had left on the morning of Day 3 to join Principal Latif in Oxford for a week-long Ibn Arabi conference. Without their help, the rest of the already slim house staff were stretched to their limits. Worse still, whenever Latif wasn't around, fewer people would step up to volunteer. Latif had a gift for encouraging people to participate, probably something to do with his sole power

to tell people to leave Braemar when they failed to participate. Now, I needed to ask for volunteers among the tree
planters to help in the kitchen and with housekeeping. The
response was effusive: ten hands went up at supper. They
all thought that cooking and housework would be easier
than planting trees. They were in for a surprise.

Though we were making good progress with the planting, the eleven thousand trees that had been planted the
year before also needed to be weeded by hand. Essentially
this involved taking off the tree tubes, pulling out the grass
(which could suppress and kill the seedlings), and putting
the tubes back on. The fiddly plastic zip ties slowed the
process.

I had carefully planned how many new seedlings we
had to plant each day, factoring in time for weeding the
previous year's trees. But now I started to feel some pressure. In order to get our grant money for the trees, we had
to plant six thousand and weed through at least half of the
previous year's.

Day 4

Unable to sleep for thinking that we might get behind
schedule, I got up at six and headed to the big house to
begin laying the table for breakfast. I wanted the volunteers to arrive to a table full of power food to get them
through the morning. Derrick joined me in the task, his
unquashable enthusiasm giving him strength where mine
had begun to wane. Together, we made the tea, toast, and
porridge and prepared the table.

I also checked to make sure we had enough goodies for morning coffee and afternoon tea breaks. In the
evenings, the Young People had been hanging out in the
Steading, pounding on handheld drums and doing whatever else Young People did. Word had it that they had also
been raiding the pantry after hours, making a sizable dent

in the Kit Kat supply.

By this time, our volunteers numbered seventy, and Adam the cook had been making daily trips into Eltondean for extra food. Reluctantly, he agreed to buy another six boxes of Kit Kats, but to balance the food budget, he was making cutbacks in other areas. He opted for instant coffee for the volunteers' morning break. The coffee drinkers were on the verge of mutiny, and I worried they'd stop working. Standing among the mutineers in the shallow, swampy section of ground at the farthest reaches of the estate, I raised Adam via walkie-talkie. He was in the kitchen at the big house, rushing around preparing lunch. I relayed the complaint about his instant coffee.

Adam's voice crackled over the device: *They came here to do a job out of the goodness of their hearts. They know what that entails because this is Braemar. It's about service to God, not about luxuries.*

He continued, but I had turned down the volume and slowly counted to ten. When I turned it back up again, Adam was still ranting: . . . *graciously accepting instant coffee, then so be it. This isn't a hotel!*

"Got it," I said, jumping in as soon as he took his finger off the transmission button.

His voice came through again: *And if they don't like it, then they can bloody well come to the house and make real coffee for themselves.*

One of the Young People who had been listening to the conversation volunteered to make the half-mile trek back to the big house. I suspected it had less to do with good coffee and more to do with the fact that it would give him a break from working.

"Okay, it's sorted. Someone's coming over," I said to Adam.

Then, he can also bring lunch out to the crew, because we're already short-handed in the kitchen, he replied.

"Understood," I said.

He continued: *It amazes me that anybody is complaining at all. When I was a lad—*

Adam was being funny now. I turned off the walkie-talkie and shoved it in my pocket. There had been nothing in the tree planting notes about coffee mutinies.

DAY 5

Volunteers continued to arrive, which meant the house and kitchen staff needed more help. But few wanted to help in the house; everyone wanted to plant trees. Those who had thought that cooking and housekeeping was easier than planting realized their mistake and returned to planting. So Rahman, Braemar's head in Latif's absence, began press-ganging people from among the tree planters while they tried to dodge him.

In addition to rising every morning at six, I had been staying up until the last dish was washed after supper. My pillow hadn't seen the back of my head until nearly eleven every night. I had hoped to get some rest between dusk and supper, but instead I always found myself picking up scattered tools and tree supplies at the end of the day. At supper, volunteers hounded me with personal requests: *Can I switch rooms? Can I have an extra pillow? Can I borrow some raingear? Can I do my laundry?* House staff also hounded me with their requests: *Remind the volunteers to leave the mud outside. Remind the volunteers they need to help clean up the supper dishes. Remind the volunteers they need to strip their beds before they leave.* It was endless.

One bright spot was the arrival of my sister, a familiar face who understood me. I drove into Eltondean to pick up Mary Linn, her friend, Jen, and her friend's mother, Andy, who were joining in the tree planting fun. Mary Linn and Jen were both military wives living in Germany, and Jen's mother had flown over from New York. Four months pregnant, my sister was staying in my room with me and my fifty egg babies. The latter were humming along in the incubator, which automatically turned the eggs with a clunk every twelve hours. My sister asked whether the incubator could be made any quieter. I suggested the noise would be good training for her when, in the not-too-distant future, she would have to get up and tend to a squalling infant.

Day 6

No one volunteered to prepare and deliver tea and goodies for the morning and afternoon breaks, so I had to do it myself. So much for the support the staff had promised me a few weeks ago. I supposed I was lucky to have had anyone show up to work at all, given the rainy weather. And, given the weather, hot drinks and goodies were especially important to keep the volunteers from packing it in and heading back to bed.

As soon as I had gotten the tree planters started at the far end of the estate, I trudged a quarter mile back to the M*A*S*H tent to light the water boiler so it would be ready for making tea by our morning break. Like the generators, the boiler was fickle; sometimes it heated water quickly and sometimes it took a couple of hours. I lit the boiler and headed back to the field to join the tree planters.

A half hour later, I hiked back to the tent to check on the water. Hottish, but still not boiling. By break time, the water had only just come to the boil. I still had to make the tea and pour it into flasks. But I realized there were only five tea bags left at the tent. I didn't have time to run back to the big house for more. So I used five tea bags for about three gallons of water. (This ratio might suit an American, but not a real British tea drinker, I discovered.) I packed the flasks and goodies in a box. Two volunteers arrived to collect it and bring it back to the volunteers in the field. I stayed behind to clean up and start more water boiling for washing the upcoming lunch dishes.

Twenty minutes later, a woman called Rahima showed up at the tent and kindly beseeched me: Had there been a mix-up? Perhaps I had mistakenly dumped used dishwater into the flasks instead of tea?

I knew that the other volunteers had chosen her as their emissary because she was a frightfully kind person and the least likely to bash me over the head with a teapot.

"Don't get me wrong," she said. "We are ever so grateful for your efforts. It's just that the tea was not quite what we're accustomed to."

I confessed my sins of using only five tea bags.

"Yes, that would explain it. Would you mind terribly if I prepared another pot?"

"There's no more hot water."

"Oh, I see," Rahima said.

My eyes welled with tears as I told her I was having trouble finding volunteers to help with refreshments. She put her arm around me and promised to find some people for the job. She also promised to drop all deportation proceedings if I promised not to make tea again. E-V-E-R!

DAY 7

At the end of the first week, many of the hardest working volunteers were scheduled to leave. And by "hardest working," I mean those over the age of thirty. This left us with a volunteer pool of mostly Young People, who were beginning to drop like aphids even though they were the most able-bodied. They never appeared before eleven in the morning, took longer and more frequent breaks, and usually skipped out quickly after supper, avoiding the washing up. It took four of them working together to plant one tree for every twenty trees staffer Derrick could plant by himself.

The previous evening I had caught two of the Young People raiding the Kit Kat stash, so I had hid what was left of it in a nondescript tin on the top pantry shelf and declared that Kit Kats would be served only during afternoon breaks.

That afternoon it rained buckets, so instead of planting we decided to begin weeding the previous year's trees. Trevor, whom I hadn't even seen in a few days, agreed to help me get the volunteers started. As an aside, he casually mentioned he had acquired 2,500 more trees to plant in a windbreak along the far side of the chicken field! Before supper, I took to my bed in self-imposed exile with a bad head cold, falling asleep to the rain pelting down on the skylight above my bed, the gentle hum of the incubator, and the groans of my sister, who had also taken to her bed with a migraine.

Day 8

I emerged from my room to more rain and fewer volunteers. Who could blame them? We all needed a day off, and no one wanted to be outside in the cold, wet dreariness. A dozen of the bravest headed out anyway, and we managed to weed five hundred tree tubes in The Brae section of the estate. It was more than I could have asked for. But stress had already taken its toll.

Whenever I ventured indoors, I was met with a chorus of *Sarah, I need . . .*; *Sarah, can you . . .*; *Sarah, what do we do about . . . .* Was I the only person on Planet Braemar who could fulfill requests and resolve issues? Clearly my delegation skills were lacking.

After supper, I vowed to enjoy a relaxing cup of chamomile tea; no washing dishes, no putting out little fires. I had just finished speaking to Rahman about the impending arrival of a fresh batch of volunteers and was headed back to the dining room for my cuppa, when both Hadiyya and Rahman called out in unison behind me.

"Oh, Sarah?"

I wheeled around.

"If I hear my name one more time, I'm going to scream! In fact, I'm already screaming!"

Rahman stepped forward and gently put his hand on my back, then guided me into the pantry, shutting the door behind us.

"I can't take this anymore! Everybody wants a piece of me every second of the day. Why can't you people sort yourselves out and let me worry about planting trees?"

"Yes, we know you've been working hard. All we wanted to tell you was to sit down and enjoy a cup of tea. We weren't going to ask for anything," Rahman said, rather sheepishly.

"That's it? You were going to tell me to relax?"

Rahman turned his eyes to the floor for a second, then looked back to meet mine.

"Uh, yes," he said.

"Oh, for fuc—" I started to say.

I covered my face with my hands. Though I felt like an idiot, Rahman understood, promising that I could focus on the trees and leave the house support to him. He also ordered me to take the following day off.

Any spiritual breakthroughs I had made thus far had pretty much gone by the wayside. I was simply coasting on "just get it done."

CHAPTER 23

Rooting

Day 9

I heeded Rahman's advice and took the day off from tree planting to give my sister Mary Linn and her friend Jen a tour of the Scottish Borders. Jen's mother, Andy, decided to stay behind and help in the kitchen. Ahava, the Israeli student who had stayed on after the Course ended, let us borrow her car. Against the better judgement of Rafi, Braemar maintenance man, who was wise in all things mechanical. He had done some engine work on the blue hatchback and confirmed it wasn't in the best condition.

"I really wish you'd reconsider. It might break down at any time," Rafi cautioned.

"Well so could I, so this car will be in good company," I said.

The three of us gals puttered off down the hill on our way to the town of Jedburgh. Jen and Mary Linn covered their eyes and gasped every time another car passed us from the opposite direction. I smiled, remembering how scary driving on the left-hand side of the road had been for me when I first arrived.

We explored the ruins of Jedburgh Abbey then got back in the car to head to Floors Castle, the two-hundred-plus room home of the Tenth Duke of Roxburghshire. But when I turned the key, the engine sputtered. After several minutes, it finally turned over, and we set off for Floors. I watched as the temperature gauge soared into the red zone. By the time we pulled into the parking lot at the castle, steam was coming from under the hood. The ticket booth attendant kindly allowed me to use her phone to call Braemar. On the other end of the line Rafi said *I told you so* and instructed me to pour water into the radiator after the engine cooled.

In the meantime, we explored the castle, a huge pile of stone consisting of one central portion flanked by two major wings. Only ten of the two hundred rooms were open to the public. The small admission fee helped pay the electric bills (God help them if they used generators). The sprawling fortress was stuffed with antiques, paintings, glassware, tapestries, and knickknacks from all over the world. Every room was like a scene from a period drama. I couldn't imagine abluting something like that every week! It would take three days just to find the vacuum cleaner if you couldn't remember where you left it.

When we returned to Ahava's jalopy, we fished plastic water bottles out of the parking lot garbage can and filled them in the public restroom. We then poured the water into the radiator. I said a short prayer before turning the key, but my supplication was rejected. The engine was silent.

"We'll have to pop-start it," Mary Linn said.

Jen and I got out to push, while the pregnant pop-starter took the controls. First, though, we had to push the car about twenty feet up a slight incline to the highest point of the gravel drive. Six people stood by and watched Jen and I make three attempts before succeeding. None offered to help. So much for my day off.

"You ready?" I shouted to my sister.

"Let 'er rip!" she yelled from the car.

Jen and I gave the car a hefty shove and kept pushing until it outpaced us. Mary Linn popped the clutch, starting the car on the first try. Hallelujah! The effort had fortified our appetites, so we headed into the nearby town for fish and chips. Now that the engine had had a chance to warm up, surely it would start again.

It didn't. For fifteen minutes we grinded the engine over and over. We shouted and cursed and prayed, much to the amusement of passersby. Again, none offered to help. I let my sister take over the controls again, she who had owned crap cars all her life and had experience with such things. She pounded the pedal and cussed so harshly that I feared for her unborn baby. But the miracle worker got it started, even if blue smoke was pouring from the exhaust. We traded places again and took off for Braemar. At every roundabout, where I had to slow, I depressed both the clutch and the accelerator to keep the engine from sputtering out. About twenty miles from Braemar, our little bombshell was really protesting. There was so much smoke pouring from the tailpipe, people behind us had to use their headlights.

"Mary, Mother of God, please get us home before this heap disintegrates," I prayed aloud.

Then I added: "Bis'mallah ir rahman ir rahim," *In the name of God, the compassionate, the merciful.*

It couldn't hurt to beseech God from both camps.

"What?" my two passengers said in unison.

"It's Arabic. We say it at Braemar before meals," I explained.

"Biz ... whatever you said," Jen laughed, and then took the easy route: "Hail Mary, hail Mary!"

I continued my prayer: "Dear Lord, if you get us home safely, I promise to listen to Rafi. I promise not to use my hair dryer anymore. I promise not to argue with Trevor.

I promise not to push the tree planters too hard. And I promise not to be such a smartass."

Outside Eltondean, the temperature gauge bounced violently to the limits of the red zone. The car started to shake, and, probably knowing that my promises were a bit too ambitious, God split the difference and let us break down right in front of the police station. The police let me use their phone to call Braemar. Rafi was just on his way out to pick up some new tree planters at the bus station in town. A half hour later he came to our rescue. He tied the dead car to the Land Rover with a towrope.

"I can't believe your luck breaking down where and when you did," Rafi said.

"Right living," I smiled.

"It's something. Anyway, I hope you'll listen to me from now on?"

"I promised God."

"Really?"

"Yes, now how do we get it home?"

Rafi explained that he would sit in the towed car while the rest of us would ride in the Land Rover.

"When I do this with my hands," he said, gesturing, "it means slow down. When I do this," (another gesture), "it means speed up."

Rafi folded his six-foot-four-inch frame into the compact blue blob. Jen sat facing backwards in the cargo hold of the Land Rover to relay Rafi's hand signals to me for the ten miles back to Braemar. It took us eight miles to realize that Rafi's thumbs-up signal meant "A-Okay," not "speed up." We never did figure out what furiously waving arms meant, but we arrived at Braemar safely anyway.

Day 10

Near the end of the two-week event, our prime goodie stash had reached a critical low. The Young People had discovered my new Kit Kat hiding place, so I had to find yet another hiding spot for the few precious bars that were left. Hadiyya had bought cheap cookies as a supplement because Adam wouldn't let us spend any more money on Kit Kats. And on top of that, Gordon, our homeless drop-in cake and bread maker, had left in the middle of the night, taking with him—it was suspected—a handful of cash from someone's wallet.

At supper, I asked a dozen people whether they could take charge of refreshment breaks the next day, but every single one turned me down with some excuse. It would be up to me.

DAY 11

I was in the kitchen by seven in the morning. No one was up yet to help lay the table for breakfast, not even Derrick. After setting the table and putting out the food, I rooted around in the pantry for some treats for the morning's coffee break. I found only about a dozen cookies; no cakes, no nothing. Celeste, Adam's wife, came in with her basket. A few days a week, she would take food back to the Steading Cottage for her family. For the past several days, she had been looking after a houseful of children, including some that belonged to tree planters. I didn't want to impose on her, but I was desperate. I asked if she could whip up some coffee cake or something. She said she would try but couldn't make any promises.

I sulked back to the pantry to grab what was left of the Kit Kats, which I had carefully hidden for the third time the night before. They were gone. All gone. I burst into tears. Celeste rushed over and put her arm around my shoulder. With hiccupping sobs, I spilled out my woes about how the staff had promised me before this whole event even got started that I had nothing to worry about. They'd help with tea and coffee breaks. I was not to worry.

They had let me down, and now there were no goodies for our breaks. Surely the tree planters would go on strike, and we'd never finish the job.

Celeste told me not to worry; to leave everything with her.

I called the Gate Lodge to talk to Trevor.

"It's me," I said, when he answered.

"Hello."

"Hello."

"You sound upset," he said.

"It hasn't exactly been a stress-free ten days."

"No."

"I need a favor."

"What is it?"

"Can you guide the volunteers this morning? We're starting in the Hoscote section, and they need to know exactly where to plant."

"I've got Daisy for the weekend, but I'm sure she'd love to help," he said.

"Thanks," I was barely able to say.

"Are you all right?"

"I will be."

"Right. Anything else?"

What I wanted to say was: *Yes, what's happened to us? Why are we still keeping each other at arm's length?* But I didn't.

"Just take the volunteers for the morning. That would be a huge help," I said.

Two hours later, I waved goodbye to my sister and her friends, on their way back to Germany.

"When you talk to Mom and Dad, tell them all about Braemar. You know, how it's not a brainwashing cult that's taking advantage of me, and how much I love it here," I said, bawling my eyes out.

While Trevor took charge of the majority of the

volunteers, I took two of them to help me in the tree nursery. Together, the three of us stuck five hundred seedlings in the blocks of soil in neatly aligned rows. The trees were leftovers that Trevor had gotten from a local forestry worker, which we wouldn't have time to plant. My two helpers kept me laughing with their jokes and imitations of various British accents. It was fun, and for once I didn't even mind the rain, even though it had turned the nursery into a mud bath.

After supper, I skipped the washing up and headed straight for the television lounge for some mindless relaxation. An hour into my film, Brewster, our champion worker, entered with a cup of tea. I didn't think the non-stop workhorse DIY guy ever took a break. He had been busting a gut in the garden for the past week.

"How is the digging in the polytunnels going?" I asked.

"Lovely. I'm really enjoying it."

"So the ground isn't too hard, then?"

"Hard as a diamond. Just the way I like it. I'll take more jobs like that."

He began sipping his tea. Loudly. I turned up the volume on the television.

"Thurrpp, ahh. Thurrpp, ahh," he sipped for several minutes.

Then he set his cup down and promptly fell asleep. He began to snore; long, snarfly sounds, as if he were choking. I turned the TV up louder. One of the staff came in and asked me to turn it down. I turned it off instead and listened to Brewster snoring.

"Dear Lord, whatever I've done to upset you, I apologize a thousand times," I said.

I returned to my room in the Steading and crawled into bed, vowing that if my situation ever got bad enough to warrant a nervous breakdown over some Kit Kats, I would quit my job, move to a foreign country, and do

something totally different. Then I realized that's exactly what I had done, and started crying again. Only three
more days, I told myself.

Day 12

Having just returned to Braemar from a conference in
England, and having heard all about my various breakdowns, Principal Latif, himself, brought goodies and drinks
to the field for our morning break. It was a sweet gesture.
Unfortunately, the volunteers had already returned to the
house for coffee. There were so few left by now, it had
made sense to send them to the house instead. I stayed
behind to finish attaching a few more tree tubes to stakes
when Latif arrived, laden with the crate of food.

"Don't tell me you're the only one working," he said,
concerned.

I stood up from the boggy earth. "The others headed
back to the house. You didn't see them?"

"I'm afraid not." He set the box on the ground.

I looked at the cache. "I'm sorry you had to lug that
all the way out here. The one day we didn't need anybody
to organize a break."

"It's quite all right. I'm sorry that you've had trouble
finding people to help."

"Not exactly what I had hoped for."

"No. Anyway, how are you?" he asked.

"Much better. We're nearly finished planting, which
leaves more time for weeding last year's trees. We might
even spare a few volunteers to help plant potatoes in the
garden."

"Thank God. You've done a remarkable job."

"Not me. The volunteers. At least the trees got put in
the ground, even if we were short-handed elsewhere."

I was amazed by how nonchalant I sounded.

"Don't hesitate to ask me directly if there's anything

you need. I assure you it will be taken care of."

I smiled. "Let me help you with that. There's still time to catch coffee at the big house."

We each grabbed an end of the crate and carried it back together. It felt good to be acknowledged by him. He seemed a different person, much lighter in spirit than when the Course had been in full swing.

Later that day, Trevor joined us to plant more seedlings in the forbidden tree field next to the chicken field. Many of the saplings had died (though not because of the Soays). One positive thing the Soays had done was to eat the grass down to the nub, making it much easier to dig the holes for the new seedlings. I was happy to be working alongside Trevor again. He, too, seemed lighter; however, I kept my hope about us being together at bay for fear of being hurt again.

Day 13

Only fifteen volunteers were left at the end, and a few had been present since Day 1. Brianna had gone home, and her country of Young People had dissolved. We woke to a sopping coverlet of wet snow, which continued to fall after breakfast. The snow made it difficult to locate the white plastic bags with the seedlings, which we had left along the track the previous afternoon. Despite the dwindling volunteer help, I showed some personal fortitude and headed outside after breakfast. If our leafless twigs were going to freeze, I thought, then they were better off stuck in the ground where the roots would stand a chance of surviving.

Five others joined me out of similar fortitude, guilt, or pity. I was so grateful that they showed up at all, that I didn't even care that two of them went back to the house for morning coffee and never returned. By late morning, the skies had turned cerulean once again. More volunteers joined us after lunch, and we finished planting the last of the six thousand trees! There was also time to plant more of Trevor's unsanctioned trees and to finish weeding seedlings in The Brae section. I was reminded how these simple things fed my soul.

DAY 14

I spent the day inspecting all the newly planted areas, making sure the tubes had been tied to the stakes correctly and the trees had been properly planted. Curiously, some people missed the point of burying the roots under the soil. Fortunately, there were few seedlings in that condition.

Most of the volunteers joined Trevor in the garden, spreading more manure in the polytunnels and planting potatoes by the bushelful in the newly-plowed field. Brewster was not happy about sharing the hard labor with others. He had already dug out all the big rocks from both polytunnels, sifting through more than ten cubic yards of soil on his own. To appease him, Trevor sent Brewster to the moors alone to dig post holes around the water supply in preparation to fence out the sheep that had caused the E. coli problem. If only Brewster had been around when we had had the Soays; I might have gotten my dream fence.

After lunch we dismantled the M*A*S*H tent. It was sad to see our mess hall and rainy day hideaway coming down.

Following afternoon tea, we had an impromptu closing ceremony at the far end of the front lawn, where we planted another oak tree. I invited Trevor to do the official honors. He got on his knees and gently shoved dirt around the roots, while I pounded in the stake and put the tree tube around the seedling. About thirty people circled around in the cool, settling mist.

"The oak is a symbol of strength. It's also a hardy and ancient species that's been growing in Great Britain for millennia. May our little seedlings still be growing here long after we're gone," I said.

Everyone clapped.

"Well, thanks everyone. It's been fun," I concluded. I could only say that now it was over.

The next day, I wandered through the planting areas again, finding three spades, one pair of pruning shears, a jack-knife, two water bottles, a five-gallon water jug, a plastic garbage bag containing a clump of Scots pine seedlings, one leather air force-style cap, and two dozen tree tubes.

I took the long way back to the big house from the lower hillside in the Sheil section, passing through the spruce plantation in Knowe Hill and emerging on the other side. I sat down on my favorite stump overlooking our little valley. The vast foreground of last year's plantings stretched out before me and up the hillside behind me. Five thousand trees had been planted in Knowe Hill alone the previous year, and all of them would need to be weeded the following year. In another few months the rosebay willow herb would be six feet high, obscuring all the tree tubes. Would the weeds choke them out? Would they survive?

A strong feeling of responsibility toward these seedlings washed over me. I wanted to see them become a forest. Tree seedlings were an invitation to have faith. I had rushed around for two weeks, fretting over details, picking up pieces, dropping others, worried we wouldn't complete the job. I had finally accomplished what I had been invited to do nearly a year ago now. But you can't rush a forest. It takes nurture, time—and a whole lot of Kit Kats.

CHAPTER 24

Slouching Toward Faith

Just after the tree planting event ended, staffer and cook extraordinaire Adam was organizing a benefit concert for Braemar in Creston Village Hall. The headliner was Arthur Brown, an ageing British music legend whom I had never heard of but everyone else seemed to know. Adam had been worrying that no one would show up, that the whole thing would flop, and that the Village Hall would be filled with the sound of one hand clapping, drowned out only by chirping crickets.

At least two hundred people filled the moderately-sized hall, including just about everyone in Creston—they weren't ones to miss a party—plus a sizeable chunk of the Eltondean population and Braemarites from far and wide. I certainly intended to strip off my Gore-Tex outerwear and have some fun. After my two-week-long trial, Adam could have sat on the stage and played a comb covered with waxed paper, and I would have enjoyed it simply because I didn't have to organize, manage, or take responsibility for any of it.

The concert was a big deal for Creston, and for Braemar. Adam, on his guitar, and his two sidekicks, on bass and keyboards, entertained the crowd for the first hour. I stood at the makeshift bar with Wakil, talking about all the funny, and not so funny, things that had happened during the previous months. I was already two glasses of wine beyond my limit of one, when Trevor strolled up and stood beside me. He ordered a glass of Chardonnay. My merlot encouraged me to take advantage of an opportunity that might otherwise have gone wanting. Suddenly, I felt a woman scorned.

"I see you managed to tear yourself away from the garden," I said to Trevor.

He looked at me and nodded. "Enjoying yourself?"

"Do you care?"

He handed the bartender a five-pound note, took a sip of wine, and turned to face me.

"I care a lot more than you think."

I snorted. "How silly of me not to notice."

Wakil raised his eyebrows.

"I suppose I deserved that," Trevor said.

"I haven't even started yet."

I took a gulp of fermented tongue-loosener, while Wakil slunk off into the crowd.

"Go on then, get it out of your system," Trevor said.

"Okay. You have been the world's biggest flip-flopping bastard since January."

"I know. I'm sorry."

"You've done nothing but sulk, be rude, and criticize me unneceral . . . unnecessesserl . . . without any reason at all. And you broke promise after promise to be nice to me."

"You're right."

"You're a selfish, rude, suffering, selfish, stupid, selfish fool!" I yelled.

The point didn't need driving home, but I tried anyway by pouring half a glass of wine down his shirt front. It would have been a full glass if he hadn't reacted so quickly.

"Yes, I have been a complete bastard. You have a right

to be angry," he said, grabbing my wrist.

"Damn right I do."

"But not to pour wine all over me."

He continued holding my wrist, looking me in the eye. Then he set his glass down and took mine from me, also putting it down on the bar.

On stage Adam had just introduced Arthur Brown to a wildly applauding and pumped up crowd. The musician instantly sent a shocking G chord through the hall and began his set. Trevor took my hand and led me to the dance floor. And we began to dance.

Soon, Arthur Brown had such control of the crowd that he had us lying on the floor on our backs and kicking our feet in the air. I kicked my legs wildly, and my skirt flopped up over my chest. Many Braemar board members were in a similarly compromising position, which was both amusing and frightening.

When Arthur burst into one of his most famous songs, "Fire," the opening line of which was "I am the god of hellfire," the crowd nearly raised the roof in a roar of applause and cheers. I found the line somewhat ironic, given this was a benefit concert for a spiritual retreat. But after seven months at Braemar, little surprised me anymore. Apparently, in the old days, Arthur Brown used to sing the song while wearing a helmet with flames shooting out of it. Too bad he had toned down his act.

For three hours Trevor and I laughed and danced, as if we hadn't just spent the past four months barely speaking to each other. During a couple of slow dances, he held me tightly, and we swayed like old lovers. I melted into his arms and the touch of his hands on my back. At midnight the band wrapped up, but many of us stayed on to chat with the band and help tidy up.

Trevor slipped out without my noticing. I wasn't sure what to think. I didn't see him until the next morning outside the garden shed, lying on his back under the tow hitch of the tractor, wrench in hand.

"Good morning," I said.

He scooched himself out from under the tractor, sat up, and smiled.

"Good morning."

"A blast last night, huh?" I said.

"Fantastic."

"So how are you feeling?"

"A little fuzzy headed but all right. How about you?" he asked.

"A little fuzzy headed but all right. So . . ."

He gazed up at the hill pasture, and we both watched the new lambs for a minute. I sat down next to him and put my hand on his knee.

"What are you so afraid of?"

He scratched his ear, still avoiding my eyes, and then he spoke.

"It's just . . . you know. It's just . . . things happened. It was a long winter, and I had a lot of time to think about things."

"And what did you conclude?"

"That I've missed you, and that I'm still uncertain if things will work."

I took "things" to mean another try at us. I didn't know what to say. I stood.

"What do *you* want?" he asked.

I was growing tired of trying to woo him back, so at that moment I wasn't sure what I wanted either.

"I miss you too," I said.

Trevor smiled.

"I'm going back to Montana in a few weeks to sell my house."

He lay back down on his back and began fiddling with the trailer hitch again.

"What's your plan after that?"

"I'd like to come back here."

"Right."

His voice sounded hopeful, like he meant "right" in a positive way, rather than *Oh bugger, do you have to?* way. I realized that although I really wanted to come back, and had only thought about leaving because of our struggles, I hadn't told him I thought about coming back. Maybe his fear was due to his assumption that I was leaving for good.

"I'm going to skip coffee today. I have to finish this. Can you help me in the garden later?" he said.

The rest of the day we worked side by side planting vegetable starts in the garden. We didn't talk much, but it seemed we both felt different, in a good way. Later, he invited me for a long walk around the estate to inspect the trees and discuss the winter of our discontent. The sheeps' antics had been a large part of our undoing. At the same time, they had gotten their metaphorical hooves under the fencing around our souls and pried away at our personal shortcomings and vulnerabilities. The opportunity to lie on our backs and kick our feet in the air in deference to "the god of hellfire" had offered us a new perspective. Were we better together or alone? Fear of the unknown seemed like a lame excuse for not trying. We stopped along the track to take in the view across our little valley. And then we kissed, not caring whether anyone saw us. It felt new, like our first kiss. We would give us another try.

I felt excited but in a more mature way, not like when we first got together. I hoped to be more optimistic as well as realistic about what a relationship would be like knowing that I would eventually run out of visa time and have to go home.

* * *

At teatime the next day, Esmé, Colin, and Matea tramped into the dining room and plunked themselves in chairs with exaggerated sighs of exhaustion. They had just come from the garden, their little faces tried desperately to look worn and overworked.

"You wouldn't believe how hard that clay soil is. We've been digging in it for one whole hour, nonstop," Esmé said.

The rest of us at the table exchanged looks and giggled. "That's the life of a gardener," I sympathized.

"I know. It's such hard work," Matea reiterated. She mimicked Esmé's sigh, then hunched her shoulders against her neck as if relieving tension.

"I much prefer animals to gardening, I think," she said, in her sophisticated five-year-old way.

"Me too. Except for sheep," I said.

Esmé took a bite of her freshly-baked shortbread cookie. "The eggs are looking really good now," she said, crumbs tumbling from her mouth.

I clanked my teaspoon on my saucer. She was referring to the chicken eggs humming away in the incubator in my room. Earlier, she had admitted to having led forays into my room with the children who had come during the tree planting with their parents. I had already told her off for it because they had been removing the incubator lid to have a closer look and letting the heat out.

"Right, that's it. You promised not to go in my room again. You broke your promise, and that makes me very angry," I said.

The children hung their heads and mumbled an apology.

"If you do it again, you're in big trouble."

I tried my best to glare at them, but it was like trying to be mad at puppies. I felt bad for scolding them. I felt even worse when I returned to my room after tea to discover what they had really been up to. On my desk were four vases of bright yellow daisies. Beside each vase was a child-scribbled note: *With love from Esmé*; *With love from Colin*; *With love from Matea*. And the fourth note: *With love from me*, in Trevor's distinctive hand.

I rushed to find the three mini musketeers and thank them. Matea and Esmé grabbed my middle for a group squeeze, while Colin just shrugged. (The fourth musketeer received his thanks later. It had been his idea for the children.)

The chicks picked five in the morning to make their entrance, waking me with the sound of muffled peeping coming from the incubator. I watched the first chick emerge. Its tiny beak chipped away at the brown shell for several minutes before the shell split and popped out a slick black chick. Two more began to hatch. Chirping shrilly, the hatched ones raised and lowered their stubby wings and flopped around, bumbling into one another and the other eggs. I lifted the lid for a better look. Immediately they sensed my presence and stumbled toward me. I quickly replaced the lid to keep them inside where it was warm, and so they wouldn't imprint on me—that is, think I was their mother.

I hurried to Ahava's room to give her the news. She must have sensed what was up because she opened the door before I could even knock. We both hurried back to my room to watch for another hour as many of the rest of the chicks hatched. After breakfast, I invited the kids to see the new babies, setting strict rules about holding them. Later, while Trevor and I formed a two-person bucket brigade to transfer a half-ton of recently delivered barley from the giant bag to the grain bin, he congratulated me on motherhood.

"Well done, my love. You must be very proud."

"I'm starting more eggs before I leave for America.

Promise me you'll look after them while I'm gone?"

"Of course, my sweet," he said and kissed me among the floating grain dust.

But there was one thing he wouldn't agree to. In total, only eleven healthy chicks hatched, nine black ones and two yellow ones. The yellow ones would eventually turn into white chickens. Trevor didn't want to "pollute" our gene pool of specially-bred black chickens with the white ones. Never mind that our flock was essentially already inbred, given that the water in the gene pool hadn't been changed in two decades.

"I'll let you raise white chicks, if you want. For about four months," Trevor said.

"What happens after four months?"

"They'll be delicious, juicy capons then."

"That reminds me, you never did try Soay roast, did you?" I said.

"I thought we were forgiving the past," Trevor said.

"Not if you're going to kill the white chickens just because they're white."

"All right, I'm sure the neighbors would love to have them."

Eugenics aside, sometimes chicks just didn't survive. One healthy-looking chick died for unknown reasons, and another—which took thirty-six hours to hatch—was obviously sickly. I left her in the incubator for two days, hoping she would improve. Though it was against my nurturing nature, Trevor had made me promise not to nurse chicks that were deformed or ill. Watching the little fluffball flop helplessly all alone in the incubator finally got to me. I couldn't bear her suffering anymore. I bundled her in a delicate pink hanky that I had found in the Steading jumble (the clothes bin) and took her to Trevor. He was planting beans in the polytunnel.

"Make it fast and painless," I said.

He stroked my hair and took the chick from me. "You're doing the right thing for the poor little beggar."

He went into the garden shed to wring the chick's neck, while I stood outside feeling like the angel of death.

"Would you like to bury her?" he asked when he emerged from the shed.

On the other side of the gravel track, where Trevor had recently scattered wildflower seeds, he dug a shallow hole. I placed the tiny bundle in the ground and gently put dirt over her, saying a silent prayer. I set a stone over the fresh soil and stood.

"I don't think I'd make a good farmer," I said.

"Why not?" Trevor asked.

I promptly started to cry, proving my point.

In addition to having a handful of surviving chicks, one of the Muscovy ducks, which we had feared had been taken by a fox, appeared in the walled garden with six yellow ducklings in tow. Trevor agreed to let them stay in the garden, instead of trying to force the family into the duck pen at night, as long as they ate the slugs and not his cabbages. The geese also produced one gosling, which Louisa named Primera for being the first to hatch. No other eggs hatched, however, so Primera's nickname became Solita. The seven adult geese guarded her like a princess. Whenever they paddled on the lake, the proud family moved as one, surrounding their beloved.

Soon, Louisa left for Edinburgh, having found a group of her Spanish countrymen to share an apartment with and where she could continue to improve her English at classes at a local college. I was sorry to see her go. Ahava and I were now Trevor's only assistants, and the two of us often got distracted by the new, young life around us: spring lambs gamboling on the hill pasture; Princess Solita's discovery of other life forms (her curiosity about her lake-mates, the ducks, was not well reciprocated); and the children, who managed to sweet-talk us into helping them weed their garden plot.

***

At the beginning of May, a representative from the Millennium Forest for Scotland Trust came from Edinburgh to inspect our tree-planting efforts. Trevor and I walked her around the entire estate, showing off the work and relating a few stories. She was thoroughly impressed that our project had attracted more than one hundred volunteers.

"Feed them and they will come," Trevor said.

She also informed us that we had to write a tree management plan and have it approved before we could receive the final grant payment. If we didn't write one, we'd have to give back the other two grant payments as well.

"Would this be the same management plan that William told me to forget about, believing they wouldn't really ask for one?" I asked Trevor.

"It's sealed, then. You have to come back to Braemar, because I'm not writing it," he said.

CHAPTER 25

Leaving

Fall had always been my favorite season, but at Braemar I had learned to love spring. Come May, the skies dried and the temperatures warmed to sixty degrees. The smell of raw earth, burgeoning with life, filled the air. Wood doves cooed, and rare cuckoo birds called out from the nearby woods. The trees exploded in buds, and the garden became transformed into an emerald mat of vegetable seedlings, surrounded by early flowers of pink, yellow, and white. Our efforts with the horse poo had paid off.

Now that he had more than doubled the planting space, and work effort, with the two polytunnels and a new potato field near the lake, Trevor was not easily drawn away from the garden for playful outings. That didn't stop me, however. I spent my last weekend in Scotland visiting Jill, a former Braemar student. Since leaving the Course that past January, she had been studying Ibn Arabi at home and had taken up watercolor painting.

We took long walks in the country park near her house, exploring the ancient oak and beech forest there. One afternoon we sat on a bench by a small lake, watching a family of swans paddle across the obsidian surface. Two ducks waddled ashore, looked at us, and grunted.

"Sorry, we haven't got any food for you, sweet things," Jill said.

"I'm definitely going to miss my birds," I said.

"This time next week you'll be home."

"Montana seems like another lifetime ago," I said.

We talked about Braemar, the Course, Braemarites, and our love for, and challenges with, all three. I told her everything that had happened with Trevor and about the tree planting and my various breakdowns.

"Seems I wasted a lot of energy worrying about things that were out of my control. And still, it all got done in the end."

"It's one thing to organize and guide the process and quite another to allow it to follow its natural course. That's where trust in God comes in," Jill said.

I had tried to understand the concept of trusting that things would take care of themselves, but I couldn't stop believing I was the driver of my own engine, relying on my wits. As was my habit, I called for God's intercession only during times of frustration, fear, or utter hopelessness.

"That phrase Braemarites are so fond of, *Inshallah, God willing*, really bugs me. Does God really care if we planted a few thousand trees?" I said.

"I should think God cares a great deal!" Jill laughed.

"But by whose will is it? God's or ours?"

"Well obviously it couldn't have been done without someone to organize it. God chose you. At the same time, you probably didn't need to fret so much over the details. Ooh, listen to me," she chortled. "I should take a page out of my own book!"

Jill picked a handful of grass and offered it to the persistent ducks, as they continued their forlorn quacking. They nudged one another closer but wouldn't take the grass from her hand. Two black Labrador retrievers suddenly ran up to us, sending the ducks flapping back to the safety of the lake. A man emerged from the wood, calling to the dogs. He nodded his head at us as he passed by.

"Why does the phrase 'God willing' bother you so much?" Jill asked.

"What's the point of God dumping a bunch of people on Earth, telling us to behave a certain way, and then controlling the outcome? Or punishing us if we don't do it Her way?" I said.

"When you put it like that, no point. But how much is God really controlling?" she said.

The way Jill saw it, "God willing" wasn't about God's controlling the outcome, but about God's desire that we find our way home to Her. Just as someone might guide a project to plant trees and not have complete control over how it gets done, so God might guide our lives to help us reach our soul's home.

"'My longing for them is greater than their longing for me,' God says in the Qur'an. He sends us here to experience His attributes," Jill said.

She meant the attributes of compassion, mercy, etcetera. These were the Beautiful names of Islam, the "Borg" names.

I told her my Braemar arrival story; how, beginning with a train that never arrived at the very start, I had only just managed to make all of my connections. In the end, I had arrived in Eltondean as scheduled, despite the apparent setbacks.

"My longing for Braemar maybe wasn't as strong as God's longing. So She stepped in to delay a train and a bus to make sure I got there," I said, half-jokingly.

Jill laughed. I continued.

"I believe God brought me to Braemar for a reason, even if I don't know what that is."

"What do you think it is?" she asked.

"I suspect a lot of things: patience, acceptance,

surrender. I'm still working on those. And maybe another was to show me the gentle side of Islam."

She nodded. "At their core, the fundamental beliefs of Judaism, Christianity, and Islam are the same. Strip away the trappings, and you are left with simply God."

"Everything is perishing but His face," I said, recalling the words in the Qur'an Braemarites often quoted.

Jill and I agreed that Islam wasn't the horrible religion our culture had projected on us. There were things we didn't like about it, but then that was true for Christianity and other spiritual practices for that matter. The different paths offered guidance; the key was to figure out how you, yourself, could find closeness with God.

There was a lot still to learn. There would always be.

Later that day, Trevor picked me up at Jill's house. He took us home via the back roads so that he could show me various places where he used to live. We scuttled around bends, where roads turned back on themselves, the farmland obscured in places by crumbling stone walls and tall beech hedgerows. He pointed out a flattened berm that was now a long, grassy path leading to Edinburgh.

"I used to go for runs along that old rail bed. I used to run marathons, you know."

"Why did you stop?"

"Dunno. You can run for miles and just let all your troubles drift behind you. I'm thinking of taking it up again."

A little ways down the road, he pulled over and opened his window. He pointed to a tiny stone chapel down the steep embankment and across a narrow river.

"That's one of my favorite churches in all of Britain. It's a sweet little place. So quiet. When I split up with my wife, I used to come here and pray to God to relieve the agony."

We drove across the one-lane bridge and made a

hairpin turn down to the church. The door was locked, but we walked across the grassy ledge on which it was perched above the river.

Trevor turned to me and pulled me toward him for a kiss.

"I don't want you to go to America. I'm afraid you won't come back."

"I have to come back. Latif told me my work wasn't finished."

"Oh. Not because of me or anything," he said.

"I suppose," I teased.

* * *

On my last full day at Braemar, I walked around the track alone, stopping at each of the planting sites and marveling at some of the seedlings that were already peering out of the tops of the tree tubes after only one month. I sat on my favorite stump overlooking the little valley. Among the many shades of green, thickets of gorse bloomed canary yellow and scented the air with a hint of coconut.

On my way back to the big house, I stopped by the chicken field to say goodbye to my flock and to Rambo, our oldest cockerel, who was gently clucking at his ladies as they scratched for the last bits of barley in the trampled grass.

"Take care of them for me, old boy. Your progeny are doing well, and soon you'll get to meet them." I said, referring to the lively chicks strutting around their brooder in the grain shed.

Rambo cocked his head, warbled, and took a few steps toward me. I reached down and held out a hand. He strutted a few steps in another direction.

Afternoon tea was served on the front lawn. Jerusha had made some melt-in-your-mouth shortbread biscuits that morning. The sun was high and bright over the hill, lighting up Trevor's mole-free front lawn, where the kids now tumbled in their shorts and T-shirts. Trevor strolled up from the garden, winked at me, and helped himself to a cuppa. After tea, I hiked up the front hill pasture to the Monument where founder Iskandar was buried. The blackfaced bundles of fleece ran away, but the lambs stopped their play to watch this curious figure: me. I stood by the Monument's steps and studied the engraving:

They are from Him and to Him they return.

"Thanks. You've got a nice place here. I'll see you around," I told him.

The next morning after coffee, everyone gathered in front of the house to say goodbye to me. I hugged them all, reluctantly bidding farewell to my newfound family. I wished Rafi the best of luck with his generators, and thanked Ahava for looking after the birds, which I knew were in good hands. Wakil gave me a big hug and asked me to bring him Golden Virginian tobacco from the duty-free when I came back.

"I won't say goodbye because this isn't goodbye," Latif said, then embraced me. "You're to hurry back as soon as possible."

I wanted to tell him how much my first impression of him had changed over the previous eight months. He was no longer the intimidating leader I had once assumed. Maybe we were both seeing things with new eyes. Instead, I thanked him for welcoming me and promised to return.

As Trevor and I drove away, the gathered group splashed the car tires with water, a Braemar tradition. Trevor drove me down Eltondean's High Street, past the pub where Wakil and I had first danced together, the night I lost my earring; past the charity shops he and I scoured on our forays into town; past the 1950s department store where I had found my contraband electric kettle (now Trevor's); past the pet store, the video store, the news agents, the Woolworth store, and the Safeway supermarket, on my way south into England to my train station.

On the train platform, Trevor and I wrapped our arms around each other. He bent down to my level so we could press our foreheads together. We gripped each other's hands. He pushed out his lower lip, exaggerating a pout, which made me smile and cry at the same time.

The train conductor made a final call. We released each other, and Trevor cupped my face in his hands.

"We shall always have Seahouses," he said, referring to where we had first held hands and walked along the seashore.

I reluctantly tugged my hand away from his, boarded the train, and found a seat by the window. We watched each other as the train pulled away from the station on its way to London and my plane home.

I would return.

Inshallah.

CHAPTER 26

Arriving—Again

Braemar had a way of embedding itself under the skin of your soul, seeping into the darkest spaces, cracking them open for light to gain an edge. Even when you do leave, if your work isn't done yet, you'll be back. I wasn't quite sure what that was for me.

During my two and a half months in America, I sold my house and visited family from coast to coast. Trevor and I wrote emails to each other daily and talked on the phone once a week. I couldn't wait to return. Montana didn't feel like home anymore. The people I had been closest to there had moved away. My soul, and heart, were at Braemar.

At the end of July, I arrived back to a garden flourishing with vegetables and flowers and an estate manager beaming with pride. My chicks were nearly grown, and a second batch had hatched, while a third cooked away in the incubator. I was pleased to my bones to be looking after the poultry and plunging my hands into the garden soil. The neighbors' spring lambs were now nearly as plump as their mothers. They tore through the pastures from time to time and occasionally escaped into Braemar property, running rampant until we would round them up again.

The tree seedlings were growing out of the tops of their tubes, which were choked with grass. The tree nursery was also overcome with weeds. No sooner had I arrived than the urge to tidy and fix and complete things began to press in. I continued to resist the feeling and instead focused on the sheer pleasure of being where I wanted to be, and with Trevor.

Trevor and I took a day off each week to explore. We strolled along North Sea beaches and ventured through quirky, backwater castles and musty Norman chapels. He bought me a used car, as well as a brand-new mountain bike, so I could grunt up and down the undulating country lanes alongside him. He had decided to take up running again. We continued to have our disagreements over which estate jobs should take priority, but we approached our differences in a less headstrong way, realizing that the details didn't matter so much as the overall goal.

The Braemar children, growing daily by the yardstick, were glad to have me back. On break from school, Esmé and Matea followed me around at every opportunity as well. Colin, nearly six, began leaving the comfort of his mother's side in favor of male staff and visitors, who would engage in sword fights with sticks and other dangerous objects. Baby sister Libby, now hurtling toward three, began losing her baby face and stepping out into the world. She even tried her luck jockeying with the others for the coveted spot at my side during weekend lunches.

Matea had also been spending time under the grow lamp. She had graduated from a precocious five-year-old to an even more precocious six-year-old. Occasionally, she invited me to join her and Ahava on private picnics in the garden. Under the shade of the overgrown rhubarb, its leaves like elephant ears, the three of us would sit. From her dwarf picnic basket, Matea produced jelly sandwiches cut into wee squares, sample-sized bags of potato chips, one-sip juice boxes, and comparatively large chocolate biscuits.

One particular day, when Esmé was at a friend's house in the valley, Matea followed me everywhere.

"Esmé's going to be sooo jealous when she finds out I'm helping you today."

After fifteen minutes of "hard work" weeding the children's garden plot, Matea insisted on showing me her guinea pigs—all eight million of them. (Real quote from Dad, Latif: "I don't understand how it happened. The first two were supposed to be females.") One by one, she retrieved a little furball from the hutch, commanding me to pet each of them. After one had received sufficient attention, she took it from me and put it back, then reached for another.

"You have to stroke them like this," she said, demonstrating.

After the sixth one, Matea announced that she had to pee. Then right there, she pulled her pants down to do her business on the grass just outside the front door to her house. I put the guinea pig I had been holding back in the hutch and said I had more work to do. Matea stumbled after me with her pants around her ankles:

"Wait, I'm still helping you!"

Trevor's children, Brian and Daisy, had also grown exponentially, and on his custody weekends, we often took them to a beach on the North Sea or to a nearby animal park where they could stuff the tame goats and sheep full of five-pence cups of food pellets. Brian grew more comfortable on his visits to Braemar, no longer whining when his mother would leave.

Children weren't the only ones that followed me around. A seventeen-year-old Spaniard had come to Braemar for the summer. Since Louisa's departure four months earlier, my Spanish had grown rusty, but Carlos spoke English well. For some reason, he was obsessed with

English grammar. He hunted me everywhere, wanting to discuss the placement of adjectives and why English didn't have gender-based adjectives like the Romance languages. He longed to engage me in analyzing the past perfect tense, and when he discovered that American and British English differed in some ways, he entered linguistic nirvana. A whole other topic to dissect! After meals, he would pursue me around the kitchen, watching as I washed, dried, and put away dishes. He carried a drying towel in his hands, though he never used it. Instead, he recited the names of the pots and pans and utensils in both English and Spanish, insisting I develop my vocabulary.

Like the children, he was sweet. Unlike the children, he was much harder to ditch. He would lie in wait by the Steading door, ready to pounce when I headed to the big house for breakfast. Trevor teased me about my new boyfriend, that is, until Latif invited Carlos to work with Trevor in the garden. Suddenly, Trevor no longer found Carlos amusing. Trevor put him on weeding duty, carefully showing him how to distinguish weeds from cultivated plants. By the end of his first day, Carlos had uprooted two hundred leek plants and a dozen rows of as-yet-to-bloom flowers, leaving behind a plot of healthy weeds.

"Ah, that explain why the straight lines," Carlos said when Trevor pointed out that weeds don't usually grow in neat rows.

He also seemed a little confused about the concept of planting. When Trevor made him stick the flowers and leeks back in the ground, Carlos simply laid the withering plants on top of the soil. Trevor scrambled to find other work where Carlos couldn't do harm. Fortunately for Trevor, he did have another helping hand, if only temporarily.

Brewster, a volunteer who had come during the tree planting, had found the hard labor of garden work so exhilarating, he returned to Braemar for two more weeks of ball-busting fun. Logging around fifteen hours a day—plenty of daylight during Scottish summers—he finished the project he started in April: digging the fence post holes around the water supply up on the moors. He was delighted to be able to hack through hard clay and rock. He also turned over dozens of cubic feet of garden soil, from which the spring vegetables and flowers had been harvested, in preparation for autumn and winter plants.

By the end of his stay, Brewster had installed a twenty-foot-long stone slab pathway in the garden, a project that had been on my wish list since the previous autumn. Around eight o'clock one evening, I went to the lake to put the ducks away. The rain was falling in buckets, and there was Brewster bashing his pickaxe into the earth. He had about five more feet of the path to go, digging out a bed in which to lay the last of the forty-pound stone slabs. He hadn't even bothered to come in for supper.

"Mustn't leave a job undone," he said.

"Surely, you can take a break to eat," I said.

"Not while daylight fades. I might stick my foot with the axe in the dark."

Before he left for home, Brewster wrote Braemar a check to pay for his stay, even though he had worked off his room and board a hundred times over. Then he hiked six miles over the moors to the A7 to catch his bus. Conversely, when Carlos returned to Spain in early September, he insisted I—and no one else—drive him to the bus depot in Eltondean, where he would carry on to London and catch his flight home the next day. When we got to Eltondean, he supposedly had lost his bus ticket, then tried to talk me into driving him to London! I sweet-talked the bus attendant into giving him another ticket free of charge, though I would have gladly paid. Someday, I thought, Carlos would become a politician.

September was a month of housecleaning, literal and figurative. The general mood was both frantic and liberating; frantic because many of the staff who had been there for a long time were preparing to move on, and liberating because many of the staff who had been there for a long time were preparing to move on. Though Braemar was ever-changing with the comings and goings of guests and residents, whenever a large movement of staff occurred, so did the emotional chemistry, for better or worse.

In addition to three house staff, also moving out were Rahman and Jelila, and Derrick. Though stepping down as indispensable maintenance man, Rafi would stay on temporarily to help the new maintenance chief get settled. For two long years Rafi had waged war on the impetuous generators, tried to instill electrical conservation among our community, and accomplished various improvement projects. He had also been a good friend to me, even though we sometimes sparred about the merits of the Six Month Course and the Steading's heating system. We had shared many a dram of whisky, a few nights out at the movies, and some pub meals. I would miss our conversations and his awesome foot massages.

September brought the Creston Valley Fair, the local agricultural show, during which Trevor and I agreed to look after Colin, Esmé, and Matea, while their parents took a break. Daisy and Brian were visiting for the weekend, too. Trevor left me with the five kids and a pocket full of pound coins to pay for entertainment and junk food while he slipped away for a "quick fag break," which lasted an hour. (How long before he would either give up smoking or give up running?) The ankle-biters took off, slipping through the entrance to the bouncy castle before I figured out where they had gone.

After jumping up and down for a half hour, my charges were certain that two ice creams each would restore their energy. I obliged; it was Trevor's money after all. Next, the older ones boarded miniature four-wheelers, and for several minutes smashed into the side barriers of the miniature racetrack in their attempt to keep the things on the road. Eventually, their parents retrieved them, and I went to watch the sheep dog trials. Some of the dogs were clearly focused, others not so much. How fun it would have been to toss in a couple of Soays.

Trevor entered some of Braemar's flowers and vegetables in the show, taking prizes for his onions, cucumbers, tomatoes, and sweet peas. The first prize for leeks was a specimen as big around as my arm, grown by a local farmer. Trevor grumbled that the farmer had probably fed it Miracle-Gro, which he thought was cheating.

"I'll have him next year. Just you wait and see," Trevor promised.

It was good to be home.

CHAPTER 27

Rewiring

Braemar's purpose was to deconstruct the ego, the internal map accreted over a lifetime that protected, comforted, and—when necessary—lied to us about the true nature of our Self. It provided an opportunity to rewire, with the Beloved as a framework. Gradually, this concept crystallized, and I began understanding more profoundly what Principal Latif had meant when he had said my "work here isn't finished yet."

When I returned for a second round at Braemar, I vowed to be better, different, more joyful, wiser. But after several weeks, I began slipping back into old habits of trying to accomplish everything; doing rather than being. I sought Latif's guidance. How not to fret or try to control? How to avoid getting dragged down into doing-ness? How could my staying here work for both me and Braemar? Latif insisted that I wasn't to overdo it.

He tried driving his point home one evening when I sat next to him at supper. After the meal, I rose, ready for action. Latif put a hand on my arm. He nodded for me to sit down. For several minutes I watched others clear the table, listened to them washing dishes in the servery, and fidgeted in my seat as people bustled between the dining room and kitchen, clearing up.

"Is this torture for you?" Latif asked.

"Yes," I replied without hesitation.

"Good."

His point was that I needed to feel okay about not having to always help with everything. To control. The lesson stuck with me for exactly twenty-four hours. The next morning, I enjoyed my after-breakfast tea without lifting a finger to help clear the table. At lunch, for the first time, I didn't even bring my own dishes into the servery to be washed. At supper, I sat as far away from Latif as possible, avoiding eye contact. When supper had finished, I helped clean up despite having put in a back-busting day in the garden. In my upbringing, one did not watch while others worked. In an attempt to rewire, the only way I could avoid helping after mealtimes was to head straight back outside to work on the estate after lunch, or flee to the Gate Lodge (and Trevor) after supper. And so I stepped back onto the merry-go-round.

As October first neared, and the start of another Six Month Course, I began craving the structure that it would bring to the household. Whereas during my first few months the year before I had quietly rebelled against the rigidness the Course imposed, I now looked forward to the Braemar Order. I still had no inclination to take the Course. First, I wasn't keen about having to follow a strict program of work and study. Second, it would mean Trevor and I having to cool any romantic involvement. Besides, in a way, I had vicariously taken the Course the year before. And I would do so again.

This year there would be two concurrent Six Month Courses: the First Course and the Second Course. A whole new set of staff, fifteen newcomers in all, arrived from Norway, England, Australia, and Scotland to be housekeepers, maintenance staff, cooks, and Course facilitators. In addition, a handful of Young People (sons and daughters of charter Braemarites) cycled through Braemar every few months or so with the intent of lending a hand while sorting out their post-high-school or post-college lives. In all, about forty of us lived at Braemar now, nearly twice that of the previous year. It meant having to reconfigure a new personal dynamic, getting to know new quirks and personalities and habits.

The Steading grew crowded with the students and Young People, and I began eyeballing the Cook's Room in the big house, now vacant after Rashid had left the previous April. The current cook lived with his wife in a cottage in the valley, so the room was vacant. Latif agreed to let me move into the big house on one condition: I had to take a Nine Day Course. I had no problem with that, and even looked forward to it, now that I had gained a more clear understanding of Braemar's Sufi-inspired studies.

The Cook's Room was on the bottom floor of the big house and came with tall and wide double-hung bay windows framing most of the southwesterly wall. Just outside the windows a handful of hens frequently pecked and scratched in the grass, their clucks and cackles providing a welcome distraction on the days I devoted to writing. (Part of the bargain I struck with Latif was that I would spend half the time working and half the time pursuing my passion to write.) The bright room was warm and comforting, and I would no longer have to stumble from the Steading to and from meals in the cold dark during the long winter.

I rifled through the attic for some spare furniture, finding a writing desk and bookshelves, along with two framed pictures both titled "An American Farm" and depicting nineteenth-century life. My bathroom, which I shared with just one other person, was on the next floor up and had a large soaking tub—and an endless supply of hot water! No more scrounging around for the perfect bath.

The Cook's Room also had its disadvantages. For one, it was directly opposite an outside door and the back staircase, which was noisy with the comings and goings of people. Though a small vestibule with an additional door created some relief from the noise and drafty cold air, my bedroom door sometimes popped out of its latch when the outside door was opened, startling me into thinking someone was entering my room. Second, the room was directly below the kitchen pantry and the servery, which was the passageway that linked the kitchen and dining room. On my writing days, or when I lay in bed ill, the footsteps back and forth, dishes being washed, and general hubbub of mealtime preparations and cleanup all went on overhead from seven in the morning until ten at night seven days a week. Around eleven at night, in search of munchables, the Young People often raided the pantry, which had a creaky floorboard directly above my bed.

Soon I began to recognize the unique character of every person's footsteps by the way he or she shuffled, hurried, plodded, or glided. I could tell when they were carrying heavy things, like a platter of leg of lamb, or tricky things, like a full tureen of soup or a soufflé. Trevor's footfalls were especially easy to detect: slow, heavy, and deliberate. I knew who was washing dishes by the way the dishes were dumped, set, or plopped into the sink. Thus, the Cook's Room was like Central Control, a direct link into the internal geography of fellow Braemarites.

Convenient access in the big house also attracted several people to my room, staff and students alike, who often popped in to chat, complain, cry, or all three at once. I became de facto counselor for a half dozen or so people, an honor mostly.

Wakil habitually dropped in on my writing days during his breaks from baking bread. Most times I enjoyed his company, feeling privileged to be a confidante and always enjoying Wakil for being, well, himself. Needless to say, I didn't get much writing done; I needed to work on the estate just to get a break. Eventually, a hand-lettered Do Not Disturb sign prominently hung on the door solved the problem. The sign also came in handy on evenings when Trevor visited.

Less frequent visitors to the Cook's Room were the children, whom I intentionally hadn't told about my move. For them, discovering my new quarters bordered on a spiritual experience. After they all had a flop on my bed, they picked up and examined every object in the room, like pilgrims with sacred relics: candlesticks, a bottle of hand lotion, dirty socks.

As a resident of the big house, I was assigned two new jobs. The first was feeding Ruby, a decrepit and shy cat who took shelter in the boiler room next to the laundry. Even though I was the hand that fed her, Ruby let only Wakil touch her. She often sat in his lap while he smoked a hand-rolled cigarette outside the back of the house. The second job was caring for the fish, who lived in a tank placed in the bay window above the sink in the servery. The tank had to be cleaned every other week, which required siphoning out the water using a flexible plastic tube. I had to suck on one end of the tube to get the water flowing from the tank and then quickly put the tube end in the sink once the water began to flow. I never did learn the art of timing, usually getting a gob full of manky fish water in my mouth.

To fulfill my other obligation of taking the Nine Day Course, I began it in early October. My fellow students were Bruce and Joy, a young Australian couple who had joined our staff for the season to help in the kitchen and look after the children when needed. We read several short works by Ibn Arabi scholars throughout the ages, most of which I had already read on my own in times of crisis. So, the Nine Day Course was more a review than a revelation. Sometimes, when the facilitator couldn't explain things to Bruce's or Joy's satisfaction, I would jump in with a translation in plain English. Apparently, I had picked up more than I realized and could sympathize with their struggles about the concepts. During those nine days, I was assigned to the estate on work days, but Trevor and I agreed to keep our distance romantically until the nine days ended. When they did, he cooked me a graduation meal of Indian curry in the Gate Lodge, which we ate by candlelight.

Because my new room in the big house was down the hall from the meditation room, it was easy to continue morning meditation with the students even after my Nine Day Course ended. Having developed the routine, I found it comforting and a mostly effective way to shut down the nafs (ego), which continued to insist they were in charge.

Zikr was now a familiar ritual for me, and occasionally I participated on Thursday nights. I had barely scratched Islam's surface, but knowing more about it kept me focused on the service aspect. For Sufis, turning one's face toward the east—toward the full glory of the rising sun—is to see God in everything. Opening up felt great, though still my mind wandered, occupied with all the things that "needed" to get done. I could not relax.

CHAPTER 28

The Birds—Brood Two

I had always taken seriously my responsibilities of managing the Braemar birds. Sometimes too seriously. Many nights I had lain awake worrying whenever some of the ducks were left outside the pen because I couldn't coax them in. Or bothered when a turkey disappeared because they would roost within reach of foxes. With the addition of new babies in all species (chickens, ducks, turkeys, and geese) came an even greater responsibility of ensuring that as many as possible grew into adults. Their care required planning as they grew from eggs to adults.

In addition to the original chicks I had incubated the previous spring, Ahava (the Israeli student from the previous year's Course who had stayed on) and Trevor had incubated more chickens and ducks while I was in America. We weren't so successful with turkeys nor they at rearing their own young. One day a turkey hen appeared with a clutch of six babies, but they all died within a few days. Trevor was convinced turkeys were too dumb and troublesome, his assertion backed by an article he had read that claimed turkey chicks tried to commit suicide by various methods, like throwing themselves at walls or flipping on their backs to break their own necks. Others preferred suffocation, allowing their fellow hatchlings to sit on them.

We had actually witnessed most of these behaviors in our own turkey chicks.

Because the chicken field was getting more crowded with incoming young, Trevor moved the dozen adult turkeys to the lake. The ducks and geese didn't like the turkeys, and the turkeys didn't like their new digs. For three weeks, every day the turkeys would wander across the estate back to the chicken field. Every afternoon Trevor would chase them back to the lake. More lakeside overcrowding occurred when a persuasive woman in the valley successfully pawned off her twelve geese on Braemar (Trevor couldn't say no), adding to our menagerie and further annoying our original flock. Our geese, having reluctantly accepted their new turkey residents, weren't having any more new neighbors, even of their own kind. So Trevor moved the newcomer geese to the chicken field, which annoyed the chickens. No one was happy.

By summer's end, our one gosling, Primera-Solita, had exchanged her yellow fluff for gray feathers, which had then turned white. In addition, a squadron of new ducklings, all hatched by actual duck hens, kept the lakeside vibrant. The yellow down of the six Muscovy babies that had hatched in the garden in May had transformed to sport sleek slate-gray feathers. In September they had grown big enough for Trevor to evict them from the garden—just in time for the Muscovy pair to hatch another brood in the garden.

With the turkeys that now lived by the lake, and the nearly two dozen new ducks, how to sort them among the two separate areas inside the duck pens at night became a source of confusion for all. The turkeys eventually sorted themselves out, roosting on top of the ducks' shelters inside the pens. The ducks seemed leery of the large birds looming over them, and probably none too happy about the turkeys crapping on them from above.

Between the adults and their shelters, and the various young scattered about in chicken A-frames and other smaller shelters at the lake, garden, and chicken field, bird duty (feeding, watering, and mucking out) had become nearly a full-time occupation.

Because the Muscovy hen had hatched six ducklings so late in the year (October), we kept mom and babies in an A-frame near the garden shed. We planned to let them out when the ducklings grew more suitable feathers and were less vulnerable to cold and predators. Every morning I fed and watered them, and one morning there were only five ducklings.

The A-frames were elongated, like giant Toblerone chocolate bars, and included a chicken wire enclosure on one end and a wooden enclosure with a hutch at the other, where they could roost at night. The frames were wrapped tightly in chicken wire to protect the young birds from predators while allowing them to get used to the outside world. The bottoms weren't wrapped in wire, however, so the frames had to be set on even ground to prevent chicks from squeezing out and predators from squeezing in. Even ground was hard to come by, and we weren't sure whether the chick had managed to squeeze out and disappear (unlikely), or a predator had gotten in (more likely).

The next morning, another duckling was missing, leaving four survivors. Small traces of downy fluff clung to the frame in one spot, along with flecks of blood. The ground underneath had been slightly excavated. Trevor had heard from a local farmer that mink had been spotted in the stream running through Knowe Hill. They were notorious predators, as were all their weasel brethren (mostly stoats in these parts).

Ducklings went missing daily, and despite our best efforts at trying to reinforce their various enclosures and night-time roosting places, we were losing. Weasels, we discovered, can pretty easily chew through chicken wire to get at what they want, and our marauder was nothing if not determined. One evening I forgot to close the little door to the roosting box in the A-frame shelter, where we kept a duck hen and her three babies. When I went to let them out the next morning, I peered inside to see the mama duck cowering in the corner. Her dead babies were scattered around her, a gruesome diorama of slaughter mocking my efforts to protect them.

Trevor's engulfing arms did little to comfort me. He offered to trap the weasels, but that wouldn't do; more would fill their niche. Besides, they were simply doing what weasels did. My responsibility was to keep them away from our birds, and I had failed. We decided that if any ducks hatched more eggs, we'd leave them to their own devices at rearing.

Autumn meant time for culling the flocks. Once again, I found myself lobbying to spare the lives of as many as possible, frustrating Trevor to no end.

One of the spared was my beloved Rambo, the sole surviving cockerel from the previous year. We now had three new young cockerels, which had quickly outgrown Rambo. They soon let him know his services were no longer needed and divided his harem among themselves. The three young cockerels claimed two of the coops for themselves and their ladies, leaving Rambo by himself in the third coop at night. In the evening, when I closed the chickens up for the night, I would open the big door to Rambo's place and sit on the threshold for a few minutes. He would sit opposite me, alone on the perch bar fluffing his feathers and cooing quietly. I would tell him how handsome he was and that I still loved him even though the other gals had ditched him for greener feathers.

With all these new birds, we realized we needed a system for tracking their ages. We decided to put a color-coded band on a leg of each chicken—and the ducks and geese we could catch—so we could cull them on a rotating basis by age. That summer's chicks, which were mostly adults now, got purple bands. We guessed the approximate ages of the remaining chickens and banded them accordingly.

A month later, two of the new cockerels had grown so big that the bands began digging into their legs. I noticed the problem when one of them, whom I named Henley, began limping. His beefy dimensions required a larger band meant for goose legs. Removing Henley's band was painful for both of us. His leg had swollen to twice its normal size. Wakil held him while I carefully peeled the wound-wire band from his scaly gam, loop by loop, with a pair of pliers. Dried blood flaked away from the fresh blood oozing beneath it. His leg had begun growing into the band, infecting his leg.

I took Henley to the vet, who knew nothing about chickens but prescribed a five-day course of antibiotics to put in Henley's water. The only way to ensure he got the antibiotics was to confine him in the grain shed temporarily. I put some rags and straw in a box for a bed and hung a heat lamp to keep him warm. For some reason, he preferred the concrete floor to his cushy bed—a real cockerel's cockerel. Several times a day I checked on his progress and lectured him about the importance of drinking his special water.

After three days his leg looked better, but Henley still favored it. The day before I planned to release him into the flock again, one of the students had gone to the grain shed to fetch the afternoon bucket of barley to feed the chickens. She claimed that she hadn't seen the large sign written in black marker: CONVALESCING CHICKEN; PLEASE DO NOT DISTURB. DO NOT CHANGE WATER! She later admitted that she had felt sorry for Henley and tried to pet him. He flapped out of her way, spilling his carefully measured water containing the antibiotic. The medicine might have been ineffective anyway, but just in case, I got more from the vet and extended Henley's convalescence another week. In the meantime, his two rivals had been making themselves comfortable with Henley's hard-won ladies.

Within minutes after Henley tentatively strutted out of the grain shed after two weeks of confinement, the other two cockerels appeared, ready to brawl. Removing Henley from the flock had upset the pecking order. The other birds no longer recognized him as one of their brethren. Later that same day the cockerels got into a fight among a patch of rhododendrons. Blood was speckled everywhere. We broke up the fight, captured the battered Henley, and took him to the laundry room to wash off the blood, most of which had come from his comb.

A local Braemarite and chicken expert said we had two choices: (1) temporarily put Henley in a wire pen protected from the others but still exposed to the flock until they got used to him, or (2) just let the boys sort themselves out. We didn't have a pen big enough for option 1; they would have to sort it out.

For three days, Henley and the largest cockerel sparred fiercely. Students and staff gave me hourly reports on how awful it all seemed, while I tried to explain that cockerels were like that. I didn't like it myself but there wasn't much else I could do. One afternoon Henley took refuge with a half-dozen hens in the dry food storage room at the back of the house after someone had left the door open. Henley shook his bloodied head, spattering red droplets everywhere. I began wiping up the mess with a wet rag when Wakil came in for a bag of rice.

"Allow me. This is no job for a lady," he said.

He took the rag and gave me a quick hug, after noticing I had begun to cry. I gently shooed Henley out of the storage room. I called a farm up the road, and they agreed to take Henley. But they didn't want him until after they returned from a weekend trip.

The next day Henley wouldn't come out of his coop, which he now shared with Rambo. (Rambo wasn't one of the cockerels who attacked Henley.) One of his eyes had become glued shut with dried blood, and he was somewhat listless. I carried him to the laundry room, where Trevor helped me gently dunk him in a warm saltwater bath to clean his bloody feathers. His head drooped into the water, as if he wanted to drown himself. We dried him off as best we could and put him back in the grain shed. I turned on the heat lamp and made him some hot porridge. By day's end, he was on his feet, standing directly below the heat lamp. He didn't seem concerned about the tiny wisps of smoke curling off his singed feathers. I turned off the lamp and smothered the sparks on his back. In a couple of days he would be at his new home, and we could be done with this regrettable episode.

The next morning, I headed to the grain shed to check on him. Henley was gone. I asked the student who had been feeding the chickens where he was—the same student who had tried to pet him. This time she claimed she had misunderstood my instructions to leave Henley inside.

The last time I saw him alive, he was peacefully eating some barley I had tossed in the beech wood for him near the chicken field. The next morning, he wasn't in his coop. Later, I found his crumpled bloody body in the leaf pile beneath a row of Leyland shrubs. I cradled the cold, lifeless mass of feathers then laid him in the grain shed and went to find Trevor. I got as far as the little wrought-iron bench tucked up against the box hedge at the side of the big house. There I sat just as the sun rose over the hill pasture to warm the day. For ten minutes, I cried. Then Trevor appeared from the garden. He sat down and put an arm around me.

"It wasn't your fault. Henley could have just as easily died from the infection."

Then Trevor took my hand and recited a poem he had once heard:

"You greeted us early with the dawn. You crowed your heart out on the lawn. With beak so shiny and comb so red, it's such a shame now that you're dead."

His sarcasm warranted a please-forgive-me bouquet of flowers and at least two boxes of gourmet chocolates, and I told him so right after I started speaking to him again two hours later. He wasn't really so callous; he just had a better grasp on the reality of raising animals.

That afternoon, Trevor dug a grave in the chicken field and put a layer of straw at the bottom. I gently laid Henley in the hole, sprinkling a handful of grain on his body, like the ancient Egyptians' ritual of leaving food for their pharaohs in the afterlife. Two dozen hens gathered around for the ceremony. I thanked Henley for being such a brave, dear boy, covered him with dirt, and walked away.

CHAPTER 29

Following Signs

On the day before Thanksgiving, Braemar buzzed in preparation for the holiday. The big house, Steading, and grounds were abluted; turkeys were dressed; pies were assembled; vegetables were chopped; and extra place settings, chairs, and tables were brought down from the attic to accommodate twenty-five additional guests. After supper on Thanksgiving eve, several of us finished preparing food for the next day's feast. Principal Latif had retired to his cottage only to return twenty minutes later, standing in the kitchen doorway looking concerned.

"Do you have water here?" he asked.

All activity stopped. We looked at one another, confused.

"Would you just check the taps?" Latif said.

Wakil walked over to one of the sinks and turned on the faucet. Cold water sputtered out before slowing to a trickle and then stopping. We tried another sink and another and another. Latif lifted the phone receiver from the kitchen wall and dialed Fairy Cottage. Same situation. Latif called the Gate Lodge. There was a pause on the other end, while Trevor checked his taps. A sputter then nothing. The Steading supply hadn't been confirmed yet, but the answer was clear.

Still not quite comprehending the implications, we all stared at Latif. With characteristic understatement, he said it may be nothing; sometimes the flow became blocked by various objects lodged in the supply pipes, such as dead frogs. But his voice had an added sense of urgency. Whatever the blockage, we had to find it and remove it quickly. To rule out a more serious problem, Latif, Trevor, and Khadir (the new maintenance man who replaced Rafi) drove up the road to Braemar's water supply on the moors. It was the blackest of moonless nights, the sky pelting hard, cold rain.

Braemar's water supply consisted of a massive underground storage tank, about sixty feet long by twelve feet wide by seven feet deep. The tank was recharged by groundwater graciously supplied by the ubiquitous rain that ceaselessly pummeled the British Isles. Winter rains in particular were important for recharging the groundwater. During summer, a pump in the valley stream below drew water up the hill to the tank to make up for the dry-season shortfall. If the level ever became low, Braemar would have to ration water until the tank recharged. If the water level ever became critically low, Braemar would be screwed.

An hour after the gentlemen's foray to the moors, Latif gathered everyone in the big house to tell us we were screwed.

Because the previous winter, spring, and summer had been wet—and because the underground tank had been overflowing—the pump had been turned off. No one had bothered to check the water level recently. After all, winter was nearly upon us, and the rains now came heavy and frequently. But the tank had become low over the summer, probably because of all the garden plots that needed watering, additional bird residents that needed watering and abluting, and this year's larger numbers of abluting

Sufis.

Trevor turned on the pump, and so now we all had to do was wait for the 38,000-gallon tank to fill. Taking into account the pump's flow rate equaling that of a garden hose, calculations showed it would take about fourteen days.

Getting water to flow through a mile's worth of empty pipe between the underground supply tank and the house required much creativity, not to mention cussing (although the latter was more to maintain emotional stability). We couldn't just fill the tank then turn on the taps. The physics of getting water to flow applies universally, whether draining a fish tank with a plastic tube or forcing water through iron pipes. You have to first draw the water from the source to the target to start it flowing on its own. It largely involved pressure—and the stickiness of water molecules—exerted by air and the water to create what's called a water column.

Our supply tank had to refill enough to build pressure and volume, and then we would have to help it along by forcing the tank water into the pipe to flow toward the buildings. We also had to release excess air pressure and sediment from the pipe. For that purpose, the pipe was equipped with seven valves along its length, four for letting out air (located at the high points in the terrain because air rises) and three for letting out sediment (located at the terrain low points because sediment sinks). We knew where three of the valves were; all we had to do was find the other four. Across about a mile's worth of undulating moorland.

And so we prepared for the Great Braemar Drought.

The next day's Thanksgiving feast went off relatively well, considering. We replaced the Willow pattern china with paper plates, and drinking glasses with disposable cups. Visitors brought cases of bottled drinking water. For several hours we tried to forget about our plight and give thanks for what we did have, as well as pray for what we didn't, such as knowledge of the whereabouts of the remaining valves.

We lived like Peace Corps Volunteers, hauling buckets of water for cooking, sponge bathing, and flushing toilets. I rigged up a camp-style bath in my room, complete with a wash basin and, for late-night emergencies, a bedpan. We borrowed a portable five-hundred-gallon tank from one of the local farmers. Because he wasn't all that bothered about the condition of his farm yard (it would often take him a few days to clean up the occasional dead sheep), God only knew what could have crawled into the tank and died. So we used water from that tank only for flushing toilets. We rounded up two dozen five-gallon buckets, and borrowed other odd buckets from local Braemarites for each bathroom in the house, cottages, and Steading with which to dump down toilets to flush.

To supply water for bathing and cooking, we procured two portable five-hundred-gallon tanks made of food-grade plastic. The students' premeditation and zikr ablutions were reduced to quick splashes of cold water on hands, feet, and face. All local Braemarites opened their bathroom doors to staff and students. Oh, how we had taken hot showers and baths for granted!

Even with rationing, our household of nearly forty people went through five hundred gallons of water quickly. Trevor spent most of every day hauling the tanks by tractor back and forth between Braemar and two neighboring farms; the owners let us use their wells to fill the tanks. Each tank took about four hours to fill. Trevor would get one started then come back to Braemar to fetch another tank and drive it to the other farm to fill. By the time he got a tank loaded on the tractor trailer and hauled it to its destination, he'd have to fetch the next tank. And so it went for him day in and day out.

While the underground tank filled at a trickle's pace, Latif and Khadir made phone calls in search of someone with a metal detector to find the remaining valves. One expensive chap arrived with an equally expensive-looking computerized contraption, which didn't find any valves but did find part of the pipeline's pathway from the tank to the big house across the moors. He marked it with yellow spray-paint to make it easier for us to know where to even *begin* looking for the valves. For three days I slogged along the windy moors in horizontal sleet, eyes to the ground through sheep and cow crap, trying to determine where the high and low points were along the undulating ground and, thus, the likely location of where to start digging for the tiny valves.

On our fourth day without water, we woke to a few inches of snow. More was forecast, dashing any hopes of finding the remaining valves. Latif and Khadir had given up on finding a valve diviner, and the few who claimed they could help wanted lots of money for the privilege.

In the meantime, I fiddled with the valves whose locations we did know to understand how they worked. Though each had a slightly different design, the principle behind their function was easy to grasp and the mechanical workings intuitive. Latif had asked whether I could bear the responsibility for getting the water flowing again. With no small amount of trepidation, I accepted his invitation as Chief in Charge of Water Flow. That forty people relied on me was worrying. That I eventually found one of the four AWOL valves late in the afternoon on the fourth day spurred me. I could do this! Maybe. Later that day, God tossed us a bone. Trevor and a couple of the students found another valve near the underground tank in a depression filled with partially frozen water and cow pee. Only two more to find! On the fifth day, however, the lack of free-flowing water began to wear.

Sufis believe that if we truly want to see God's face, we see everything as a sign of Her existence. Latif took God's signs seriously, and so he gathered everyone in the Mead Hall in the afternoon of day five to question whether we Braemarites had been focusing enough on God. Was our devotion wanting, our sincerity for closeness to God lacking? The drought was punishment. He instructed us all to ask God for forgiveness and guidance. I resented being collectively blamed, the object of God's wrath. It quite simply seemed that someone had forgotten to check the underground tank and turn on the pump. Who was that someone? The maintenance person? The estate management team? God's great hand? Did it matter?

Though angry at Latif for the verbal spanking, I thought about what he said. Had we been more consumed with love and compassion rather than the wrath and judgment that had settled in again as we settled into our new community members, would we now be experiencing drought? I wondered. The whole point of life in the Sufi tradition is union with the Beloved, which on Earth is impossible without demonstrative compassion for our fellow beings. In this sense, we were all responsible for a full and flowing reservoir of our lifeblood. But how exactly would our love for one another have intervened to prevent a water crisis? To paraphrase Freud, sometimes a drought is just a drought. I was willing to ask God for forgiveness and guidance, as instructed, in case Latif was right about our lack. What was my personal drought? Lack of compassion? Lack of obedience? Maybe God was sending us a sign; call it punishment, if you like. Or, call it our being given the opportunity to discover our strengths and growth areas by sharing in a common struggle for a basic life need. Maybe this was a gift to see the perfection in our perceived—and projected—imperfections.

Nothing rallies cooperation more than crisis. The next morning, Latif sent every able-bodied person out to the moors clutching spades. The yellow spray-paint that had marked the underground pipeline was now buried under four inches of snow. Trevor took a break from hauling water to help dig. A local farmer had told Trevor he recalled seeing many years ago "something that looked like what you're looking for" near the fence separating his grazing land from the open moors. Fifteen of us gathered in a circle and watched Trevor and two young lads jab their spades into the ground. Clods of clay, infused with ice crystals, sprayed all around us. Five minutes of their fervent digging revealed a box about a foot below ground. The box was formed by bricks and covered with a square plank of rotting plywood. We whooped and hollered and cheered as the lads removed the plywood to reveal a valve! I wanted to kneel down and kiss it.

We moved along to the next probable location for the last missing valve, and after a half hour of digging around for it, voila! All seven valves were now accounted for after six days of hunting. And that was the easy part. Now we had to get the water flowing.

The solution was to prime the pipe by filling it with water ourselves so that the water in the tank could more easily "stick" to the water in the pipe, creating the required water column and starting the continuous flow. The only way to fill the pipe with that much water was to empty all the portable water tanks we had been using for our temporary supply into each of three pipe sections. To do that, we had to connect each pipe section with a portable water tank via a garden hose. To do that, we had to find a way to connect the garden hose to a three-inch-diameter opening on the portable tank on one end and a way to connect to the quarter-inch-opening on the underground pipe at a valve opening on the other end. Two valves were identical, but the third had a different style opening, which meant finding two different ways to hook up the hose. How much more challenging could God's signs get?

We scrounged various hoses and metal connectors from the workshop and garden shed, rigging up a leaky, but workable, system for two of the valves. For help with the other end to connect the portable tank to the garden hose, we turned to a plumbing store in Eltondean. We explained our dilemma to the owner, but unfortunately he was fresh out of Braemar Water Crisis Thingies. We thanked him for indulging us at closing time and were about to leave when I spotted the solution: a heavy-duty shop vacuum with a hose about the same size as the opening of the portable tank. The shop owner was reluctant at first, but I put on my most sorrowful eyes and begged him to let us borrow his shop vacuum hose. He relented, probably just eager to get rid of us crazies so he could go home for his tea.

The vacuum hose fit perfectly, thanks to a generous helping of duct tape. Adam, Trevor, and I sat in the cold, dark evening on the hill above the big house and opened the pipe valve and the water outlet on the portable tank. We waited as the water began to flow from the tank into the underground pipe section that ran down the hill to the big house. It took an hour, and it was like putting blood back into a dying patient.

Over the next twenty-four hours, we hooked up the portable water tanks to the other sections of pipe, putting a total of thirty-thousand gallons of water into the mile-long underground pipe. Using walkie-talkies, Adam, Trevor, and I each took a position along the pipeline, opening each of the valves in sequence to clear trapped sediment and air. Then, we held our collective breaths and gathered in the laundry room of the big house to test whether we had succeeded. We opened the taps in the laundry room sinks. Murky water sputtered from the faucets, beautiful and wet. After twenty minutes of flow, we declared victory. At lunchtime, I announced to the whole house that running water was again ours; we might even have hot showers by nightfall! Everyone cheered and hugged and thanked us.

The adage about counting unhatched eggs is one well worth paying mind to. Two hours after lunch, the water stopped flowing again. It appeared that all we had succeeded in doing was draining the pipe of the water we had just put in it. We hadn't succeeded at establishing the water column from the underground supply tank.

Trevor resorted to canons, renting a diesel-powered pump to force water into the pipes, which would also be more effective at forcing out trapped air, the likely culprit of our first failure. Again, we filled each pipe section with water with the help of the diesel pump, opening all the air and sediment valves in sequence. We bled the valves of air five more times just to be sure there was nothing left in the pipe to prevent the flow. It took another two days. Surely, God could see that we were paying attention now.

By day eleven, the underground supply tank was nearly full. We turned on the laundry room faucets and crossed our fingers. Water sputtered into the sinks. After an hour of letting the water run, we again declared victory, although with subdued enthusiasm. Systematically, we began turning on the water mains at each of the cottages and the Steading, allowing time for their water tanks to fill. To get water to flow again in the bathrooms on the top two floors of the big house, we had to run a garden hose up through the bathroom windows and attach it to each of the sinks, reverse-filling the pipes via a spigot outside. It was messy but it worked. By teatime, water was restored throughout all the buildings, just in time for the students to leave on their annual pilgrimage to Turkey. At least they could shower before crowding into vehicles for the three-hour drive to the airport.

Whatever our community's collective misdeeds or forgetfulness, the dry spell had taught us a lesson: Even if it's raining in abundance on the outside, remember to watch out for signs that your internal tank might be getting low. And take precautions to keep it full.

CHAPTER 30

The Turning

Building a relationship with God requires building relationships with others, oneself included. There is no better place to immerse yourself in a relationship than in an intimately connected community. God help you if you don't know your boundaries. But sometimes that is what's needed to grab your attention.

To live in a community is to live on those rough edges. This is where growth happens. You could say where shit happens, growth happens. This is true both organically, as in the benefits of spreading eight million tons of horse apples in the garden, and psychologically, as in noticing what crops up when the crap of the mind—the nafs, the ego—layers our experience. Some people are open to experience, and the lessons come fast and easy. Most of us resist, struggle, give a bit, grow some, resist more, struggle, and so on. We're reluctant to weed our own garden yet quick to admonish others for not weeding theirs. Braemar provided plenty of opportunities to examine and recognize what were weeds and what were flowers. Sometimes even the pursuit of God, however, brings out the worst in people.

Usually, Braemarites faithfully abided by the Braemar Order, those expectations governing participation, respect, hygiene, and proper attitude. Sometimes, however, the very people who scolded others for lapsing in attention to God had no qualms about using a kitchen cutting board to roll a cigarette then smoking it while preparing supper. Sometimes people had shouting matches in the big house. Not often, but rebellion happened and usually only whenever Principal Latif was away.

Latif's job was to help cultivate Braemar's garden, which necessarily meant pulling weeds. Depending on the offense, some weeds were temporarily exiled from Braemar; in extreme (though rare) cases, permanently. He had ultimate authority over who stayed and who went, so when he asked you to weed your garden, you did it. If atonement was in order, it usually included a full ablution of your personal self and your room, as well as reciting a few repentant prayers.

I had grown to love and respect Latif and never dreamed of flouting the rules (the big ones, anyway) for fear of displeasing him. Then one day, that changed.

Right after the Great Braemar Drought, Latif and the students had gone to Turkey on their annual pilgrimage, leaving about fourteen of us behind to manage the place. Normally this wouldn't be a problem except that the group would be gone until December 20, and we were expecting more than a hundred guests for the holidays. Members of the global Braemar community were coming to the mother ship to celebrate the last Christmas and New Year of the twentieth century. There were guest beds to make up, holiday food to prepare, and the entire Steading, big house, and cottages to clean.

The weather had turned bitter, and I was caring for the birds again while the students were away. The garden taps froze, so each morning I hammered through the ice on the lake to fill water buckets then hauled them to the bird pens. Trevor had taken a two-week job planting trees near Eltondean, and I didn't even see him during that time. He needed extra money for his growing kids. For several days I washed and folded mountains of towels, sheets, and linen table cloths. The students hadn't had time to do them before leaving for Turkey, mostly because of the water crisis. I also helped prepare meals, and even soloed meals here and there. Day after day and night after night, I was often the last one in the kitchen finishing the chores while everyone else had retired for the evening.

Whereas I had started to turn my focus toward the task at hand—feeling the texture of the cotton sheets and all that—all I could feel was every aching bone in my body and the resentment that came from the impression of being the only one who was actually doing any work. Sure, a few people had taken ill, but there were at least ten pairs of hands who were perfectly capable of making light work. Yet, many often sat at the table after meals while three or four of us cleared the table and washed up. And the mountains of laundry didn't seem to reduce in size except for the dent I was making.

I worried that when our Turkey pilgrims returned they'd be faced with two weeks' worth of chores and only a few days to do them before the onslaught of guests. I didn't say anything to anyone; I just assumed my fellow seekers would eventually start doing their fair share. What were they doing all day?

Anger and sleeplessness turned into a sinus infection and migraines. What I needed was fresh, raw garlic to help fight the infection. But garlic was forbidden at Braemar because, someone once told me, the smell drove the angels away. After having participated in several sweaty zikrs now, I came to understand that if garlic were on our menu, any angels with a Braemar landing permit would want to change their flight plans. Instead of garlic for warding off illness, Braemarites soaked onions in honey then drank the juice. So one morning, I diced an onion and put it in a bowl with honey. I covered the bowl with clingfilm and taped a large note on the top. With a thick black Sharpie I wrote: SARAH'S; DO NOT EAT.

After lunch that same day, several people got up from the table and walked away without even clearing their own plates. That was the final straw. I stood.

"That's it, I'm not washing one more bloody dish for you people!"

I stomped out of the room and headed to the kitchen. I needed to drink the sweet oniony juice and go back to bed. But my healing concoction was gone. Just then, our stand-in cook walked into the kitchen. The regular guy had gone to Turkey.

"What happened to my onions?" I asked him.

"I put them in the lunch," he said.

My face flushed in anger. "What, you can't read? I left a note."

"Um, I didn't see it?"

I stomped back down the stairs to my room and crawled into bed. Celeste came in, clearly distressed to see me in such a state. It wasn't like me to yell at a tableful of people.

"I'm fed up with everyone and everything!" I sputtered.

Spittle flew from my lips as I told her how I was tired of others being lazy freeloaders. What had happened to the Braemar Order? If everyone helped, none of us would be overworked.

Celeste reminded me of the story about the sisters Mary and Martha from the Gospel of Luke. They had invited Jesus to their house for supper, and while Martha scrambled around getting ready for their exalted house guest and making all the food and doing all the work, Mary sat at Jesus' feet and enjoyed his company. This pissed Martha off. She told Jesus to tell Mary to get off her fat lazy behind and help out, and Jesus told Martha to chill out.

"The moral of the story," Celeste said, "is that there are more important things than running around all busy like. Don't let your service to others distract you from the ultimate reason for your work, which is to contemplate God. What good are you to the community if your service is contaminated with resentment?"

Her words echoed what Hadiyya (who had left Braemar) had told me the previous year. I knew this was my self-imposed burden, and I still hadn't learned when to stop. Celeste told me to get some rest; that the work would get done; that people would step in when they were ready.

"Don't overwork yourself. You're only human."

Celeste was right, of course. But I wasn't going to feel better until I got revenge. After all, I was only human.

So later that afternoon, I drove into town and bought a bulb of garlic.

In our sacred kitchen I chopped every clove of that forbidden fruit into fragrant chunks. I used the cook's favorite knife. And I didn't clean it afterwards. I used a yellow cutting board, which was supposed to be used only for fruit. I didn't clean that either. I put the garlic in a large mixing bowl and poured honey over it. I set the bowl on the table under the window next to some cooling loaves of bread. I even tried wafting the garlic odor onto the bread.

What I didn't do was put a note on the bowl telling others not to eat it. When the cook prepared supper that night, I hoped he wouldn't notice it was garlic and use it. With great delight I was going to watch them all eat forkful after forkful of poisoned stir-fry! And, I was going to relish every stinking second of it. Angels would stop coming. People would fall ill. I didn't care. Those slackers deserved it!

Only none of that happened. After supper the garlic was still in the bowl where I left it, and still there after lunch the next day. The next evening, in defeat, I drank the sweet juices myself. (But I didn't wash out the bowl!) Later, I felt a lot better both physically and emotionally, if not a little humbled. Turned out that some of the "slackers" had actually been cleaning rooms, making up beds, creating menu plans, and procuring extra mattresses and dishware for the hundred plus guests that would soon be arriving. And they had spent time in meditation, restoring themselves with the strength needed to manage the upcoming holidays, setting intentions for maintaining order in what had the potential to be quite chaotic. They knew their limits and practiced self-care, while my mind had been frantically rushing from one task to the next, forgetting that the quality of the action—and the thoughts while doing it—mattered much more than the quantity of boxes ticked.

Loving and serving others, I finally began to learn, required both action and contemplation; knowing when to work and knowing when to rest. I don't know whether angels like garlic or whether garlic really does cure infections. But sometimes, even in service to God, a simple rebellion can cure what ails you.

* * *

Two weeks later, Christmas arrived, my first at Braemar because I had spent the previous Christmas with friends in England. The holiday was appropriately discussed in the Course study and during morning staff meetings. Latif reminded us of Christ's gift of forgiveness, compassion, and love, stressing the importance of servitude. There was something transformative about sharing a traditional Christian holiday with a wider community of Jews, Christians, Buddhists, questioners, and one or two Muslims. I discovered that different schools of Islam believe different things about Jesus, including that some believe Jesus was an exalted prophet sent by God to guide the children of Israel, and that Jesus will come again.

I also began to grasp for myself a clearer understanding of the nature of Jesus, which, despite having been raised a Christian, had always eluded me. For one thing, I had never understood what it meant that Jesus died for our sins. What had begun to make sense was the symbolic meaning of his death, wrapped in that simple phrase from the Qur'an that Braemarites brought out on frequent occasion: Die before you die. Jesus' death, it now appeared to me, was death of the ego, which was necessary to reveal our true nature, our divine selves. The nature of his resurrection was symbolic of the fact that our spirit nature never dies. Die before you die was God's revelation to Muhammad and St. John's call to be born again. I had to chuckle about having become more clear about Jesus via my experience with Islam.

Following Christmas, we set our intention and focus on welcoming the New Year. Visitors who had come for Christmas stayed, and dozens more from around the world trickled in to the Braemar mother ship. More than a hundred of us were going to be celebrating, not just a new year, but a new millennium. Mattresses and cots occupied extra spaces in nearly every room in the big house, Steading, and cottages, looking like a relief shelter for disaster victims.

Braemar's coup de grace, however, had begun to take root several weeks earlier in the wood shop. It was a manifestation of Latif's dream to build an outdoor pavilion for such gatherings. He and Adam had been drawing and contouring their vision for some time. In mid-November the rest of us had been introduced to their concept of Millennium Henge. Before the Turkey trip, Latif had organized an old-fashioned barn-raising, erecting the basic frame for the henge on the front lawn. For a few weeks the skeletal frame had stood open to the heavens. Just after Christmas it became time to complete the masterpiece.

The circular henge consisted of about a dozen upright square timbers, ten-by-tens that stood eight feet high, supported by steel plates on the ground. Similar to its prototype, Stonehenge, Braemar's version was strengthened by additional timbers that lay across the tops of the uprights. Poles formed the roof's ribs, running from the tops of the timbers to the center of the circle. Custom-fitted white sail cloth formed the roof and sides, transforming Millennium Henge into a giant yurt. The roof peak was open to accommodate a tubular metal chimney that vented a wood stove in the center of the henge.

For the flooring, we first put down heavy-duty plastic sheeting, which the children enjoyed slipping and sliding on in their stockinged feet. We scattered straw to a depth of about six inches, which the children rolled in and tossed fistfuls of at one another. Next, we laid down woven coconut fiber mats, and on top of those, Turkish carpets, which our guests had brought to Braemar from their own collections. Excess carpets were hung from the walls around the entire perimeter, giving the inside a feel of dense, warm comfort. We placed rocks around the central wood stove to form a hearth. Boughs cut from an ancient sequoia near the house were draped across the hearth rocks. We strung light bulbs from the structure's ribs and covered them with paper lanterns. Resident handymen created twenty-five round table tops, which were supported on logs two feet above the ground. Around the tables we placed pillows, mats, and low stools. Each table was covered in a crisp, white linen cloth, crowned with a vase of flowers, and scattered with tea lights. Iron Age Britain meets Turkish souk.

In the kitchen, four Braemarites with cooking talent oversaw the creation of a culinary marvel, surpassing all other celebratory meals. Behind the big house they made a fire pit with spits big enough to roast three whole lambs, which sizzled and spat all day on December 31. By early evening, dozens upon dozens of plates of food began accumulating on the dining room table in the big house. There were mounds of glistening hummus dented with Turkish olives; piles of salad greens and bowls of cucumbers bathed in yogurt sauce; two twenty-pound Atlantic salmon, topped with grilled onions on a bed of greens; braised leeks and carrots lightly coated in parmesan cheese and toasted to a delectable brown; and more.

I dressed in my best clothes for the meal then helped everyone carry the food to the henge. At the door, I had to stop and catch my breath. A hearty fire crackled in the wood stove, its permeating warmth captured by the deep burgundy carpets hanging from the walls. A subtle forest fragrance wafted among the earthy odor of wool. The tea lights on the tables flickered across the place settings, magnified through drinking glasses in a kaleidoscopic dance. A lump formed in my throat; my eyes teared, overcome with the vision. In true Sufi fashion, Braemarites had transformed a simple tent into a divine sanctuary of beauty.

One hundred and sixty Braemarites gathered around the tables; backs, elbows, legs, and feet all gently bumping neighbors as we wiggled for room on wobbly cushions. We gave thanks to God, the Compassionate, the Merciful. I added my own silent prayer of gratitude for the opportunity to share this once-in-a-lifetime event with fellow seekers on a collective journey to closeness with the Beloved. The weather was mild and dry outside but ironically rather damp inside. The fire and our body heat created condensation on the ceiling, which dripped on random diners, including me. Esmé, who wanted to spend the last hours of the century by my side, counted the intervals between drips and giggled every time one landed on my head. Sadly, Trevor had taken ill. We delivered a plate of food to him in the Gate Lodge, but he didn't want any company. I felt bad, but we seemed to have drifted apart once again since the water crisis.

Around eleven o'clock, we cleared the tables and moved them aside. In Braemar tradition, five minutes before midnight, we gathered in a circle and held hands in silence. The clock failed to chime, but we knew it was midnight from the distant crackle of fireworks in Eltondean. Latif spoke first.

"Welcome, everyone, to the twenty-first century." He clasped his hands in prayer position and bowed in salaam.

The moment was simultaneously eternal and fleeting, suspended between two centuries, momentarily pulling in opposing directions, what Carl Jung had called the "tension of the opposites." For me, at that moment, the opposites were shadow and real self, ego and soul, human and divine, earth and heaven. Poised on that threshold, it felt like we had left one room but hadn't quite entered the other, the liminal space where matter and spirit intersected. It was then I first realized that is where we find God, in transition moments; on rough edges; in places and at times where we least expect it; not always when things look bright and rosy. I didn't want to let go of that knowing.

We clung to those last few seconds before rupturing the silence with celebratory shrieks. The person holding my right hand let go; the one on the left pulled me toward her for a hug. For several minutes we circumambulated our moist, dripping shelter, kissing and embracing one another and extolling good wishes.

Several people journeyed up the front hill to the Monument where Braemar founder Iskandar was buried. Home-made oil-burning tiki lanterns stuck in the ground lit the way from the garden gate to the Monument. Braemar's traditional Hogmanay talent show followed, though without the sillier skits of previous years in favor of singing and instrumentals.

At four in the morning, running out of steam but not quite ready for bed, I headed to the servery to do my bit of washing up. There was Latif, hands plunged in the sink, and Sam Banks, a member of the board of directors, deftly working a dish towel around a wine glass. I grabbed a towel and joined in, not bothered by the stacks and stacks of dishware to clean up. It would get done, without my having to control it or resent doing it.

I may have come to know a miniscule more about myself and the essence of God, but the work hadn't changed. We would always need to take care of our basic needs, to keep the drought at bay, to clean up, to care for one another and other creatures. Truly being of service—to yourself, to others, to God—is performing with love because it's the right thing to do. Knowing when to quit before resentment creeps in is also being of service. To yourself.

I went to bed at 5 a.m. and rose again at 9 a.m., ready for new beginnings.

In the afternoon on New Year's Day, we played "Turning" again, the video Braemarites always watched before their Turkey pilgrimage. It was my third time watching, and each time I understood the message a little more. Like on the potter's wheel, or the woodworker's lathe, we are shaped and molded by experience, forever turning, being turned, toward the Beloved.

On the evening of New Year's Day, we had one final celebration in the Millennium Henge: the world's largest zikr. Fully abluted and dressed in our best, we sat in silence on the Turkish carpets until everyone was present. Even Trevor, now recovered, joined in. There were too many people to fully carry out the movements, but whenever possible, we stood and swayed instead. Coiled like a python in the middle of the henge was a giant tesbi, a string of prayer beads that Muslims use to keep track of their supplications to God. I had caught a glimpse of this tesbi once in the closet of Iskandar's old room, now the Braemar library. It was twenty-five feet long, its wooden beads nearly the size of soccer balls and strung together with a thick rope. The beads had been worn smooth by many hands, and on New Year's Day, it would see many more.

We began the zikr with the Arabic words *Bis'mallah, ir-rahman, ir-rahim*, in the name of God, the Compassionate, the Merciful. Slowly, the tesbi was unfurled. Bead by giant bead, we counted the repetition of *Allah* until the tesbi had made one round through the entire group. Toward the end of the zikr, we stood, and then, like a living tesbi ourselves, we moved in a flowing river through the circular henge, bestowing peace among our community.

Just like the moment when the new millennium had arrived, I hovered at the intersection of spirit and matter, suspended in time with my fellow Braemarites in an indescribable mystical experience, straddling the edge—that rough and loving and beautiful edge—of Unity with God.

CHAPTER 31

Recharging

One cloudless, cold day in January Rafi, the former maintenance man, returned for a brief visit. He invited me, Trevor, and Wakil to go for a plane ride. He needed to log some flying time to keep current on his pilot's license. The four of us packed into his sturdy Volvo station wagon and headed for the flat country southeast of Edinburgh. By "plane," we thought Rafi meant a Cessna-style vehicle with solid wings and an enclosed cabin. When we arrived at the little airport we discovered our assumption was wrong.

"Where are the planes?" Wakil asked, as we pulled into the parking lot.

"Right there," Rafi said.

He pointed to scores of colorful microlights parked on the field. The Flintstone-style contraptions were essentially tricycles with lawnmower-size engines and kites for wings.

"We're going in one of them?" Wakil said, tapping on the car window, wide-eyed.

"Of course, what did you think?" Rafi said.

"Uh, a real plane, maybe?" I said.

"I'm not going in one of them," Wakil said.

"Don't be silly, you two. They're perfectly safe, aren't they?" Rafi asked Trevor for confirmation.

"If you say so," Trevor said.

"Isn't the wind a little gusty today?" I asked.

"You need a bit of wind for lift," Rafi said.

He opened the car door and proceeded to get out. The rest of us sat there, unmoving and silent.

"Oh come on, you lot! We came all the way up here to fly. You're not going to back out now," Rafi said, annoyed.

The three of us slowly got out of the car and trailed behind Rafi toward the double-wide trailer that served as the airport office and passenger lounge. While Rafi took care of the paperwork (signing something that probably said the microlight people weren't responsible in the event that anybody plunged to their death), the rest of us had a farewell cup of tea and sat on the sofa.

"Don't think I'm gonna go," Wakil said.

"You have to. We are," Trevor said, pointing at me.

I had been thinking the same thing as Wakil but didn't say so.

"You go first, then, if you're so brave," Wakil said.

Then the two began arguing that the other should go first, which ended in name calling. Because only one passenger can fly at a time—and Rafi hadn't flown in a while—we eventually persuaded Wakil to go first. Trevor's comments about the "shabby looking wings" didn't help, but I ended the debate by telling Wakil he could get it over with sooner. He agreed.

The preparation time leading up to his flight was the quietest half hour we'd ever spent with Wakil. He tried on various flight suits and helmets until he found one that could zip up over his Guinness gut. Then the four of us headed for the "plane." Rafi and Wakil strapped themselves in.

"It was great knowing you, Wakil," Trevor said, patting him on the shoulder.

Wakil was so afraid, he couldn't even muster his usual

retort of "bugger off." As they motored to the runway, Wakil gripped the handholds and looked back at us one more time. Trevor and I laughed at their comical ascent into the atmosphere, which looked like the scene in "E.T." where the little alien flies with the boy on his bicycle. A half hour later they returned, and Wakil couldn't stop talking.

"It was brilliant! Bloody hell, I reckon that was the best thing I ever done in me life!"

Wakil stripped off the insulated flight suit and handed it to me. When I put it on, it bunched up around my ankles, and the helmet more than doubled the size of my head. Rafi and I could talk to each other through an intercom built into the helmet.

So that we could take off properly, I had to dangle my feet outside the tricycle. I was about to face all three of my cardinal fears at the same time: (1) Small aircraft. Once airborne, we gained altitude pretty quickly. At about a thousand feet up, I looked down. (2) Heights. When I realized that looking straight ahead was easier on the stomach, I began enjoying the ride more—until Rafi flew over the Firth of Forth. (3) Crashing over water and drowning.

Though it was frightening to feel so vulnerable, being exposed so high above the ground was also exhilarating. After about twenty minutes the early winter sun began sinking low. I was freezing, still a little apprehensive, and ready to be on terra firma again.

Trevor was next, the cockiest one about flying and the most scared when his turn came. As they motored to the runway, Trevor grabbed Rafi around the chest. Both were big men; it was a wonder the thing ever got off the ground. They stayed up a long time, returning after the sun had settled below the horizon. Back on the ground Trevor was stunned into silence. He loved it, and Rafi was pleased that his three chickens hadn't backed out in the end. So were his three chickens.

It wasn't long before the urge struck for me to soar to other new heights.

When the holidays had ended and our guests had departed so too had the ecstasy I had felt during the Braemar reunion and celebrations. Feelings of overwhelm and the self-induced pressure to get it all done came back in full force. I worried about being driven to the edge of another breakdown. It was clear my need for control hadn't been tamed. Would it ever? I didn't want another crisis to undo what little I had gained in personal growth. Plus, if I were going to pursue a creative writing career, I had to get away from this place, where distraction lurked around every corner.

When I told Principal Latif all of this, he had agreed that leaving for a while was a good idea. I admitted that it felt like running away. Shouldn't I stay and conquer instead? Isn't that the way? To push through? His reply was a clear "no."

He suggested that I was finally learning my boundaries, when to admit I had had enough. Being able to walk away, to surrender to what is, without feeling bad about it was the real measure of gain.

"It's not defeat," Latif said. "It's wisdom."

He even helped me find my retreat. (Oh, the irony of retreating from a retreat!) Latif seemed more pleased for me than I was about leaving. But I took his message to heart and began preparing my mind for something different.

"I hope you're not leaving because of me," Trevor said, gently bushing the side of my face with the back of his hand.

Between the stresses of the water crisis and all the activities going on at the holidays, Trevor's and my relationship had cooled somewhat. We still struggled to find a way to work peaceably together and also to allay our fears that one day I would eventually have to leave Scotland because I couldn't get a visa forever. Neither of us wanted a long-distance relationship. I tried to assure him the move wasn't about him, although it partly was. Now I was the one putting my desires in check so as not to be hurt when the time came for me to leave the country.

In late January Trevor reluctantly agreed to help me move into a two-bedroom cottage at Buccleuch Farm, six miles farther up the valley and on the edge of Glenmeade Forest. The hundred-acre farm and its hillock pastures were an oasis among the vast, dense spruce plantation. It was fully furnished and included a large kitchen, bathroom with a deep tub, and sitting room with a fireplace. Best of all, I had a washer and dryer, a microwave (no such thing at Braemar), and TV all to myself. I could cook what I wanted, eat what I liked, watch TV with no interruption, and even leave dirty dishes in the sink overnight. No battling for the washer or dryer or bathtub.

The landlords lived in their big house just up the driveway from the cottage. Their children were away at school, and the husband spent most of the year abroad for work, leaving the wife on her own to manage twenty sheep, four dogs, three cats, three chickens, three peacocks, two goats, and two horses. I added five more chickens to their coterie, bringing with me from Braemar an old hen and her four late-hatched chicks.

Working on a novel, I wrote four to six hours every weekday and at least two hours a day on weekends. In the afternoons I went for long walks around the pastures or up the forest road or explored the nearby hiking trails, sometimes discovering abandoned homesteads or hidden forest waterfalls. The dogs loved me. Every time I set foot outside, they were there wagging tails in anticipation of a walk.

Every night I tried to build a fire and then sat in front of the television. Sometimes I even turned the TV on. And sometimes the fire stayed lit for more than five minutes. My proficiency at fire-starting hadn't improved. Eventually, Trevor rescued me with a bag of coal, and my fires went from bad to satisfactory. At my request, Trevor rarely came over. I needed space, and we settled for visiting on Sunday afternoons when I came to Braemar for lunch.

Occasionally, I invited Braemarites over for meals, many of whom remarked how relaxed I had seemed after "going native." Not just a visiting American anymore, I had become a valley resident. But the thrill of living alone turned into loneliness. Whenever the phone rang in my little cottage, I would pick it up after the first ring, eager for human contact and an invitation: Would you like to come for supper tonight? Would you like to play bridge on Saturday evening? Would you like to go to Edinburgh with me tomorrow? Other times, six miles wasn't far enough from Braemar: Could you come up and clean the fish tank? Could you help out in the office on Wednesday? One of the chickens looks ill; what should we do?

The delivery man became my boredom barometer. Whenever I caught myself watching him from my window as he unloaded twenty-five-pound bags of goat chow into the barn, I knew it was time to have someone over for a meal or to go into Eltondean and poke around the shops.

In general, I missed contact with people. Despite the trials of communal living, I grew to understand the importance that relationships play in personal growth and how isolation can sometimes destroy us. I also began to miss Trevor's company more than I wanted to admit. We began talking on the phone a couple of times a week, and he confessed his own personal failures in his previous marriage and how he wanted to do better with me. I softened, again wondering what it would feel like to just live each day as it came without worry about the future. If he and I were meant to be together, love—I wanted to believe—would find a way through visa issues and whatever else. Trevor started spending an occasional night with me at my little cottage, and we eased back into being a couple.

In late March I prepared to move back to Braemar just when the Six Month Course ended. Oddly, the day before, Braemar's water stopped flowing again, but not because the tank had run dry. Instead, air kept getting trapped in the pipes from the previous incident. Trevor warned me to stay in the cottage a few extra days while he sorted it out.

"I want make sure you're happy and healthy, not too stressed like last time," he said.

It took only one full day, after which he deemed it safe for me to move back into the Cook's Room in the big house. It was just as I had left it, and once again I woke periodically to the sound of footsteps overhead during late-night pantry raids and to mice scuttling behind the walls.

***

In early April we hosted another volunteer tree event, which we dubbed the Annual Tree Bash. It was much reduced in scope. The Bash was ten days instead of fourteen, and included twenty volunteers instead of a hundred, most of them a teenage brood of charter Braemarites on their spring break from school. We planted a few thousand more trees and continued weeding the previous years' planting. In all, a blissfully uneventful event, with Trevor and I working side by side most days.

As summer drew near it began to feel like my work at Braemar was done—whatever it was that God had brought me here to do. I didn't want to think about life after Braemar, yet I knew my time was coming. What was next? I wasn't ready to go back to America, so I decided to embark on a sixty-two-mile pilgrimage to avoid thinking about it.

It was my friend Jill who had first told me about St. Cuthbert's Way. We had planned to walk the footpath together some day, but physical reasons prevented her from joining me. Nevertheless, she wanted to honor my journey, so the day before my walk began we paid homage to St. Cuthbert at Durham Cathedral, where he was laid to rest. Cuddy, as he is affectionately known, was a seventh-century animal-loving monk of local significance. Legend tells of his proclivity for praying in the middle of the night waist deep in the North Sea. When he emerged from the water, sea otters would wrap themselves around his feet to keep him warm. (Would that my Soay sheep had been so devoted!) St. Cuthbert's Way linked Melrose, Scotland, where Cuddy had served as abbot, with Holy Isle, a.k.a. Lindisfarne in England, where he had also served.

In the cathedral I knelt upon one of the crocheted pillows that surrounded his stone tomb and prayed to the saint to increase me in knowledge. In morning meetings, Latif had often discussed trying out this type of supplication to beseech God to open our eyes to the wisdom of the moment. I also asked Cuddy for guidance and safety on my six-day journey, which I would be walking alone.

CHAPTER 32

The Way of Saints

DAY 1

At six o'clock on a May morning Trevor dropped me off at the start of St. Cuthbert's Way near the ruins of Melrose Abbey, where Cuthbert had entered the monastic life around AD 650. I set out with my daypack stuffed with snacks and raingear, and a walking staff that Trevor had carved for me from an ash tree branch. The trail started up a long flight of steps, eventually ending at the base of a steep hillside that helped form the three Eildon Hills. I wound my way through thickets of gorse—large, spiny shrubs with yellow pea-blossom-like flowers that smell like coconut. The scent incongruously evoked summer on the beach in my mind's eye, while my real eyes took in the rumpled Scottish Borders landscape on a blustery day. Diverting from the Way, I climbed the north hill and gazed across the valley toward the Cheviot Hills, where the journey would lead in a few days.

In the village of Bowden I stopped at the twelfth-century church and sat in a pew, sketching the stained-glass window in my journal. I thought about my ancestors and wondered when the first of them had come to Christianity and what that looked and felt like for them. A sudden turning on of hope for what was probably a miserably difficult existence? Or a gradual coming home to the greater possibilities that love offered? Outside, I sat on a bench to eat my peanut butter sandwich and basked in a rare episode of sunshine. The parish priest arrived and asked whether I was on the Way, nodding toward my backpack and staff. We chatted for a few minutes, and then clouds hid the sun. I fished my raingear out of my pack.

"It wouldn't be the Way if the Lord didn't throw in a few obstacles," the priest said, holding his palm toward the sky. He wished me luck and entered the church.

By now, I was used to obstacles in this land. I spent the rest of the day—six hours—wriggling into and out of my raingear, never quite fully in synch with the off-again, on-again rain. As soon I got it on, the rain would stop. When I took it off, the rain would start again. God was having fun with her obstacles.

The Way passed near the village of Dryburgh, home to another abbey ruin that I loved. I took a detour just to see it again and sat on a bench in what had once been the cloister garden. I wondered what life had been like for the monks, then realized I already had a pretty good idea: hauling water, growing and cooking food, sleeping, praying, bathing, and eating together twenty-four hours a day. Not much had changed over the centuries for people in serious pursuit of God. How did they work out their differences? Probably not by nipping down to the pub for some dancing and a few beers.

The detour to Dryburgh left me pressed for time to make it to Maxton Parish Kirk by five o'clock, where Trevor would pick me up. Because the beginning and ending points of the first two days were close to home, Trevor wanted to pick me up and drop me off between home and the trailheads, saving me money on meals and accommodations and breaking the Way into more manageable sections.

By the time I reached Maxton my feet ached, and all I wanted was to quit walking. Just as the day's journey had started up a long flight of steps, so it ended. The wooden steps, slick from rain, climbed up around the side of the church to the parking lot and were locally known as Jacob's Ladder. Christians, Jews, and Muslims all have variations on that theme about the meaning of Jacob's dream of a ladder reaching between Heaven and Earth, angels moving up and down it. English Sufi writer Martin Lings likened Jacob's Ladder to "the 'straight path,' for indeed the way of religion is none other than the way of creation itself retraced from its end back to its Beginning."

I reached the church's parking lot just as Trevor pulled up in his car. To me, in that moment, he was the perfect man, arriving in his chariot to bring me home to a hot meal, a hot bath, and a warm bed. The straight path to a loving partner.

DAY 2

Trevor dropped me off in the exact spot where he had picked me up the day before in the church parking lot, exactly where my feet had last touched the ground before having gotten into his car. I begged him to drive me two miles farther so I wouldn't have to start the day walking on the hard surface of the road because my feet still ached.

"You'll hate yourself if you don't walk every inch of the Way," he claimed.

We argued for a few minutes, then he got out of the car, walked around to my side, opened the door, and tugged at my arm to pull me out. He put my pack on my back and handed me the walking staff.

"Don't forget this. See you at five in Crailing."

He kissed me and quickly drove off. I shook my fist, while he waved at me in his rearview mirror. I hobbled along the country road, thoughts of Perfect Man fading in my mind. At least the sun was shining. Finally, the Way picked up again on a proper earthen path, and I arrived at a grave marker of a woman who had apparently had greater moxy than me where aches were concerned. The English had killed her lover at the Battle of Ancrum Moor in 1545, and the marker's inscription told of her response:

Fair maiden Lilliard lies under this stane; Little was her stature, but muckle [big] was her fame; Upon the English loons she laid mony thumps; And when her legs were cuttit off, she fought upon her stumps.

Lilliard's determination renewed my strength. I began thinking about all the times at Braemar I pushed through difficult work in difficult weather, under sometimes difficult emotional conditions. How many times had we needed to redo a job because our efforts had failed? How the work never ended, nor would it ever end because that is the nature of work, of survival. The nature of seeking.

In Ancrum I stopped at a nature center called Harestanes, which was also the home of the Borders Forest Trust, the organization that had helped Braemar get the grant to plant trees. They were also the ones who had responded to an email nearly two years earlier from a woman in Montana who had been looking for a break from her dull life. "Check out this place called Braemar," they said. She had, unwittingly embarking on a journey she had never imagined. At that moment, there were no regrets, only gratitude for the experience. Until I reached the River Teviot.

Water began to hurl from the sky in sheets, and the next several miles I spent thinking about surviving to day's end. Rain, wrestling with raingear, and aching, soggy feet. Many days at Braemar had been like this.

At the village of Crailing, the sun emerged just long

enough for me to take off my raingear and pack it away for what I hoped was the final time. Then the darkest cloud I had ever seen engulfed the sun behind me. I struggled back into my raingear and quickened my pace. A mile or so later, the black mass in the sky, full of lightening and rattling the earth with thunder, caught up to me. For an hour the downpour seeped into my "waterproofs." Just as I was about to reach my meeting point with Trevor, the rain stopped. On the drive home we hit a hail storm. At home, I relished every second of my bath and a home-cooked meal, my last for the next few days.

DAY 3

Rain. My feet hurt before I even get out of bed. I didn't want to go, but Trevor refused to listen to my complaints, dumping me off at the exact same spot where he had picked me up the day before.

"It's for your own good," etcetera, and "You'd hate yourself if you didn't walk every inch," etcetera.

I didn't think I'd hate myself, but that didn't matter to him. The only shred of mercy he showed was walking with me for the first quarter mile. As soon as the rain began to pelt down like nails, he ran back to his car. I stuck my tongue out at him as he drove past waving and smiling at me.

I had five miles of road walking in this eleven-mile day. Fortunately, the rain stopped several minutes later, and I sat on a log by the roadside to sketch Cessford Castle ruins in the distance. The fifteenth-century fortified tower once housed the Kers, ancestors to the current Duke of Roxburghshire. The Kers were also Borders Reivers who served as wardens to what was called Middle March, the region of the disputed England–Scotland border.

The sun was still playing in and out of the clouds when I reached Morebattle village. I stopped to buy a bottle of orange juice at the post office that also doubled as a small shop. Two elderly women stopped to chat and ask, Are ye doing the Way?

I confirmed that I was.

"You had better put sun cream on your nose because you have freckles just like me, and I'll get burned if I don't," one said.

I looked at the brooding clouds racing toward the sun, hell bent on extinguishing it.

"The rain might stay clear of you while you cross the mountains," the other woman said with such certainty that I did put on more sun cream.

She was right. But that didn't stop the ritual of donning and removing—approximately eight million times—my raingear, while the rain threatened but stayed away. The dressing and undressing had become a habit by now.

Just outside of Morebattle was the steepest ascent on the entire sixty-two-mile Way and the highest point—Grubbit Law ("law" is Scots for "hill"). I stopped at a stream, removed my boots and socks, and stuck my feet in the cool water to relieve the swelling before climbing the mountain. Halfway up I stopped to sit on a rock and eat my turkey sandwich. A ewe and lamb approached and stared. Whether out of loneliness or loopiness, I held out my hand with some trail mix (they refused) and tried engaging them in conversation.

"I used to have sheep. Bloody nuisance, but cute."

The ewe cocked her head. The lamb lost interest and tried to suckle, but the ewe kicked her away.

"Funny thing about those Soays, they were a lot like me. Didn't like being confined and pretty much did whatever they pleased. No matter how hard I tried to control them, they always outwitted me. They always came back, too. Maybe I should have trusted they would come back and not worry so much when they wandered. Do you think God feels the same way about me?"

The ewe scrunched her top lip, turned, and walked away, her lamb close behind. Funnily enough, the Soays we had now lived on a farm within a few miles of where I sat. I waved in their general direction and continued to the top of Grubbit Law—1,070 feet. Gazing back toward journey's beginning, I saw the Eildon Hills at the far end of the horizon and rain all around, except on me! With the aid of Trevor's hand-carved staff, the up-and-down, up-and-down crossing of the swales warmed me despite the brisk breeze. Okay, so Trevor was now back in my good books. Though not the thousands-feet-high Rockies of Montana I had backpacked, this hike was equally challenging, but with foxes and sheep instead of grizzlies and mountain lions.

About a mile and a half before Kirk Yetholm, my destination for the night, the skies opened, anointing every crevice of my body. Raingear was pointless; the hostel was nearby. I was the first one to check in that afternoon. Later, I met four other walkers, some on the Pennine Way and others on St. Cuthbert's.

Maggie, a 72-year-old Glaswegian, sat next to me and my cup o'noodles supper in the common room. She arrived by car and had all the fixings for a gourmet stir-fry. I declined her offer to share in hopes of losing some of the ten pounds I had gained since first arriving in Scotland twenty months earlier. Maggie was attending a food fair in Jedburgh and filled my ear about the nasty business of genetically engineered foods, in particular slamming the Americans for their evil-doings on the genetic modification front. I agreed with her. When she found out I was American and not Australian (had my accent changed?), she apologized for "all the horrible things" she had said. I assured her I had taken no offense, and we talked about Scotland.

Just as I was crawling into bed, two women in their fifties arrived and took the bunks across from mine. They, too, were walking the Way. Elsie was practically in tears, as she lowered her backside unsteadily onto the mattress and gingerly removed her boots. I recognized the agony in her contorted face and got up to rifle through my pack. I handed her a tube of soothing foot cream, which Trevor had bought for me. The peppermint oil, arnica, and other naturopathic goodies were supposed to ease long pilgrimages. Mary was in better shape; she walked regularly. Elsie hadn't walked more than two consecutive miles in her whole life. That day they had walked nearly seventeen miles.

Before going to sleep, I gave thanks for my health.

DAY 4

Maggie offered to drive me to the town of Wooler, the next destination, because it was bucketing rain. God showed no signs of turning off the heavenly spigots just to please a few pilgrims.

"I would hate myself if I didn't walk every inch of the Way. Besides, my boyfriend would be disappointed if he found out," I said.

"How's he to know? No sense in catching your death just to please a man."

She had a point. Tempted, I declined.

I slithered into the still-damp waterproofs, wrapped my backpack in a plastic garbage bag, and forged on. In about a mile, the path headed up a steep bank through pastures and moorland into the Cheviot Mountains. Here, I met Mary and Elsie, who had set out a full hour before me. It had taken me only twenty minutes to catch up to them. I asked how they were (still blistered and exhausted) and offered encouragement (you'll be fine; try counting the sheep). I was torn between walking with them and carrying on at my own pace. I didn't want to be slowed down because it was thirteen miles over the mountains in the most remote part of the journey.

"We'll catch up again later," I said, picking up my pace.

I crossed the border into England, which didn't look any different except that it was raining harder. Most of the day was hill after hill, up and down, wet skies, mud-sucking bogs, and bedraggled sheep. When I reached a small, dense patch of spruce, I thought someone must be playing a joke: the waymarker pointed directly into the unsightly plantation when it could have gone around it. Maybe there was something I didn't know. I pulled out the map, and yep, right through the block of tightly spaced, spooky wood. Sometimes the only way around the dark unpleasantness is through it.

I climbed over the fence stile into the plantation and spotted the path, under about eighteen inches of water. Even the wet-loving spruce seemed to hate the rain. Their roots formed humps above the ground's surface, as if trying to keep their feet dry. The root humps created a bank for me to walk on and kept my feet less wet. Not that it mattered. My boots made squishy noises with every footfall; water seeped in from the stitching. In about one hundred yards, I was out of the woods.

Constant rain has a way of eating holes in your soul.

"I'm trying to walk, here!" I shouted at God. "A little sunshine would be nice!"

Constant rain also does things to the brain. I began to have conversations aloud with some of the more significant people in my life, mostly past boyfriends—and Trevor. I apologized to them for some of my less saintly acts, defended my position for others, and examined what might have been different. Did St. Cuthbert think about such things? Maybe not the boyfriend, part . . . well, who knows? But probably the part about feeling remorse for poor behavior and a softening of the spirit, a smoothing of the rough edges, motivated to be better.

With this new thought, the rain began to feel like one giant ablution.

Near a farmstead in a lonely hollow, I was startled by a gigundous bull in the field where the path traversed. He was only about ten yards away munching grass by a stream. I walked quickly past, nearly running into another bull, as big as a hippopotamus but with the courage of a mouse—thankfully! At the sight of me, he ran in the other direction. I laughed, forgetting about the other bull just yards behind, which could have killed me at any second.

In the settlement of Hethpool, consisting of four Arts and Crafts style cottages, I stopped to admire a hillside of oak trees planted by Admiral Lord Cuthbert Collingwood, second in command to Horatio Nelson at the Battle of Trafalgar. Collingwood planted acorns at every opportunity, concerned that the Royal Navy would run out of oaks to cut down to rebuild their aging fleet. Though I disagreed with the admiral's intention behind planting the trees, I tipped a virtual bicorn to him, fellow tree-planter and Cuthbert namesake.

Continuing on at the top of another Cheviot hill, two couples caught up to me, walking briskly past and dressed head to toe in the latest outdoor gear. One of the women invited me to walk with them. I thanked her but declined on account of being a slow walker.

"We're slow too," the other woman said, as they sailed past me.

Putting my head down to guard against the lashing rain in my face, I tried to keep up with them for about a quarter mile. I looked up just as I was about to pass a waymarker that pointed to St. Cuthbert's Way uphill to the right. The others charged on ahead along a flat gravel road. I stopped to consult the map and confirmed that the Way did indeed head up the looming, steep, soggy, steep, blasted, steep, God-forsaken, steep, cloud-enshrouded (did I mention steep?) mountainside! The gravel track the others took was a shortcut to town. I shook my fist at the two couples, now a long way ahead.

"Cheaters!" I shouted.

They didn't hear me.

"I am not a cheater. I'm walking every inch of this damn trail, and I'm going to enjoy it if it kills me," I mumbled.

The mantra *I am not a cheater* carried me up the mountainside to the saddle. Higher hills surrounded me, and some had the ruins of Iron Age forts. But my feet were too swollen to walk the extra mile to explore. On the other side of Yeavering Bell, one of the mountains, was the ancient site of Gefrin, where around AD 627 a missionary called Paulinus arrived to baptize the people into a new religion called Christianity. They would have been among some of the region's first Christians.

In the saddle below Yeavering Bell, my feet throbbed to be born again. I stopped to baptize them in a puddle. The chilling plunge sent ripples of dull pain up my spine to my head. My feet were wrinkled and pale from being soggy all day. Oh, for the healing powers of St. Cuthbert! How did he cope on his travels throughout these hills? No Gore-Tex or sturdy hiking boots to comfort him. Maybe high-tech clothes were more of a burden compared with natural woolens? On his pilgrimage ministering to the people of these harsh Northumbrian hills and valleys, Cuthbert had no idea where he'd spend each night, or even whether he'd find food for the day. What faith he had to plod on, feet clad in nothing but cloth and leather. No cheater, he! It made my troubles seem too trivial to think about, considering I had a warm, dry bed at day's end, and I was pretty certain a hot pub meal was in my future.

At two o'clock, I reached another mountain pass, a long flat meadow at the top of the mountains from which I saw the town of Wooler below. The rain subsided, finally offering the opportunity for me to stop and eat trail mix without it turning into goop. I sat on the ground at the junction of two stone dykes, out of the wind, and opened my rain jacket.

"Thank you!" I shouted to the sky.

Only a few miles to go. In the hostel in Wooler I found a spare peg in the warming room to hang my sopping raingear. One of the guests offered to make me a cup of tea when he saw the apparition of myself enter the common room. It was a holiday weekend, so the hostel was filled with vacationing families. For supper I treated myself to a half pint of Guinness and fish and chips at a nearby pub. After a hot shower, I dropped into bed. I shared a room with a woman and her twelve-year-old daughter, also called Sarah. The girl gnashed her teeth and talked in her sleep. All night her mother kept saying in a loud whisper, "Sarah, stop that!"

Sleep eluded me.

Day 5

The last full day of my pilgrimage began with the brightest sunshine I had seen in weeks. I headed out wearing shorts for the first time since my summer in Montana. The Way drew nearer to the sea now, and I could smell it in the air. Taking a two-hour detour, I strode across the sandy flats of Weetwood Moor to see cup and ring designs that had been carved into a slab of rock some 4,000 years ago. The rings were concentric circles; the "cups" were carved, shallow bowls—big enough for my fist—at the center of the circles. No one knows what they mean, but circles imply all sorts of mystical significance: the circle of life, labyrinths walked by the ancients, returning to our spiritual home.

Back on the Way, I encountered Mary and Elsie again. They had made it over the Cheviots with some struggle. The sun was the only thing that had encouraged them to get out of bed this morning—that and knowing they would finish the walk.

I decided to travel with them to the end. We talked about Braemar (they had asked what brought me to Britain), getting into a discussion about Muhammad and Jesus. It reminded me how little most Christians knew about the Muslim faith, and although Braemar wasn't affiliated with any particular religion, I realized how even my recent (yet limited) education in Islam had begun to affect me in a positive way.

Mary proclaimed her faith in Jesus and asked me how I thought Muhammad differed. I told her I believed Muhammad loved Jesus; that for Muslims, Muhammad was not a savior in the same way that Jesus was for Christians; that Muhammad did not replace Jesus, but rather Muhammad was another of God's prophets; that all of the prophets brought unique messages to humanity; that some Muslims believed Jesus was one of God's most exalted prophets and that he would come again; that just because I had spent some time living in a spiritual community that studied the teachings of a Sufi saint (alongside other spiritual practices) did not make me a heretic. Mary, in particular, seemed skeptical.

For the first time I found myself defending Islam to a Christian. Neither angry nor defensive, I simply wanted the ladies to understand what my experience had given me, what God had revealed by bringing me to Braemar. Our limited knowledge of Truth wouldn't fit on a pinhead compared with God's true nature. The unique spiritual journeys we all take are God's infinite manifestations to be celebrated not disparaged. To accuse others of taking the "wrong" journey not only showed ignorance but grave arrogance by presuming to know how others should lead their lives. I wanted them to understand that my own spiritual life had been enriched from exposure to other traditions, and I loved God more strongly than ever because of it.

Mary said nothing. I left it for God to show her whatever she needed. We changed the subject.

I realized that people of all faiths could feel threatened by other beliefs; that it was normal, comfortable, to perceive the world as black and white; that it seemed logical that believing one thing precluded believing another. Could one hold a belief while also accepting that she could be wrong and simply choose to believe one thing over another because it felt right? For me now, the answer was yes. Comfort and logic can be veils to Truth.

We arrived at St. Cuthbert's Cave, an overhang of huge limestone boulders just below the top of a ridge among neatly planted rows of conifers. Two men were there who had been a day behind me the whole time and finally passed me when I slowed to talk with Mary and Elsie. They weren't finishing the entire route, however (cheaters!). Instead they were going as far as the coast and skipping the last two miles out to the abbey on Lindisfarne Isle. The walk across the sands to Lindisfarne is the most sacred part of the Way. How could they skip it? I didn't ask, but a voice in my head supplied the answer: *We're all on a path of our own choosing and need.*

Cuthbert had served a few years at Lindisfarne and was buried at Lindisfarne Abbey after his death in 687. The abbey soon became a pilgrimage because of reports of miracle healings taking place at his tomb. In 875, and with Cuthbert's remains, the monks fled Lindisfarne to escape invading Danes. When the monks dug up his body, it had not decomposed at all—a phenomena allegedly common among saints (though who goes digging up their bodies to find out?). They took the remains and his relics on a seven-year, cross-country run for their lives, reportedly once hiding his remains in this very cave where I now enjoyed lunch with my new pals.

The three of us ladies continued up and over the ridge of the Kyloe Hills and stopped to take in the clear view down the valley. The North Sea sparkled in the distance. Lindisfarne was visible through the haze. If this walk had been a film, this would be the moment when the choir of angels reached their crescendo, and the audience's collective throat tightened. The lush grasses in pastures below made for fat sheep and cattle. In the sky surly clouds pressed the sea at the horizon. Overwhelmed with the beauty—the perfection—of it, I brushed away a tear.

I took a short detour to a higher spot to experience my *mons gaudium*, my "hill of joy," described by pilgrims throughout the centuries as that moment when you finally see your goal. I sat on a rock and began sketching Lindisfarne in the distance, telling Mary and Elsie that I would catch up with them later. I watched them make their way down the long slope toward the sea.

Later I walked as fast as my swollen feet could carry me to catch up to them, passing an opportunity to soak them in a stream. For five days I had walked alone, with the exception of that morning, and now I craved the company of fellow pilgrims. I wanted to be a witness for Mary and Elsie as they set out across the sands to complete their sacred adventure to Lindisfarne. I never did see them again.

In my rush to find them, I nearly missed a waymarker to the right. Believing there was no way the ladies could have gotten that far ahead of me, I thought they might have missed this waymarker and carried on straight down another dirt track instead. They had said they had gotten off track several times. Part of me wanted to look for them and bring them back. *We're all on a path of our own choosing*, I reminded myself. I resisted this habitual urge to shepherd the lost—to control—and instead chose the obscure St. Cuthbert's Way through the tall grass.

By the time I reached a wide spot called Fenwick, a cluster of a few houses along a trunk road just off the senses-mutilating A1 super-highway, I had already walked twelve miles. My feet were about to go on strike. I crossed the highway and hobbled down a country lane toward another dangerous crossing, the East Coast Main Line railway along which the Flying Scotsman traveled at more than 100 mph.

On the other side of the tracks the Way cut through a field growing two crops; on one side was corn, the other, wheat. The farmer had plowed a very distinct path down the middle separating the corn from the wheat. The wheat was waist-high, and I brushed my hands along the feathery tops as I walked along. Strangely, it felt like a brief taste of Paradise, and I didn't want that moment to end. During that singular experience, every hardship I had endured in the past two years was suddenly worth having led me to this very place, to this simple act of walking through a field of wheat rippling in the sea breeze. Everything was as it should be. I was warm and dry; even my throbbing feet were no hardship. I was content. Loved.

When I reached the end of the wheat, I wanted to turn around and do it again. Like the New Year's Day zikr in Braemar's Millennium Henge, when it was over, I yearned for more. This was the longing Rumi wrote so much about in his poetry: *When the soul lies down in that grass, the world is too big to think about.*

I continued another mile or so to the causeway that linked the mainland with Lindisfarne. After five days of essentially having been alone, the hordes of people I encountered here on this stupendous Sunday afternoon was simultaneously assaulting and exhilarating. A string of cars inched along the causeway back to the mainland to beat the rising tide. I waited at the car park, hoping to see Mary and Elsie. They had either not yet arrived or had already set out across the sands. I waved toward the island just in case they were watching.

My B&B near Beal was still another two or three miles up the road. I sat down for about a half hour and could barely get up again. Never in my life had I been in such all-over physical agony. With every step my feet screamed, sending sharp bolts up my legs, trunk, and neck to my brain: *Get off your feet!* My brain returned the messages: *Only another few miles to go. I promise!* The skin on my legs, arms, and face were tight and red with sunburn.

I walked another mile and sat down again to gingerly pry my boots off; my feet looked doubled in size and were blistered everywhere. I pulled my tennis shoes out of my pack, while a woman approached me from behind.

"Are you a pilgrim?" she asked.

I smiled at the warmth in her voice. Yes, a bloody knacked, cream-cracked, feel-like-I've-been-whacked pilgrim! She asked whether I was okay and dug in her purse for bandages, handing me four. She really wanted me to have them even though I told her that they wouldn't help at this point. She, too, had sore feet, she said. She had taken the train to Beal from Berwick and walked across the causeway to Lindisfarne. I looked at her bare feet, high heels in hand.

"I'm afraid I chose rather unsensible shoes today," she said.

She walked with me until my turnoff to the B&B, her conversation helping to take my mind off the full-body throbbing. We wished each other well, and nearly in tears, I told her how grateful I was that she had stopped to help.

She embraced me and carried on her way.

I had one more mile on a dirt road to go. A couple in a convertible passed by not bothering to offer me a lift despite that I was hobbling badly now. They didn't even slow down for the puddle, instead hitting it square on and sending water in a perfect spray all down my right side. The woman looked back at me with a sheepish grin. I didn't even have the strength to flip her off. I was starting to get used to the knowledge that God sends all kinds our way. How we choose to experience them is up to us.

When I reached the B&B, the couple was unloading luggage from their convertible. They saw me and hurried inside. The hostess greeted me at the door and motioned for me to follow her up the stairs. I looked at them as if they were Mt. Everest. She offered to carry my pack, which dripped with muddy water.

"Have you had your tea?" she asked, meaning supper.

I asked how far the nearest pub or restaurant was. She surveyed me from head to toe.

"I'd better fix you something here. Scrambled eggs and toast all right?"

"Sounds heavenly. Do you have a tub?"

An hour-long soak did little to soothe the muscles after seventeen miles. I had to lift my legs out of the tub with my hands because my legs wouldn't move on their own. I descended the stairs like a toddler, on my butt, one step at a time. I limped to the dining room for my eggs and toast. As hungry as I was, I could barely lift the fork to my mouth, stabbing my cheek several times in an attempt to feed myself. Afterward, I crawled on my hands and knees back up the stairs to bed.

Day 6

I got up at quarter till five to walk back to the car park by the causeway, two miles, to meet Jill by six o'clock. She was going to walk with me across the sands to Lindisfarne. The morning was cold, with heavy rain clouds looming. I wore shorts anyway, expecting to wade through shin-deep water in places across the sands.

I walked along the road to the causeway, feet protesting all the way. Jill drove past me about a half-mile before the car park, then realizing it was me, backed up and stopped. I got in, telling her that I wasn't cheating because I've walked every inch of the Way so far and then some. Besides, this wasn't even part of the Way. She looked at me as if she thought I was beginning to lose it.

We parked and suited up for the quickly approaching rain. Though it was customary to walk these last two miles barefoot, the chill was too much for my already abused feet. We both kept our boots on and began following the telephone-pole-like markers driven into the sand and marking what was believed to be the original path to Cuthbert's abbey. The rain turned to hail, which felt good on my sunburnt legs. It blew over quickly, though, and we dodged pools of seawater undrained from the outgoing tide, walking in silence. I thought about the previous five days. I had walked more than sixty-two miles, mostly alone, pushing through the hardships. All the obstacles were now transformed into badges of victory.

When we reached the island, I proclaimed, "I did it!"

Jill hugged me.

We walked into the village, stopping to visit the abbey ruins then going inside St. Mary's church. We gathered with a dozen others in the choir seats behind the altar for a short morning service, where Bible passages were read and hymns were sung. I closed my eyes and soaked up the singing voices around me, contemplating how it had been from this place, and Iona on Scotland's west coast, that my ancestors had been taught about a foreign man who had died six hundred years earlier, leaving behind a message about peace, love, and forgiveness.

We ate breakfast at a local B&B, meeting up with Trevor. Over bacon and eggs I told them about my pilgrimage. Trevor smiled.

"I'm proud of you. Aren't you glad you walked every inch of the Way?"

I was. And I realized that although I could walk through life alone if I chose—I had the requisite fortitude—I rather enjoyed sharing life with others. Messy, persnickety, pious, irreverent, blaming, accepting, depressed, joyful, scatterbrained, clear-headed, stubborn, easygoing, nutty, lovable people.

CHAPTER 33

Wrapping Up

After my pilgrimage along St. Cuthbert's Way, I lived another five months in Great Britain, splitting my time between house-sitting for various Braemarites and traveling. Jill and I spent two weeks during midsummer in the Orkney and Shetland Islands, and I visited friends in England. Mostly, I lived at Braemar, wrapping up miscellaneous business for the tree planting project, writing the forestry management plan, putting up signage for the walking trails, and caring for new seedlings in our budding tree nursery. We also had two new broods of the chicks to raise.

Sometimes I helped Trevor in the garden, which, with no small effort, he had brought back to life for a second season. I tried abandoning my restrictive need for organization and tidiness, opting to pay more attention to doing whatever task grabbed Trevor's fancy in the moment. During times of particular grace, I could find awe in the mundane. I could feel the handle of the hoe and imagine the tree from which it had been carved. The stinking mound of straw from mucking out the duck pens became the sweet smell of life and love for my winged beloveds.

Sufis say that physical life is the expression of the soul's development, the outward expression of inward unfolding. Battling cold, shoveling crap, gathering fire-wood, chasing sheep, becoming undone by tree planting projects. Outwardly these were just experiences. Inwardly, they told the story of my soul's longing for closeness to God.

I now knew that I would never achieve that sense of completion I had always craved. I would never reach a point where everything would be finally done—or my idea of perfect. It simply is not the point of life. I was beginning to warm to that idea.

Even having acquired this knowledge, I had my moments of backsliding—and still do! Sometimes hoeing gave me blisters, and shoveling mucky straw threw my back out. On forgetful days I complained or got angry or felt overwhelmed. On better days I remembered that I was human. And, I could choose. To fume about injustices or be anxious about a future event that may never happen are choices that do not always serve our better selves. Judgment and expectation are the gateways to misery and disappointment.

I came to realize the path was more spiral than linear. As we are turned, we may reach greater heights of know-ingness, but we still go round and round, covering the same ground, just from a different perspective. Enlightenment is the realization that life does not change, only our thoughts about it. We will chop wood, carry water, plant trees, carry sheep, cook, clean, and do it all over again day after day. My work on Earth would be complete when God called me home.

Wakil was my greatest teacher in this. His slovenly self was yet a model of perfection in its imperfection. God doesn't always deliver what we need in a nice, tidy pack-age. One day Wakil would be full of praise for God, mak-ing beautiful bread in the kitchen; the next, he could talk a blue streak against a fellow Braemarite while nursing a bottle of whisky in bed and vowing never to cook again. His visceral honesty, sometimes harsh, was real. He never hesitated to express even his most base humanity because he knew it was fleeting. Wakil understood the need for constant reminding of who he really was. He practiced his zikr.

A new Course started in October. A new set of students arrived in wonderment equal to their trepidation. While laying the table for supper one evening, I found myself instructing one of the newcomers, a young American woman called Diana, to place the Willow pattern plates with the picture facing upright. She looked at me and grimaced. I knew that look: *Does it matter?*

"You'll find that Braemar is all about paying attention. It's just one of the many ways that we practice being in service to one another, to ourselves, and ultimately to God," I said.

I put my hand gently on her shoulder and smiled. She smiled back, but I could see a hint of worry in her eyes. A few days later Diana and I passed each other in the back stairwell. She was on her way to report to the housekeeper for her afternoon work assignment. I was on my way to show another student how to take over the task of caring for the birds. Diana stopped me.

"This is turning out to be harder than I thought," she said. "What's the secret to surviving this place?"

The secret! It is that we are Love. That is all we need to know, and the sages and prophets have been telling us that for ages. It's no secret.

I thought for a second about the most useful advice I could muster for Diana. Easier to give than to live.

"Learn your boundaries. Find your joy without getting dragged into others' drama. There will be drama."

It sounded lame, but she seemed satisfied. I added,

"Your experience is whatever you make it, for better

or for worse."

"Thanks, that helps," she said, and continued up the stairs.

I lingered for a moment, in the servants' stairwell, a fitting place for that brief exchange. One servant to another. Then I skipped down and out the back door.

I had asked God to nudge me toward something, to improve my dead-end life. She had given me the opportunity to bare my soul; to learn what was Real; to remember that I am the manifested consciousness of God. She had given me Braemar.

My work here now complete, I was ready to return to America to start my next great adventure.

EPILOGUE

The grass was waist high and wet. Without the proper outerwear, the four of us were soaked from our waists down within the first fifty yards. I hadn't walked the Braemar trail through White Wood in more than a decade, and the trail hadn't been mowed in a long time. Trevor had always kept it clear, but he had long since left Braemar, and subsequent estate managers obviously had had different priorities. Instinctively, I knew where the trail had been, and my husband and two young adult stepchildren followed in my tracks. We were visiting Scotland and had come to Braemar this Sunday afternoon in June for a quick visit.

My last trip to Braemar had been eleven years earlier to participate in an annual Forestry Fortnight, an offshoot of the tree planting project. During that previous visit, on the brow of the hill above the Gate Lodge, fellow Braemarite Derrick and I had planted a rowan tree in memory of our friend and former student Jill, who had recently died from breast cancer.

On this current visit, my husband and stepkids waded among the tall grass in the wood, sidestepping muddy areas and leaping over boggy spots. The trees, no bigger around than twigs and no taller than fifteen inches when we had first stuck them in the ground, were now solid trunks—up to a foot in diameter and taller than a house.

"Here's where one of the volunteers got stuck in the bog. It took three of us to pull him out," I recalled.

Through Knowe Hill and The Brae we continued. I related more stories for the kids about how our band of Soays were impossible to keep contained; how the estate manager, Trevor, had made me drive the tractor on my second day down this incredibly steep hill; and where we had built a gate and scratched our initials in the wet concrete. The initials were still there, though we had to clear away the moss to find them.

We continued along what we thought was the main track on our way back up the hill toward the old Gate Lodge. Suddenly, I didn't recognize anything. I had lost my bearings. The track hadn't seen a tractor in ages, and the trees were so tall on both sides, you couldn't see across the Creston valley anymore. The trees had completely transformed the landscape.

"Maybe we should cut up across the sheep pasture back to the big house," my husband said.

I wanted to keep trying to follow the track, to find my way through it. As rewarding as it was to see how much the seedlings had grown into a young forest, I was also overcome with nostalgia. Never again would I be able to sit on my favorite stump in Knowe Hill and gaze at the view across the valley.

The other three clambered over the gate and began trudging up the steep pasture toward the big house. I hung back for a few minutes, wiping away some of the memories that coursed down my cheeks in droplets.

I caught up with my family, and we wandered through the big house and the Steading, peeking inside the two old rooms I had once lived in. I recounted how two guy pals had sandwiched me in bed one night, comforting me after I had lost one of my favorite earrings up on the moors. My husband shook his head and clucked his tongue in mock disapproval.

"Under the subflooring in this room, with carpet glue,

the estate manager and I wrote our initials inside a big heart," I told the kids. "And here, he kissed me for the first time."

"Too much information," my stepdaughter said. Her brother groaned.

At teatime in the big house, a few old friends filled me in on the whereabouts of various Braemarites, the different courses now offered, and who had come and gone. Principal Latif had retired and moved to Edinburgh, but Wakil was still there.

"Hiya, love," he said, when I gave him a big hug.

He said it as if he had just seen me yesterday. He was never one for sentimentality, so I didn't take offense at his non-demonstrative response for not having seen me in so many years.

After tea and just before we were getting ready to leave, I stepped inside the meditation room. The Qur'an in micro print, the one with the stunning calligraphy in Arabic phrases swirling around the borders, still hung on the wall in the same place. I recalled some things I had heard often during my Braemar years:

Show us things as they are. Help us to see the soul's truth with the heart, not with our eyes or our mind. To see things as they truly are reveals the Reality of God.

How threatening that calligraphy had seemed when I had first lain eyes on it. With different eyes, I now saw the love of an artist who knew the Reality of God, inviting all who gazed upon his work to do so with an open heart.

"Ready, darling?" my husband said from the doorway. He held out his hand.

"Yes," I said, looking back for one last gaze at the big room, remembering everything I had learned in this place and everything it had given me.

And what had become of Trevor?

Reader, I married him.

Post-Epilogue

Since writing the Epilogue, our dear friend Wakil died during the spring of his fifty-seventh year. His heart had finally been cracked open for the Light to pour in. Someone said the hospital room was so packed with friends and family to say goodbye, that no one could move. He is buried on the hill above the big house next to Iskandar's Monument, a spot Wakil had chosen himself. The autumn after Wakil's Marriage with God, Trevor and I returned to Braemar and planted five dozen daffodil bulbs on his grave.

Acknowledgments

Women Who Write of Virginia, who read multiple original drafts many years ago, and the non-human critters of "Braemar," who taught me the most valuable lessons about living in the moment. Denis Ledoux (The Memoir Network), Sarah Yuen, and Nevin Mays (Nevin Mays Editorial) for your editorial input, and Anne Dubuisson for sharpening the axe (AnneConsults.com). Reviewers: Mary Bisbee-Beek (Arbor Farm Press), Ruth Elias, Jacqueline Jeynes, Will Koehler, and Eleanor Wray. Michelle Argyle for the cover and book design (Melissa Williams Design).

Author Bio

S.A. Snyder has worn hats as a writer, editor, reporter and columnist, writing instructor, and communications consultant. In a previous life she was a forester and wildlife biologist. Her experience covers topics as diverse as environmental sciences, electrical and mechanical engineering, telecommunications, travel marketing, finance and insurance, adaptive recreation, health and wellness, workplace safety and security, and general business. Sarah's latest adventures include oral storytelling, public speaking, and inspiring others to discover their true potential.

Also by S.A. Snyder

Scenic Routes & Byways: Montana, 3ʳᵈ Edition
(Rowman & Littlefield)

Forthcoming by S.A. Snyder

NON-FICTION

Hu Let the Sheep Out:
Life Lessons from Animals I've Known

The Value of Your Soul:
Rumi Verse for Life's Annoying Moments

FICTION

Aislinn Zafirah Trilogy

In this comedy of errors, an animal rights activist must help her reincarnated, beastly, mother solve the mystery of her death.

Luna River

A tragic story of mother and child, loss and redemption, set in Wyoming.

Connect with S.A. Snyder

Visit www.lunarivervoices.com to:

- Sign up for the newsletter
- Download book club discussion questions
- Watch YouTube videos of Sarah's live storytelling
- Take a quick quiz to determine whether you're ready for your own retreat or adventure
- Prepare for your retreat or adventure
- Learn more about Ibn Arabi and the Sufi poet Jelal ad-Din Rumi
- Connect via social media, find links to retreats in Scotland, and more

To book S.A. Snyder for speaking, storytelling, or reading engagements, visit www.LunaRiverPublishing.com.